Norbert Gutenberg/Richard Fiordo (eds.)

Rhetoric in Europe: Philosophical Issues

Rhetorik in Europa,
herausgegeben von Norbert Gutenberg und Peter Riemer
Band 1

Norbert Gutenberg / Richard Fiordo (eds.)

Rhetoric in Europe: Philosophical Issues

Frank & Timme

Verlag für wissenschaftliche Literatur

ISBN 978-3-7329-0319-1
ISBN (E-Book) 978-3-7329-9688-9
ISSN 2510-389X

Herstellung durch Frank & Timme GmbH,
Wittelsbacherstraße 27a, 10707 Berlin.
Printed in Germany.
Gedruckt auf säurefreiem, alterungsbeständigem Papier.

www.frank-timme.de

Contents

Dr. Norbert Gutenberg, Saarland University /
Dr. Richard Fiordo, University of North Dakota

Introduction to Philosophical Problems in European Rhetoric

In a land liberated from the Sicilian tyrant Thrasybulos around the Fifth Century BCE, from the seminal reflections of Corax of Syracuse through the insightful advancements of Corax's student Tisias, as the legendary history of Ancient Greek rhetoric recounts, Isocrates surfaced. From Corax and Tisias, the clever "crows" of Ancient Greek rhetoric, emerged Isocrates. Isocrates refined the courtroom school of rhetoric Corax and Tisias spawned into a philosophical rhetoric. About 2,400 years later in Saarbrucken, Germany at the Saarland University at an international congress honoring Isocrates and the European rhetorical tradition, an assemblage of scholars casting modern light on ancient rhetorical monuments wrote and delivered learned papers on diverse areas of rhetorical studies. The scholarly work that follows focuses on the topic of rhetoric and philosophy.

The scholarly contributions to the tradition of rhetoric from Isocrates and Europe demonstrate the ideas from Isocrates that students should practice composing and delivering speeches on an array of topics, that civic education was essential to serve a democracy, and that the fruits of education are sweet. To Isocrates rhetoric embodied not only a verbal and symbolic expression of thought but also philosophically an outward feeling and an inward conception of reason, feeling, and imagination. He endorsed a living rhetoric—one that a capable rhetor adjusts continually to changing conditions and by fitting discourse to an occasion. Rhetoric allowed us to persuade ourselves and others, to address practical problems, to direct public affairs, to transcend the brutishness of the animal kingdom, to surpass the lives of barbaric societies, to foster the core of a liberal arts education, and to live the civilized life.

One of the many fine expressions of noble ideas to be found among the rhetorical treasures Isocrates bestowed on posterity is this never-ending wisdom reflected explicitly or implicitly in the conference papers dedicated to philosophy and rhetoric. When we are about to say anything, Isocrates instructs us first to weigh it on our minds because "with many, the tongue out-runs the thought." Sounding like Ludwig Wittgenstein 2,400 years later, Isocrates advises two occasions for speaking. The first occasion is when we know the subject thoroughly. The second occasion is when we must speak. Isocrates and Wittgenstein would likely be intellectual friends on Wittgenstein's philosophical point that "what can be said at all can be said clearly, and what we cannot talk about we must pass over in silence." The scholarly contributors to the rhetoric and philosophy portion of the 2013 Saarbrucken conference on rhetoric address this and other profound philosophical concerns in rhetoric.

In Verse 18 of *To Dominicus*, Isocrates offers sound guidance: "Spend your leisure time in cultivating an ear attentive to discourse, for in this way you will find that you learn with ease what others have found out with difficulty." The articles in this book offer wise discourse on rhetoric, discourse designed to help people in social and political contexts learn the easy way rather than the hard way. Highlights of the dozen English articles delivered fully in this book follow in uniform order:

In "Isocrates and the Rhetorical Creation of Europe: The Medium as Message," Charles Marsh, Oscar Stauffer Professor, at the University of Kansas addresses Isocrates and the creation of Europe through rhetoric. His article demonstrates the idea that Isocrates helped create the concept of transnationalism that, eventually, led to Europe both as an idea and a political union. Marsh shows the importance of Isocrates' rhetoric in helping to establish the idea and reality of Europe.

In "Rhetoric and Politics: Some Approaches on the Social Psychology and Sociology of Rhetorical Discourse Analysis – Presentation of a Case Study," Virgílio Amaral, Post-doctoral Researcher in the Centre for Social Studies at the University of Coimbra, examines rhetoric and politics. The study focuses generally on the Social Representations Theory and specifically on the relation between Social Representations Theory and the analysis of the rhetorical speech within politics. The main objective of this study was to investigate the role of the sociology of absences in order to understand aspects of current political behavior in Portugal, such as difficulties in gaining agreement among its left-wing parties so that a sociology of emergences might be pursued.

In "Argumentum *ad hominem* – Good Argument or Fallacy? An Analysis of Croatian Parliamentary Debate," Gabrijela Kisicek, Senior Research Assistant in the Faculty of Humanities and Social Sciences at the University of Zagreb analyzes Croatian parliamentary debate in terms of the value of *argumen-*

tum ad hominem. Traditionally, many logic textbooks have treated *ad hominem* argumentation as fallacious and dismissed it as a logically unacceptable way of supporting a conclusion. This general assumption is challenged and a range of examples provided in which arguing *ad hominem* can be viewed as a legitimate and non-fallacious argument.

In "From *Democratia* (δημοκρατια) to *Res Publica*: Adaptation and Evolution of Classical Rhetoric," Panagiotes Kontonasios (Classics PhD, National and Kapodistrian University of Athens), examines the adaptation and evolution of classical rhetoric. His main purpose in the study is to explore how Roman rhetoric emerges and enriches Ancient Greek rhetoric. Stressed in the article are the particular characteristics of the polity of the *res publica*. The paper addresses the fact that free rhetoric dominated in the early Roman polity before Rome turned to militarism.

In "The Concept of *Doxa* in the European Reinvention of Rhetoric," Erik Bengtson, PhD Fellow in Rhetoric at Uppsala University, explores the relationship between rhetoric, opinion, and knowledge. Since the birth of rhetorical theory in ancient Greece, the discussion of rhetoric has involved a struggle between *doxa* and *episteme*, where *doxa* is understood as mere belief or opinion while *episteme* is understood as true knowledge. He aims to resolve an ancient issue pertaining to *doxa* and *episteme* in the European reinvention of rhetoric. The concept of *doxa* is shown to be a fertile focal point for a transnational discussion on rhetoric and knowledge related to the classical rhetorical tradition as well as the modern tradition of continental philosophy.

In "Richards' Non-Aristotelian 'New' Rhetoric: Grounds for a Microscopic Rhetoric and a Macroscopic Hermeneutic" Richard Fiordo, Professor of Communication at the University of North Dakota, examines the rhetorical theory of I. A. Richards. He interprets Richards' rhetorical theory as anti-Aristotelian and links his new rhetoric to general semantics. Specifically, the thesis is that Richards' microscopic perspective on rhetoric can serve as grounds for a macroscopic hermeneutic. The study uses the dynamic of Hermes from Ancient Greek mythology to interpret Richards' rhetorical adjustment of communicators to messages and their interpretation. Overall, the study develops a system for interpreting words and symbols in diverse contexts.

In "Stoic Influence in a Ciceronian Rhetorical Tradition: Kant, Arendt, and Perelman's 'Rule of Justice'" Brandon Inabinet, Assistant Professor of Communication Studies at Furman University, maintains that Cicero's rhetorical ethic was based on Isocrates, Aristotle, and the Stoics. Cicero, he argues, created a political theory of communities ethically oriented toward cooperation, while acknowledging divisions. He concludes this article with the view that a sophisticated ethical theory of rhetoric today must recapture practical theories of Cicero to deal adequately with the present cultural strife in Europe and abroad: that is, to anticipate and take into account current discourse across borders, environmental concerns, and intergenerational audiences.

In "Rhetorical Toleration: John Locke on Ethics and Fallacy Theory," Mark Longaker, Associate Professor of Rhetoric and Writing at the University of Texas at Austin, calls worthy attention to John Locke on ethics and fallacy theory. He contends that Locke's rhetorical approach to political toleration should be compared to philosophical defenses of toleration. He uncovers how Locke's philosophical arguments contrast with his rhetorical view of toleration. In the article, he argues that toleration—both early-modern and present-day—depends upon argumentative forms that contribute to a conversational ethos.

In "The Parliamentary Model of Rhetorical Political Theory," Kari Palonen, Professor of Political Science at the University of Jyväskylä, sets forth the thesis of a parliamentary theory of knowledge. Quoting Quentin Skinner, he holds with Skinner that Hobbes's Leviathan can be thought of "as a speech in Parliament." Furthermore, "great works of political philosophy are recognizably contributions to a debate." In other words, Palonen elucidates a parliamentary model of rhetorical political theory. As a complement to the "rhetorical turn" in parliamentary studies, the author argues that what is needed also is a reactivation of a "parliamentary turn" in political theory.

In "Do the 'Critical Questions' Have Only Dialectic Relevance? Some Remarks on the Rhetorical Value of CQs in Legal Argumentation," Serena Tomasi, Professor of Rhetoric, University of Trento – CERMEG (Center of Research on Legal Methodology), asks whether critical questions have rhetorical value in legal argumentation and answers by showing how court rhetoric functions through critical questions. While the Italian Supreme Court has recently set logical standards for evaluating expert opinions, the Court's guideline appears generic and fails to avoid the most practical difficulty of providing a reasonable justification. The Italian Supreme Court has recently set logical standards for evaluating expert opinions. The Court's guideline appears quite generic and fails to avoid the most practical difficulty of providing a reasonable justification. The critical analysis set forth in this study involves a broader argumentative framework for the judicial evaluation of scientific evidence.

In "Can Rhetoric Help in Creating a European Episteme for the Digital Age? The Example of Publication Processing and Analogical Semantics," Carole Lipsyc, Head of Development, Adreva, Paragraphe Laboratory, University of Paris, asserts that rhetoric offers an inspiration for solving some of the challenges that digital publishing faces when treating complex semantic objects. On an epistemological level, the author analyzes the influences that both rhetorical and non-rhetorical approaches to digital publishing could have on cognition and on social interactions. The critical analysis used in the article constitutes the philosophical tool of symbolic form. Optimally, this study proposes that a rhetorical approach to digital publishing could inspire a European way of building the emerging digital society, a way that would take into account ethical and responsible dimensions.

In "'One Speaks To Be Listened To': Schleiermacher's Philosophical View of Rhetoric and Orality," Norbert Gutenberg, Professor of Speech Communication at the Saarland University, and Richard Fiordo, Professor of Communication at the University of North Dakota, analyze and interpret Schleiermacher's philosophy of speech in human cognition and social relations. The rhetoric of Friedrich Schleiermacher is reviewed in terms of modern speech communication theory and didactics. Schleiermacher focuses our attention on attention: that is, we speak to be heard, to be listened to, to be provided with attention, and to be confirmed existentially. Schleiermacher's rhetorical perspective of a teacher as someone who "disposes of high-grade knowledge" and who advances "the principle of communication" is explained.

As readers examine the articles in this book in their entirety, these sublime words of Isocrates from Verse 41, once again found in *To Dominicus*, might be considered for the sound counsel they provide: "Always when you are about to say anything, first weigh it in your mind; for with many the tongue outruns the thought. Let there be but two occasions for speech—when the subject is one which you thoroughly know and when it is one on which you are compelled to speak. On these occasions alone is speech better than silence; on all others, it is better to be silent than to speak." His words might echo beneficially in the inquisitive minds of the readers of this volume. Isocrates' philosophical thoughts on rhetorical discourse might thus inspire readers through the meaningful contributions of the authors of this scholarly work on European rhetoric in honor of Isocrates.

DR. CHARLES MARSH, UNIVERSITY OF KANSAS

Isocrates and the Rhetorical Creation of Europe: The Medium as Message

Abstract: The idea that Isocrates helped create the concept of transnationalism that fostered Europe both as an idea and as an eventual political union is common fare in rhetorical studies. De Romilly (1992) writes that "Isocrates was perhaps the first in antiquity to focus his political theories on the idea of Europe" (p. 2). Isocrates anticipated "the idea of Europe" (Hariman, 2004, p. 231) and used the words Europen *and* Europes *13 times in his essays. But, to date, critical exploration of Isocrates' role in developing the idea of Europe has primarily dealt with the content of his works – with his eloquent and relentless focus on panhellenism and the related conflict between Europe and Asia. This essay, however, will focus on medium rather than message. It will focus on Isocrates' pioneering use of a new medium—written documents/syggrammata—and the role that the new rhetorical medium played in forming Europe.*

1   Introduction: Overview

The most famous passage in the Isocratean canon, the so-called Hymn to Logos (Jaeger, 1944/1971), which first appeared in *Nicocles* (5–9) and was repeated in *Antidosis* (253–257), holds that speech/logos is a civic and political unifier, by means of which "we have come together and founded cities and made laws and invented arts" (*Nicocles* 6). Yet before Isocrates, who was "the first individual who could be termed a 'writer' in the modern sense of the term" (Lentz, 1989), logos and its community-building powers traveled primarily orally: Cities, alliances, arts, and laws were built through face-to-face communication. Isocrates expanded logos to the tangible, transportable text and used it preach his message of panhellenism to distant leaders including Archidamus of Sparta, Dionysius of Syracuse, and Philip of Macedonia. Isocrates "indicates that his works are to be understood as being sent out or even published throughout the Greek-speaking and -reading world" (Too, 1995, p. 127).

Marshall McLuhan's (1964) famous dictum that "the medium is the message" (p. 23) denotes the idea that a pervasive medium's cultural and neurological impacts far outweigh the importance of the content that it conveys. Writing, as McLuhan (1964) has further noted, helps build broad common cultures and, through the printing press, leads to nationalism. Not only did Isocrates' new medium bolster panhellenism by geographically and chronologically extending the community-building powers of logos, it transformed the human mind, catalyzing such culture-shaping disciplines as ethics, law, philosophy, and more (Havelock, 1982). As Havelock (1982), Ong (1982), and other scholars of orality and literacy have noted, brain capacity previously devoted to memory in oral cultures now was liberated for more extensive forays into what Socrates called the examined life. As Haskins (2004) puts it, "The critical eye now dominates the easily seduced ear" (p. 23).

A generation ago, structuralist critics dissected texts into *histoire, narration, and récit* (Genette, 1972)—or, in Rimmon-Kenan's (1983) terminology, *story, narration,* and *text*. Heretofore, scholarly accounts of Isocrates' formative role in the idea of Europe have focused on *histoire*/story/content. Ideally, the contribution of this essay will be to show the importance of Isocrates' *récit*/text/ new medium in helping to establish the idea and reality of Europe.

2   The Concept of Europe in the Greece of Isocrates

Isocrates was born in Athens in 436 BCE. The son of a financially successful flute-maker, he became a logographer—a writer of speeches for Athenian litigants—then opened a school that, in the words of Jaeger, "has exercised a far greater influence on the educational methods of humanism than any other Greek or Roman teacher …" (1944/1971, p. 46). Isocrates lived and taught in the Athens of Socrates, Plato, and Aristotle and died at age 98, shortly after writing the essay *Panathenaicus* and a letter to Philip of Macedonia.

Regarding the genesis of Europe, Meier (2012), in *A Culture of Freedom: Ancient Greece and the Origins of Europe*, poses a question that must be addressed in this essay. "Where does Europe begin?" he asks. "Where, indeed, does anything ever begin?" (p. 3). Throughout the work, Meier cautiously traces the origins of Europe to ancient Greece, and he concludes that, although "[t]here are no hard-and-fast rules about where to locate historical ruptures" (p. 46), "[w]ithout the Greeks, Eurasia would never—and certainly not permanently—have been divided into two separate continents" (p. 21). Sacks (1995) notes that by the eighth century BCE there was a rough understanding that Europe and Asia "were two different continents, separated by the Aegean sea"—but that the Greek word *Europe* and its derivatives primarily referred to central Greece (p. 94).

An early sense of being European may have been fueled by a perception of otherness, of being not-Asian. In the fourth century BCE, for example, Aristotle, in *Politics*, holds that Asians "lack spirit" (1327b) and are "servile" (1285a) in comparison with the Greeks. Modern histories often cast the seminal battles of Marathon, Thermopylae, and Salamis not just as battles between Greece and Persia but between two cultures, West and East, Europe and Asia. The subtitle of Lloyd's *Marathon* (1973) is *The Story of Civilizations on Collision Course*. The subtitle of Bradford's *Thermopylae* (1993) is *The Battle for the West*. The subtitle of Strauss' *The Battle of Salamis* (2004) is *The Naval Encounter That Saved Greece—and Western Civilization*. Meier (2012) asserts that in the wake of these fifth century BCE battles, "the Greeks began to conceive of themselves in opposition both to the barbarians and to Asia…. [T]he contrast between the Greeks and Persians was increasingly being perceived as a contrast between Europe and Asia" (p. 36). For an educated Greek individual in the time of Isocrates, according to Jaeger (1939/1973), a map "of the surface of the earth was divided into two roughly equal parts, Europe and Asia" (p. 158). As we shall see, however, such a map probably guessed at the northwestern reaches of Europe. Isocrates himself writes of "[a]ll the world which lies beneath the firmament being divided into two parts, the one called Asia [*Asias*], the other Europe [*Europes*]" (*Panegyricus*, 179).

Isocrates' use of the word *Europe* and derivatives is revealing. *The Thesaurus Linguae Graecae* database indicates that he used *Europen* or *Europes* 13 times in his essays. Although he seemed to use the word to indicate the Greek city-states and their surroundings (*Panegyricus* 117, 176, 179; *To Philip* 151), often in contrast to Asia (*Helen* 67; *Panegyricus* 149; *Archidamus* 54), in *Panathenaicus* Isocrates does seem to distinguish between Greece/Hellas and Europe:

And so it resulted from the policy which we pursued that Hellas [*Hellada*] waxed great, Europe [*Europen*] became stronger than Asia, and, furthermore, the Hellenes who were in straitened circumstances received

cities and lands, while the barbarians who were wont to be insolent
were expelled from their own territory and humbled in their pride ...
(47)

"[E]ven if it is still imprecise and uncertain," De Romilly (1992) concludes,
"this very manner of speech is a first step towards our modern notions of Europe" (p. 4).

Barry Cunliffe's book *The Extraordinary Voyage of Pytheas the Greek* (2002)
documents the scant knowledge Isocrates and his contemporaries had about
the Europe beyond Greece and the familiar Mediterranean ports. Pytheas was
a fourth century BCE Greek explorer who left an account, now lost, of a land
and sea exploration that involved a journey into terra incognita: probably
across the neck of the Iberian peninsula and a circumnavigation, with frequent
stops and land-based explorations, of what is now Great Britain. In approxi-
mately 330 BCE—eight years after Isocrates' death—Pytheas became "the first
Greek to travel ... to the limits of the inhabited world and to publish a sober
description of what he saw" (p. viii). At that time, the "familiar world was
largely restricted to the Mediterranean and Black Sea fringes and the rivers of
Egypt and Mesopotamia" (p. 35). The "north Atlantic shore" was "shrouded in
mystery" (p. vii), in part because a hostile Carthage largely controlled the Strait
of Gibraltar from 500 to 250 BCE (p. 53). With some of the tin necessary for
bronze being imported from Britain, the Greeks knew of mysterious lands to
the far northwest, but, in the time of Isocrates, those lands were "beyond the
known world" (p. 18). In short, much of the landmass of Europe was unknown
to Isocrates and his contemporaries.

3   Proto-Europeanism: Isocrates and Panhellenism

Throughout his essays, Isocrates worked toward a panhellenic confederacy.
"His own political writings, read throughout Greece, gave him greater influence upon popular opinion than belonged to any other literary man of the
time," declares Jebb (1876), "and he used this influence principally to enforce
one idea" (p. 13). That idea, of course, was panhellenic unity. Citing the example of an idealized past, Isocrates reminds his readers that "our ancestors will
be seen to have preserved without ceasing the spirit of concord towards the

Hellenes…" (*Panathenaicus*, 42). Isocrates, writes Ober (2004), "proposed to reconcile two senses of 'we' available to his Athenian audience—'we the few and good' and 'we the demos'—with a third, much broader conception of 'we the Hellenes'" (p. 23). Of Isocrates' dual loyalties to Athens and to a larger Greece, Norlin (1928/1991) concludes:

Love of Athens is the one passion of his dispassionate nature; and second only to this is his love of Hellas. Or rather, both of these feelings are blended into a single passion—a worship of Hellenism as a way of life, a saving religion of which he conceives Athens to be the central shrine…. (pp. ix–x)

In *To Philip*, Isocrates asserts that "throughout my whole life I have constantly employed such powers as I possess" to foster panhellenic unity in the face of the threat from Persia (130). Later, in *To the Rulers of the Mytilenaeans*, he declares, "I have myself composed more discourses on behalf of the freedom and independence of the Greeks than all those together who have worn smooth the floor of our platforms" (7).

According to Too (1995), Isocrates is "the author who more than any other sets out and effects an apparently *panhellenic programme*" (p. 138). Similarly, Hariman (2004) concludes, "Isocrates was a *proleptic* thinker. He worked out … the idea of Europe" (p. 231).

In championing Isocrates as the first effective advocate for panhellenism and consequent European identity, however, both Isocrates himself and modern critics have, logically, focused on the content of his essays: He focused on "*subjects* wider and nobler than the concerns of any single city" (Jebb, 1876, p. 43). His "one *fundamental preoccupation* [was] the ideal of pan-hellenic unity" (Marrou, 1956/1982, p. 87). Isocrates was "perhaps the first in antiquity to focus *his political theories* on the idea of Europe" (De Romilly, 1992, p. 2). Isocrates "adopts the old *theme* of pan-Hellenism in order to criticize the contemporary historical situation" (Haskins, 2004, p. 125). (Emphasis added to preceding quotations.) Such terms as *subjects*, *theories*, and *theme*, of course, focus on the content—the panhellenic message—of his essays. As McLuhan (1964) maintains, "[I]t is only too typical that the 'content' of any medium blinds us to the character of the medium" (p. 24).

Rather than addressing the content of Isocrates' essays, however, this essay addresses the medium of that persistent panhellenic message and that medium's role in developing panhellenism and the concept of Europe as a geographic and cultural entity. Again, the contribution of this essay, ideally, will be to show the importance of Isocrates' *récit*/text—his new medium of the written essay—in helping to establish the idea and reality of Europe.

Classical scholars have generally attributed to Isocrates the development, within Western civilization, of distributed documents in general and the critical essay in particular. Isocrates' own introduction to *Antidosis* sets forth his confident realization that he is escaping the confinements of the oral culture of Athens and Greece:

If the discourse which is now about to be read [*anagnosthesesthai*] had been like the speeches which are produced either for the law-courts or for oratorical display, I should not, I suppose, have prefaced it by any explanation. Since, however, it is novel and different in character, it is necessary to begin by setting forth the reasons why I chose to write [*graphein*] a discourse so unlike any other.... (1)

Antidosis, thus, is something new and different: It is not a speaker-delivered oration destined for law courts or the Assembly. Rather, the discourse adopts a new medium for a new audience: It is a tangible text to be read (*anagnosthesesthai*) by readers anywhere. Later in the essay (12), in fact, Isocrates cautions his new audience not to tire themselves by reading the long essay in one sitting.

Just as he refers to readers in his introduction to *Antidosis*, Isocrates—via the verb *graphein*, to write—refers to himself as something new: a writer. Isocrates, maintains Lentz (1989), is "the first individual who could be termed a 'writer' in the modern sense of the term" (p. 123). "Isokratic prose was meant to be read rather than to be spoken," Jebb (1876) concludes. "This is the basis of its character, distinguishing it from the earlier rhetorical prose, and fitting it to influence the literary prose of the modern world" (p. 426). Echoing Jebb and Lentz, Too (1995) holds that "Isocrates is the ancient author who more than any other establishes writing as a medium of political expression and activity ..." (p. 114). Perhaps fearing this new competition for his own chosen oral medium, Isocrates' contemporary Alcidamas (van Hook, 1919) attacked Isocrates as one of "certain so-called Sophists [who] are vainglorious and puffed up with pride because they have practised the writing of speeches" (p. 91).

4   The Impact of Isocrates' New Medium

As a medium, Isocrates' writings took the form of *syggrammata* (*Antidosis* 14, 33); Liddell and Scott (1889), in their standard Greek lexicon, define *syggramma* (plural, *syggrammata*) as "a writing, a written paper" (p. 753). Isocrates also used the term *biblion* (*To Philip*, 21), which Liddell and Scott (1889) define as "a paper, scroll, letter" (p. 150). The *récit*/text of this tangible new medium helped establish the idea and reality of Europe in three ways: It expanded the spatial potential of logos; it expanded the temporal potential of logos; and, as a pervasive new print medium, it altered human nature in ways conducive, in the opinion of McLuhan and other scholars of orality and literacy, to nation-building.

The portability of Isocrates' new medium enabled his panhellenic message to be studied by contemporaries throughout Greece. In spatial terms, it expanded the sphere of reception. For example, Isocrates directed essays—understood to be read by others (Jebb, 1876, p. 426; Too, 1995, p. 150)—to Nicocles of Cyprus, Philip of Macedonia, Dionysius of Syracuse, Archidamus of Sparta, and others. Isocrates' panhellenic message, in Haskins' (2004) words, thus "exceeds the spacio-temporal limits defined by the law courts, the Assembly, and the festival, the three explicit institutions of rhetorical practice in the Athenian democracy" (p. 72). Too (1995) reviews Isocrates' repeated efforts to cast himself as a modern Agamemnon, a uniter of the Greek city-states, and she concludes:

> Isocrates' literary career is to be seen as modelling itself upon Agamemnon's military enterprise … At stake in this self-characterisation is the claim to define Greek identity through language, for Isocrates' rhetorical and linguistic programme assumes a political agenda, arrogating to itself the right to determine the *logos* which defines the Greek community. (pp. 138, 139)

Isocrates' *syggrammata*, unlike their oral counterparts, were "intended for written circulation" (Morgan, 2004, p. 148).

Beyond spatial boundaries, Isocrates' new medium expanded temporal boundaries in several senses. For example, written compositions that were not scheduled for a particular Assembly or court session allowed a more flexible composition process. T. Poulakos (1997) holds that "one of Isocrates' most important contributions to the history of rhetoric [was] the gift of time" (p. 70):

> With time on its side, eloquence would have a chance to develop its intrinsic qualities even as it continued to cater to an external situation…. [T]he new spaciousness of public deliberation … became affable to ethical considerations. (pp. 70, 71–72)

This "gift of time" increased writers' ability to revise and refine their messages. Isocrates himself "turned into a writing orator whose very compositions functioned as arguments for producing, studying and practicing rhetoric in the written mode," J. Poulakos (2004, p. 79) writes. Indeed, Isocrates discusses revising early drafts of his essays in *Panathenaicus* and *To Philip*. Yet Isocrates' gift of time included more: Readers also received the gift. No longer dependent on the speaker, a reader could pause as often as he or she wished to ponder the words of the writer. Again, in *Antidosis*, Isocrates urges readers not to read the essay in one sitting (12). Isocrates' new medium afforded his audiences more time to consider the merits of his panhellenic message. Isocrates, in Too's (1995) estimation, "replaced the earlier politics of the voice by a politics of the written word" (p. 150).

The gift of time bestowed by Isocrates' new medium also encompasses the spread of Greek philosophy and rhetoric throughout the later Roman Empire as well as the re-emergence of classical texts from the so-called Dark Ages of the fifth to 15th centuries. In *A History of Western Philosophy* (1945), Bertrand Russell notes that Greek culture was a powerful formative influence on Rome. Of rhetoric in particular, Kennedy (1972) concludes that the "rhetoric seen in Latin literature is largely Greek" (p. 4).

Regarding the role of Isocrates' new medium in preserving Greek and Roman culture during the Dark Ages, Muir (2005) finds it appropriate that "[t]he first classical text to be translated from the Greek into English was Isocrates' *To Nicocles*" (p. 183). In *The Classical Tradition*, Gilbert Highet (1959) makes much of the influence of those recovered classical texts in reviving the idea of Europe:

"But much of [classical learning] was covered by wave after wave of barbarism; silted over; buried; and forgotten. Europe slipped backwards, backwards, almost into savagery. When the civilization of the west began to rise again and remake itself, it did so largely through rediscovering the buried culture of Greece and Rome. Great systems of thought, profound and skilful works of art, do not perish unless their *material vehicle* is utterly destroyed…. What happened after the Dark Ages was that the mind of Europe was reawakened and converted and stimulated by the rediscovery of classical civilization (p. 1, emphasis added)."

Writing, of course, is not only more portable than speech; it also is more durable. One key idea preserved by Isocrates' new medium was his own radical belief that nations are built on shared cultural ties rather than shared blood ties (*Panegyricus*, 50). The new medium, thus, not only helped to develop the idea of Europe: Centuries later, it helped to revive and infuse the idea.

Finally, Isocrates' new medium helped transform human consciousness in ways conducive to change and the exploration of new ideas, including nationhood and, perhaps, international alliances. Havelock (1986), Ong (1982), and other scholars of orality and literacy have held that members of oral cultures devote such quantities of intellectual energy and neurological storage capacity to memorizing cultural history and norms that little ability or inclination remains for analytical thought. In fact, Thomas (1992) notes that the Greek word for truth, *aletheia*, means the opposite of forgetfulness, *lethe* (p. 115). Havelock (1982) was among the first to assert that oral cultures use speech to preserve cultural norms, thus discouraging the growth of new ideas such as nation-states:

"[T]he religion, law, and custom, the ethical and historical consciousness of an oral culture are not in themselves capable of incorporation in visible models. Their close conservation depends upon strictly verbal description handed down between the generations. Description here passes into prescription. What is done becomes what ought to be done."
(p. 127)

Such strictures certainly operated in the Greece of Isocrates: "Oral methods continue[d] to be trusted, just as oral tradition was considered the perfectly normal source for the past at least till the fourth century and to some extent beyond" (Thomas, 1992, p. 89). Ong (1982) thus describes the probable fate of new and complex ideas within a culture that lacked Isocrates' new medium:

> "In an oral culture, to think through something in non-formulaic, non-patterned, non-mnemonic terms, even if it were possible, would be a waste of time, for such thought, once worked through, could never be recovered with any effectiveness, as it could be with the aid of writing. It would not be abiding knowledge but simply a passing thought ..."
> (pp. 35, 73)

McLuhan in particular insists on the link between writing and the birth of nationalism. In his landmark *Understanding Media* (1964), he titled a key chapter "The Printed Word: Architect of Nationalism," and he asserts:

> "The hotting-up of the medium of writing to repeatable print intensity led to nationalism.... Our western values [are] built on the written word.... [A] single generation of alphabetical literacy suffices in Africa today, as in Gaul two thousand years ago, to release the individual ... from the tribal web.... It can be argued, then, that the phonetic alphabet, alone, is the technology that has been the means of creating 'civilized man'—the separate individuals equal before a written code of law."
> (pp. 37, 85, 86)

In a later interview, McLuhan (*Playboy*, 1969) declared, "Our own Western time-space concepts derive from the environment created by the discovery of phonetic writing, as does our entire concept of Western civilization" (p. 33).

5   Conclusion

Certainly a case could be made that Isocrates used, in addition to *story* and *text*, the third aspect of narratives—*narration*—to indirectly advance the idea of Europe. Because his medium of the written essay was new, Isocrates paused frequently in his narratives to explain to students and other readers why he was doing what he was doing. We already, for example, have read his explanation of his new medium in the first lines of *Antidosis* and have noted his emphasis on revising successive drafts. According to Jaeger (1944/1971), Isocrates "often seized an opportunity to break off the thread of his argument, and to explain what he was saying, how he was saying it, and why" (p. 55). "Isocrates' orations," Morgan (2004) explains, "are both individual arguments set in a historical context and rhetorical modes meant to be emulated by his students" (p. 126). Because Isocrates urged his students to address topics that embraced more than the narrow interests of an individual city-state, he thus used both story and narration to advance panhellenic ideals. As he wrote in *Antidosis*, "[W]hat discourse could have a nobler or a greater theme than one which summons the Hellenes … to be of one mind among themselves?" (77).

The purpose of this essay, however, has been to focus on the third aspect of narratives: text. Isocrates' new medium allowed his redefinition and expansion of the concept of community to overcome space and time. Furthermore, his new medium helped introduce to the human intellect capacities conducive to building culturally united nations and even continents. In this case, medium indeed was the message in McLuhan's sense—and yet it was more. In Isocrates' essays, the medium enhanced the message it contained.

References

Aristotle (2005). *Politics*. (H. Rackham, Trans.). Cambridge, MA: Harvard University Press. (Loeb Classical Library: Original work published in 1932.)

Bradford, E. (1993). *Thermopylae: The battle for the West*. Boston: Da Capo Press. (Original work published in 1980.)

Cunliffe, B. (2002). *The extraordinary voyage of Pytheas the Greek*. New York: Walker & Co.

de Romilly, J. (1992). "Isocrates and Europe". *Greece & Rome, 39*, 2–13.

Genette, G. (1980). *Narrative discourse: An essay in method* (J. Lewis, Trans.). New York: Cornell University Press. (Original work published in 1972.)

Hariman, R. (2004). "Civic education, classical imitation, and democratic polity". In T. Poulakos & D. Depew (Eds.). *Isocrates and civic education*, 217–234. Austin, TX: University of Texas Press.

Haskins, E. V. (2004). *Logos and power in Isocrates and Aristotle*. Columbia, SC: University of South Carolina Press.

Havelock, E. A. (1982). *The literate revolution in Greece and its cultural consequences*. Princeton, NJ: Princeton University Press.

Havelock, E. A. (1986). *The muse learns to write: Reflections on orality and literacy from antiquity to present*. New Haven, CT: Yale University Press.

Highet, G. (1957). *The classical tradition: Greek and Roman influences on Western literature*. New York: Oxford University Press.

Isocrates (1986). *Isocrates in three volumes, Vol. 1*. (G. Norlin & L. van Hook, Trans.). Cambridge, MA: Harvard University Press. (Loeb Classical Library: Original work published in 1928.)

Isocrates. (1991). *Isocrates in three volumes, Vol. 2* (G. Norlin & L. van Hook, Trans.). Cambridge, MA: Harvard University Press. (Loeb Classical Library: Original work published in 1929.)

Isocrates (1992). *Isocrates in three volumes, Vol. 3* (G. Norlin & L. van Hook, Trans). Cambridge, MA: Harvard University Press. (Loeb Classical Library: Original work published in 1954.)

Jaeger, W. (1939/1973). *Archaic Greece: The mind of Athens* (G. Highet, Trans.). New York: Oxford University Press. (Original work published in 1939.)

Jaeger, W. (1944/1971). *The conflict of cultural ideals in the age of Plato* (G. Highet, Trans.). New York: Oxford University Press. (Original work published in 1944.)

Jebb, R. C. (1876). *The Attic orators from Antiphon to Isaeos*. London: Macmillan and Co.

Kennedy, G. (1963). *The art of persuasion in Greece*. Princeton, NJ: Princeton University Press.

Kennedy, G. (1972). *The art rhetoric in the Roman world*. Princeton, NJ: Princeton University Press.

Lentz, T. (1989). *Orality and literacy in Hellenic Greece*. Carbondale, IL: Southern Illinois University Press.

Liddell, H.G, and Scott, R. (1889). *An intermediate Greek-English lexicon*. Oxford: Clarendon Press.

Lloyd. A. (1973). *Marathon: The story of civilizations on collision course*. New York: New American Library.

Marrou, H. I. (1982). *A history of education in antiquity* (G. Lamb, Trans.). New York: Sheed and Ward. (Original work published 1956.)

McLuhan, M. (1964). *Understanding media* (2nd ed.). New York: Signet.

Meier, C. (2012). *A culture of freedom: Ancient Greece and the origins of Europe* (J. Chase, Trans.). New York: Oxford University Press.

Morgan, K. (2004). "The education of Athens: Politics and rhetoric in Isocrates and Plato". In T. Poulakos and D. Depew (Eds.). *Isocrates and civic education*, 125–154. Austin, TX: University of Texas Press.

Muir, J.R. (2005). "Is our history of educational philosophy mostly wrong? The case of Isocrates". *Theory and Research in Education, 3*, 165–95.

Norlin, G. (1991). "General introduction". In G. Norlin (Ed.). *Isocrates in three volumes: Volume I* (G. Norlin, Ed. & Trans). Cambridge, MA: Harvard University Press. (Loeb Classical Library: Original work published 1928.)

Ong, W. J. (1982). *Orality and literacy: The technologizing of the word*. London: Routledge. Isocrates & Europe – 18.

Playboy (1969, March). "The Playboy interview: Marshall McLuhan". Retrieved Sept. 14, 2013, from http://www.nextnature.net/2009/12/the-playboy-interview-marshall-mcluhan/.

Poulakos, J. (2004). "Rhetoric and civic education: From the sophists to Isocrates". In T. Poulakos and D. Depew (Eds.). *Isocrates and civic education*, 69–83. Austin, TX: University of Texas Press.

Poulakos, T. (1997). *Speaking for the polis: Isocrates' rhetorical education*. Columbia, SC: University of South Carolina Press.

Rimmon-Kenan, S. (1983). *Narrative fiction: Contemporary poetics*. London: Routledge.

Russell, B. (1945). *A history of western philosophy*. New York: Simon and Schuster.

Sacks, D. (1995). *A dictionary of the ancient Greek world*. New York: Oxford University Press.

Strauss, B. (2004). *The battle of Salamis: The naval encounter that saved Greece – and Western civilization*. New York: Simon & Schuster.

Thomas, R. (1992). *Literacy and orality in ancient Greece*. Cambridge, England: Cambridge University Press.

Too, Y. L. (1995). *The rhetoric of identity in Isocrates*. Cambridge, UK: Cambridge University Press.

van Hook, L.R. (1919). "Alcidamas versus Isocrates: The Spoken Word versus the written word". *Classical Weekly*, 12:12, 89–94.

DR. VIRGÍLIO AMARAL, UNIVERSITY OF COIMBRA

Rhetoric and Politics: Some Approaches on the Social Psychology and Sociology of Rhetorical Discourse Analysis – Presentation of a Case Study

Abstract: Based on the Organon of Aristotle, Perelman (1997) is recognized as the contemporary philosopher responsible for the New Rhetoric studies, involving the exercise of rhetoric to dialectic reasoning (as opposed to analytical reasoning). Political rhetoric and argumentation are linked to dialectical reasoning. In this study, rhetorical and political issues with respect to the speeches that occurred after the Portuguese Democratic Revolution of 25 April 1974 are discussed. The work is interdisciplinary and combines contributions from the sociology of knowledge, philosophy, contemporary history, and social psychology. In addition, the study is part of a larger research that analyzes broader political discourse in the context of the revolutionary era. A number of specific approaches are covered, such as discourse analysis rhetoric (Billig, 1991; Potter, 1996; Castro, 2002; Van Dijk, 2006) in regard to the critical incident problem of the control of the media, who at the revolutionary time, objected to the two major left-wing parties: the Portuguese Socialist Party and the Portuguese Communist Party. Identified are a number of social political constructions of the time (Berger and Luckman, 1966/1973). The main objective of this study was to investigate the role of the sociology of absences (Santos, 2006) in order to understand aspects of current political behavior in Portugal: for example, the difficulties of getting agreement between the left-wing parties (Santos, 2011) to pursue a sociology of emergences (Santos, 2006, 2011).

1 Introduction

The conflicts covered in the political arena between different positions are accompanied by discursive processes of legitimation and validation of each party, corresponding to the delegitimization of opposing positions, with persuasive aims and to obtain the support of public opinion. These processes configure a clear case of validation of polemical social representations, according to the typology of social representations proposed by Serge Moscovici (1988).

In this work, we intend to address the issues of Rhetoric and Politics, the purpose of the discussions that occurred after the democratic revolution of April 25, 1974 in Portugal, which ended a dictatorship of fascist nature that lasted almost 50 years.

This study focuses on the issues of Rhetoric and of its use in the political arena, is part of a research project of an interdisciplinary nature, carried out at the Centre for Social Studies, University of Coimbra, which aims to understand the processes of social construction of the political reality of the time, better and how it is reflected today in the Portuguese political scene, such as the great difficulties of understanding of the forces of the Portuguese left political spectrum. This work combines elements from the Sociology of Knowledge (eg. Berger & Luckman, 1966/1973; Habermas, 1987; Bordieu, 1989; Babo-Lança, 2006; Santos, 2006; Santos, 2011), Philosophy (eg. Foucault, 1971/1997; Perelman, 1997; Perelman & Olbrechts-Tyteca, 2006) Contemporary History of Portugal (eg. Medeiros Ferreira, 1994; Rosas, 1994; Reis, 2004; Cabrera, 2006; Varela, 2001) and Social Psychology (eg. Moscovici, 1988; Billig et al., 1988; Billig, 1991; Potter, 1996; Burr, 1998; Bar-Tal, 2000; Castro, 2002; Van Dijk, 2006).

The method of analysis used is based predominantly on theoretical and methodological studies proposed in the area of Social Psychology, the main area of affiliation of the author.

Understanding, today, the discursive processes in the context of the revolutionary era, means exercising asociology of absences in order to understand, as mentioned, some aspects of present political behavior, i.e., exert a sociology of emergences (Santos, 2006; Santos, 2011).

2   The Rhetoric in the "public sphere": the case of politics

In the field of "public sphere" (Habermas, 1987), in particular in the political terrain, i.e. the analysis of political discourse, the media is vital in the contribution to the social construction of a political reality and the way it is construed, to suit every political position in confrontation.

The analysis of political texts, whether produced by politicians (Cabrera, 2006) or whether produced by the media (Babo-Lança, 2006) is crucial for the identification of political and ideological beliefs, which meet four functions (Bar-Tal, 2000): epistemic function of knowledge about the political positions regarding the world and the social environment, a function of training, maintenance and reinforcement of social identities, a function of preservation of the community, group or social system, and a function of orientation and legitimization of behavior .

Alongside of legitimate beliefs of every political position, created through political speeches, are the opposite of those beliefs by the political opponents.

However, on any subject of public controversy (Nogueira, 2001) identical linguistic content can manifest itself in many different meanings, according to the discursive structures and strategies used by the parties, each discursive formation can claim for itself the "veracity" of his version on an event. Discursive Approaches in Social Sciences and Humanities can articulate with the positions structuralist and poststructuralist (Focault, 1971/1997; Burr, 1998), according to which the meanings associated with language are not fixed, but open to question. The focus of discursive approaches, following the postmodern epistemological approaches (Foucault, 1971/1997; Nogueira, 2001), is that social knowledge is anchored in exactly the ways of creating meaning, rooted in the designations ("linguistic" categories) adapted by "knowers". Discourse currents understand, therefore, that rather than predict or control phenomena, as with the positivist tradition, it is necessary to investigate the meaning of such matters (Burr, 1998; Nogueira, 2001). In this sense, the discursive approaches are suitable for the study of controversial contexts or categories that generate public controversy, such as the political controversy.

3   Methodological Considerations on the Theoretical Analysis of Rhetorical Discourse in Social Psychology

Perelman (1997), the philosopher responsible for the movement of the New Rhetoric studies, claims the foundations of such an approach are with Aristotle. Aristotle, in Organon, distinguishes between two types of reasoning: analytical reasoning, which aims to relate the truth of the premises to the conclusions, and the dialectical reasoning, based on assumptions that are made up of generally accepted opinions, to make others accept theories that can be controversial, aiming at persuasion.

The rhetoric is associated to the dialectical reasoning. Thus, for example, the field of political argumentation, philosophical, literary and even legal "is the credible, the plausible, the probable, in that [...] escapes the calculation of certainties" (Perelman & Olbrechts-Tyteca, 2006, p.9).

We adopt in this work the discursive perspectives on rhetoric in Social Psychology, as Psychology of Rhetoric of Billig (1991), Critical Discourse Analysis of Van Dijk (2006), and analysis of the mechanisms of constructing arguments (Potter, 1996; Castro , 2002).

Discussing some of these discursive approaches, Castro (2002) identifies three common aspects:

1) intra-subject variability: A single subject or sender of a message can convey varying versions of a subject, depending on the audience you want to persuade

2) Function: The variability of transmitted versions may have different functions persuasion: from the interpersonal to the ideological functions

3) Construction: A speech precisely builds a version aiming to persuade an audience

Below, we describe briefly the theoretical and methodological assumptions of current discourses in Social Psychology, in conjunction with the rhetorical analysis (Billig et al, 1988; Billig, 1991; Castro, 2002):

1) The language may be used as a way of building reality; linguistical descriptions not only serve to explain the world, but also to build it

2) The social thought—and political—is essentially argumentative; speech commonsense has a persuasive meaning, so that their contents and their persuasive functions are articulated

3) Therefore, in discourse analysis, understanding the persuasive functions can be a way to identify and reconstruct the meaning of what is said

4) In relation to any issue, there are always two themes or contradictory positions. The thought of commonsense as well as political thought, is dilemmatic

5) As a consequence, what is implied in a speech only becomes evident when, in speech analysis one is confronted with another (dialectical analysis of discourse). In rhetorical terms, any action is more than the expression in favor of a position, it is also, implicitly and explicitly, an argument against the opposite position (Billig, 1991)
6) To understand a position, it is important to understand the argumentative context in which it is expressed (see tactical reasons, strategic, etc.).

It also takes into account the analysis model proposed by Potter (1996), incorporated by Castro (2002), and some aspects focused by Van Dijk (2006), which allows the identification of mechanisms inherent to rhetorical persuasive speech: taking the argument to its extremes in order to persuade a predisposed audience, or its inverse, the minimization; description of arguments using evidence, the arguments for inoculation (want to show the audience that there is no interest in the subject of the arguments presented); mechanism of distance (assuming neutrality and not wanting to prove anything); presenting credentials in argument (use of subject categories with particular knowledge on the subject in order to make the message credible).

This paper seeks to address the rhetorical speeches around a critical incident in the context of post-revolutionary April 25—the "Republica Case"—served by two political parties, the Socialist Party and the Portuguese Communist Party.

4   Objectives of this study: the study framework

Through political rhetoric, both parties sought to impose certain "meanings" (Bourdieu, 1989) around ideological polarities (Van Dijk, 2006), arising from two views about the nature of political legitimacy: an "electoral legitimacy" claimed by the Socialist Party; since the first free elections in Portugal after the fascist dictatorship—the elections for the Constituent Assembly (Assembly that drafted the first constitution of the country after the revolution)—and a "revolutionary legitimacy" claimed by the Portuguese Communist Party. Through the analysis of political rhetoric used by the two party formations in question seeking to understand, as stated, some processes of social construction of political reality at the time (Berger & Luckman, 1966/1973; Moscovici, 1988), which impacts even nowadays (Santos, 2011).

The dictatorial regime before the democratic revolution obviously not only had political implications, but also social and economic. Fascism became a monopoly capitalist ideology and structure, which led to the exploration of much of the working class (Rosas, 1994). The revolution and the end of the regime symbolized, on the left-wing, the end of that oppression. In part because of this, and as regards Varela (2011), "terms like 'socialism', 'classless society', 'revolution', 'democracy' were part of the lexicon of propaganda all Portuguese political leaders of the PPD (Democratic Popular Party), PS (Socialist Party), PCP (Portuguese Communist Party) the extreme left" (p. 125), which still continues in todays lexicon, e.g., in the designation of the portuguese Social Democrat Party: "Portugal is the only country in Europe that has a liberal party called Social Democrat" (Varela, 2011, p.125).

As that author also states, in a historical perspective and "The speeches, political programs, documents are relevant for what they say, but also for not saying" (ibidem) adds to these considerations, for the historical understanding of the revolutionary period. It also will be necessary to understand the context and argumentative strategies in which what is said gets a precise meaning, with functions not only rhetorical, but with historical implications, such as the difficulties of understanding between the political parties of the left spectrum (Santos, 2011).

Such conflicts between, on the one hand, the Socialist Party and forces with the similar ideas or more to the right, and on the other hand, the Portuguese Communist Party and similar forces or more to the left showed up in so many other incidents critics of the time (Medeiros Ferreira, 1994;). It was, for example, the case of controversy concerning the "Lei da Unicidade Sindical" ("Trade Union Law of Oneness"), around pluralism versus centralism to adopt a framework for trade union representative of the diverse workforces. Regarding this incident, terms like "Unity" or "Democracy" acquire different meanings depending on the argumentative strategies used by these two party formations (cf. Varela, 2011, pp. 142–145).

A historical event of primary importance was the right-wing coup on March 11, 1975. Beyond the political repercussions or political-economic (as nationalizations that followed, including the Banking and Insurance, and the expropriation of farmland, policies carried out by the 4th Provisional Government), became the argumentative positioning of the Portuguese Communist

Party, related to its political priorities, and their understanding of a new phase of the revolution (cf. Brito, 2010, p. 139).

In fact, from the events of March 11, according Seabra (2007) "all public interventions, all speeches Cunhal (historical leader of the Portuguese Communist Party) dramatized [...] confrontation with the reactionary forces, for the country to realize [...] we were in the midst of a revolution that would be taken until the end against those who oppose it" (p. 242).

Not only are terms such as "Revolution" or "Socialism" that acquire different meanings in the argumentation of the parties in question, but also the term "Democracy". To the Socialist Party, from the elections of April 25, 1975, the word "Democracy" would correspond to a "pluralist democracy" of parliamentary base (Reis, 2005). For the Communist Party "Democracy" would be "a bourgeois democracy that Portugal does not serve" (Cunhal, apud Varela, 2011, p. 203), defending himself another kind of Democracy.

It is therefore in this context, both historical and from the point of view of political rhetorics, one can understand the political rhetoric around the Critical Incident in the case concerning the control of the media between the Socialist Party and the Portuguese Communist Party.

5   The "Republica Case": Two versions in confrontation

During Salazarism the newspaper "Republica" symbolized (along with the "Diário de Lisboa"), the legal press, a possible resistance to the regime. According to Mesquita (2005), the newspaper "came to 25 April [...] with the prestige of being the only Portuguese daily that assumed, explicitly, as an organ of the democratic opposition" (paragraph 14).

During the revolutionary context that pitted the Socialist Party to its left, an incident occurred which opposed most journalists and the director of the newspaper to most other workers of Republic, which led to the kidnapping of the former by the latter.

A journalist of a leading weekly publication at the time in Portugal ("Expresso") (quoted in Portugal's Socialist 05.23.1975, p. 15) described the general framework given in the public opinion as follows:

"There are two conflicting theories. The position of the Editorial Board and who, on behalf of the newspaper's independence and freedom of the press, want to continue the same body and the same editorial direction. Another theory is that of other workers, that too in the name of freedom and independence would not want to continue the direction."

In the present work, we do not intend to get to the veracity of the facts and versions presented, but single out the rhetoric analysis about the "Republica Case", a corpus of news texts published in official organs informative of each parties—the "Portugal Socialista" , official organ of the Socialist Party, and "Avante", the official organ of Communist Party—how those who sought to legitimize the exercise of power, and how the content served by each political formation ("Socialism", "Democracy", "Freedom") took on different meanings depending on the context and the argumentative strategies used.

6   Method

<u>Period</u>: May to July 1975

<u>Corpus Analysis</u>: official press organ of the Socialist Party (Portugal Socialista) and Portuguese Communist Party (Avante)

We selected 26 news items, 13 of every newspaper, given the following selection criteria: they are opinion articles about the case, correspond to political speeches on the situation in the country and / or on the case, or correspond with the news content relevant to understand the historical background, social and political environment in which it occurs.

<u>Procedure:</u>
- Identification and contrast between arguments presented by each of the political forces.
- Reconstruction of speeches by interconnecting arguments (content) and their functions.
- Identifying mechanisms rhetoricians used, based on the Potter system (1996).

7 Results

7.1 Some used rhetorical mechanisms (examples) (Potter, 1996; Castro, 2002)

1. Construction of the argument using extremes (Objective: mobilization)

Defend the independence of the "Republica" is to defend the Portuguese democracy, is to defend the revolutionary process in which the Socialists are particularly active, is still the defense of national independence.

[…] "Nor the pouring rain, nor the presence of military and armored vehicles demobilized people," or "Men who do not sleep when they are concerned the rights of the People." (Portugal Socialista, 22/05/75)

The reaction is still too hard. The conspiracy continues. (Avante, 5/22/75)

Our party was the target of daily provocations […] The reaction was mobilized […] candidates of our party beaten, invaded work-centers […] The Communists received death threats. (Avante, 10/7/75)

2. Construction of the argument using facts (objective: strengthening the argument)

[…] Editorial in the period leading up to March 11, the constant attacks on inter-union, the anticommunist campaign of that newspaper became spokesman […] (Avante, 22/5/75)

Everything serves to manufacture anticommunism. The 1st of May, the single union, the occupation of a radio, the internal conflict of the "Republic." (Avante, 7/10/75)

3. Arguments by inoculation

   [...] Because we are opposed to this global condemnation of the role of parties here and there that you begin to sketch. But these trends will gain ground rapidly, if the action of the parties did not enter in the revolutionary process. (Avante, 5/22/75)

4. Resource credentials of the individuals directly involved in the case

   [...] Want to reorganize the antifascist fighter Raul Rego (director of the newspaper) (Portugal Socialista, 5/23/75)

   [...] Undisputed figure of resistant and anti-fascist fighter who has just been elected to the Constituent Assembly and to whom April 25 owes so much (Portugal Socialista, 5/21/75)

5. Presentation of Credentials

   [...] No more than the Communists fought for the freedoms and rights of citizens. Ensuring [...] distribution of the glorious Avante! [...] Unique example of the struggle for freedom of the press [...] (Avante, 6/12/75)

7.2 Synthesis on rhetorical mechanisms on the "Republica Case" (mechanisms mainly be used by each of the Parties)

- Communist Party: Action minimizing the rhetorical mechanisms for the Republic event. Polarization of social and political reality, building with this polarization image of a PS divisive and reactionary, countering the image of a PCP unifying the masses. There is also recourse to the mechanism of distancing case against the Republic, serving up this mechanism extremes to the facts.
- Socialist Party: Appeal to the mechanism extremes to the facts. The Socialist Party is entitled defender of freedoms threatened—in particular press freedom—and serve up this rhetoric for extrapolation. Often uses the resource credentials for credible opinions (eg the anti-

fascist Raul Rego, director of the newspaper). Looking to join the audience for their theses making some allusion antifascist militants or sympathizers. They do not have the credibility of the PCP (Communist Portuguese Party) as a party, due to the years of illegitimacy, looking for singular facts to emphasize

8 Analysis and discussion of results: provisional findings

Looking for an interpretative analysis of the moments in which the discourses convey and provide a possible interpretation of the political concepts of time, based on the Billig assumption (1991) that advocates a certain position always opposes another. This means that the analysis of the contents of the arguments necessarily articulated with their functions, allows us to elucidate—to later—the meanings of concepts current in the revolutionary period in Portugal, as "Socialism", "Democracy" and "Freedom" and, as we proposed, the purpose of the Republic case, by two parties: the Socialist Party and the Portuguese Communist Party.

The Meanings of "Socialism", "Democracy" and "Freedom" and the problem of Political Legitimacy

Dichotomies / Ideological Polarities

Freedom of opinion	Freedom of working-class
Reformist Socialism	Socialism
Party pluralism (Electoral Legitimacy)	Legitimacy revolutionary
Democracy Policy (Party pluralism)	Popular Democracy

These results basically clarify the divisions of the left who are still in Portugal, given that show two completely different programmatic visions between the two major parties of the Portuguese left.

This stresses also, we believe, the usefulness of rhetorical analysis of speeches in the "public sphere", in particular in the political domain—a domain privileged, in democracies, for persuasive speech that argues exactly the same kind of societies that political formations project. Finally, this research is also useful in the study of historical rhetoric for the analysis of the evolution of Portuguese society, particularly in implications of the past even at the present, despite the passage of time.

References

Babo-Lança, I. (2006). *A Configuração dos Acontecimentos Políticos: O "Caso República" e as Manifestações nos Açores em 1975.* Coimbra: Minerva.

Bar-Tal, D. (2000). *Sharing Beliefs in a Society: Social psychological analysis.* Thousand Oaks: Age.

Berger, P. e Luckman, T. (1966/1973). *A Construção Social da Realidade.* Petrópolis: Vozes.

Billig, M. (1991). *Ideology and Opinions. Studies in Rhetorical Psychology.* London: Sage.

Billig, M., Condor, S., Edwards, D., Gane, M., Middleton, D. & Radley, A. (1988). *Ideolological Dilemmas.* London: Sage.

Bordieu, P. (1989). *O Poder Simbólico.* Lisboa: Difel.

Brito, C. (2010). *Álvaro Cunhal: Sete Fôlegos do Combatente (Memórias).* Lisboa: Edições Nelson de Matos [2ª Edição].

Burr, V. (1998). "Realism, Relativism, Social Constructionism and Discourse". In I. Parker (Ed.): *Social Constructionism, Discourse and Realism.* London: Sage.

Cabrera, A. (2006). *Marcello Caetano: Poder e Imprensa.* Lisboa: Livros Horizonte.

Castro, P. (2002). *Natureza, Ciência e Retórica na Construção Social da Ideia de Ambiente.* Lisboa: Fundação Calouste Gulbenkian / Fundação para a Ciência e Tecnologia.

Focault, M. (1971/1997). *A Ordem do Discurso.* Lisboa: Relógio D'Água Editores.

Habermas, J. (1987). *The theory of communicative action. Lifeworld and system: A critique of funcionalist reason, Vol. II.* Cambridge: Cambridge University Press.

Medeiros Ferreira, J. (1994). "Portugal em Transe (1974–1985)". In J. Mattoso (Ed): *História de Portugal* (Vol. 8). Lisboa: Circulo de Leitores.

Mesquita, M. (2005). *O Caso República. Um incidente Crítico.* Consulted in 29 of July of 2009, http/webjornal.blogspot.com/2005/05/o-caso-*Republica*-um-incidente-critico-um.html.

Moscovici, S. (1988) Notes toward a description of social representations. *European Journal of Social Psychology,* 18, 211–250.

Nogueira, C. (2001). "Análise de Discurso". In L. Almeida e E. Fernandes (Eds): *Métodos e Técnicas de avaliação: Novos Contributos para a Prática e Investigação.* Braga: CEEP.

Perelman, Ch. (1997). *O Império Retórico: Retórica e Argumentação.* Lisboa: ASA.

Perelman, Ch. e Olbrechts-Tyteca, L. (2006). *Tratado de Argumentação*. Lisboa: Instituto Piaget.

Potter. J. (1996). *Representing Reality: Discourse, Rhetoric and Social Construction*. London: Sage.

Reis, A. (2004). "O Partido Socialista na revolução". In V. Canas (Ed): *O Partido Socialista e a Democracia*. Oeiras: Celta.

Rosas, F. (1994). "O Estado Novo (1926–1974)". In J. Mattoso (Ed): *História de Portugal* (Vol. 7). Lisboa: Circulo de Leitores.

Santos, B. (2006). *A Gramática do Tempo: para uma nova cultura política*. Porto: Afrontamento.

Santos, B. (2011). *Portugal: Ensaio contra a autoflagelação*. Coimbra: Almedina.

Seabra, Z. (2007). *Foi assim*. Lisboa: Alêtheia.

Van Dijk, T. (2006). "Ideology and discourse analysis". *Journal of Political Ideologies*, 11 (2), 115–140.

Varela, R. (2011). *A História do PCP na Revolução dos Cravos*. Lisboa: Bertrand Editora.

Dr. Gabrijela Kisicek, University of Zagreb

Argumentum *ad hominem* – Good Argument or Fallacy?
An Analysis of Croatian Parliamentary Debate

Abstract: Traditionally, many logic textbooks have treated ad hominem argumentation as fallacious and dismissed it as a logically unacceptable way of supporting a conclusion. This general assumption was challenged by Johnstone (1952) who provided a range of examples in which arguing ad hominem can be viewed as a legitimate and non-fallacious argument. Since the middle of the 20th century, scholars of argumentation have come to hold that an ad hominem argument should be examined contextually, and thus evaluated much more precisely before legitimately dismissing it as irrelevant (e.g., Walton, 1998; Groarke & Tindale, 2004; Salamon, 2007; Woods, 2007). Research reported in this study focuses on the analysis of political discourse, specifically on parliamentary debate. Data include ten debates over the period of one year (June 2011 to June 2012). These debates centered on various topics and the main goal of our analysis was to identify ad hominem arguments and to evaluate them in the political debate context. Results indicate that the relevance of ad hominem varies with the topic of the debate. For instance, when economy, finances and investments were discussed, then ad hominem arguments were for the most part legitimate. Results further indicate that in discussions of topics concerning the Croatian national identity, independence and sovereignty—which evidence a comparatively more emotional style of debate, ad hominem arguments were for the most part logically irrelevant, and may therefore be viewed as fallacious. The findings of this study are presented as evidence for the viability of a larger scale empirical research project which, eventually, will compare argumentation ad hominem in political discussions across national boundaries.

1   *Ad Hominem* Arguments – Fallacy or Legitimate Argument

Ad hominem or arguments against the person are very common in public discourse and are directed to undermine credibility of an opponent. For that

      41

reason, they are usually classified as ethotic arguments, "that is, arguments that deal with some feature of the character of the speaker" (Tindale, 2007, p. 82).

Identification and explanation of *ad hominem* arguments have been attributed to the philosopher John Locke (1632–1704), but the idea of argument against the person can be traced to Aristotle's work. Nuchelmans (1993) writes about the term *ad hominem* as originating in Aristotle. Two kinds of argument are discussed. Both share common features and are often referred to by similar or identical expressions. One is traced to Aristotle's works On Sophistical Refutations (165a37) and Topics (101a25), which refers to "arguments that are based on propositions which have been conceded by the adversary" (Nuchelmans, 1993, p. 38, cited after Walton 2006). This type of argument from commitment is also known as *ex concessis* argument and *disputatio temptiva* by Boethius (480–524 CE). The other meaning is close to that of the personal attack type of argument and "was picked up by Aquinas (1225–1274) from passages in Aristotle's Metaphysics, (1005b35, 1062a2), where Aristotle distinguishes between proof in an absolute sense and proof relative to a particular person" (Walton, 2006).

In the 17th century logic textbooks were using the term *argumentum ad hominem* "referring to arguing about any subject-matter at all from the concessions of one's interlocutor, a usage attested as a scholastic commonplace" (Nuchelmans 1993: 41, cited after Hitchcock, 2006). Also in the 17th century, Galileo uses the expression "*ad hominem*" for an argument whose author derives a conclusion not acceptable to an opponent from premises accepted or acceptable by the opponent but not the arguer (Finocchiaro 1973–74, cited after Hitchcock, 2006). The personal attack type of *ad hominem* argument is described by Locke in his Essay Concerning Human Understanding as "pressing a man with consequences drawn from his own principles or concessions (Cited after Tindale, 2007, p. 82)."

Traditionally, *ad hominem* arguments are considered to be fallacious on the grounds of being irrelevant for discussions based on attacking an arguer's character rather than the claim he is making. However, what seems to be generally accepted in logic from the beginning of the 20th century has been questioned in the work of many scholars. The first theorist who claimed that there are situations in which attacking a person's character is not just irrelevant but it can be reasonable was Johnstone (1952, 1959). He opened a question on how to distinguish a reasonable from a fallacious *ad hominem* argument. Logic textbook authors Copi and Cohen (1986, p. 98) think of *ad hominem* arguments to be fallacious because personal character of a speaker is logically irrelevant to truth of the claim and correctness of an argument. However, they make an exception for arguments in legal discourse where *ad hominem* can be a relevant and legitimate argument: "There is one context in which an argument that appears to be *ad hominem* is not fallacious. In the court of law or other formal proceedings, when sworn testimony is given and it is believed by the opponents to be perjury, deliberate falsehood, the unreliability of the person giving the testimony may appropriately be exhibited."

Argumentation scholars in the 20th century treat the *ad hominem* argument as a fallacy of diversion but emphasize the difficulty in recognizing the strict line between the fallacy and legitimate argument. Among those argumentation scholars are informal logicians Johnson and Blair (2006) who treat *ad hominem* as a fallacy but also write on the difficulties of making a strict difference between relevant and irrelevant attacks on a speaker's character. Relevant attacks on a speaker's character can be seen when we question or refute arguments from authority or expert opinion (Mizrahi, 2010), when candidates for public position are examined (previous accomplishments, good moral character etc.), and when we examine arguments based on a person's testimony.

To recognize the legitimate use of *ad hominem,* it is relevant to take into account several aspects of argumentative discourse: context, situation, participants in the discussion, stages of the argumentation process, etc. Considering the context, Walton (2002) writes about *ad hominem* arguments in legal discourse depending on the stage of a trial and concludes that *ad hominem* is irrelevant in the argumentation stage but relevant in the sentencing stage. Salamon (2007, p. 121) also includes legal discourse as a context in which *ad hominem* is a legitimate argument, e.g. credibility of a witness. In addition, she mentions two more situations for legitimate *ad hominem* to occur: arguments against the pronouncements of scientific cranks and arguments against the exaggerated claims of salespersons. Hoaglund (1981:9) tries to answer the question of how we can tell whether *ad hominem* is fallacious or not. "The *ad hominem* material tends to be fallacious when it directs attention *ab re* or away from the issue being considered. An *ad hominem* argument can be valid when the person or his circumstances are the issue, in which case it is *ad rem.*"

Determining the difference between fallacious and non-fallacious *ad hominem* was the goal of Brinton's (1995) work in which he draws attention to three elements important in argumentation: the person, the person's advocacy of a claim, and the proposition or the claim itself. Understanding the difference between the three elements is helpful in recognizing the difference between fallacious and non-fallacious *ad hominem*. Referring to Britnon, Tindale (2007, p. 86) writes:

> From this perspective, fallacious cases of *ad hominem* would be ones that denied a claim or proposition in question solely on the basis of person's advocacy of it—which is to say that all good *ad hominem* argument could do is to show that a person's is not a good reason for believing the claim; it does not show that the claim is false. The individual participating in or witnessing the debate must decide, on the basis of his scrutiny of all the factors, whether the *ad hominem* material is pertinent to the issue or not.

Yap (2013, p. 99) claims that although character traits might be logically irrelevant to the argument, they could be relevant in the argumentation process in general because they contribute to establishing credibility of a speaker and his expertise: "It is not fallacious to call someone's credibility as a witness into question when they have been known frequently to lie, or have strong motives to lie. Similarly, we can question someone's expertise if they have no training or experience in that field." However, it is important to distinguish between undermining the credibility of a speaker using *ad hominem* argument and pure insult. While calling someone names, offending or humiliating a person, does not contribute to a civilized communication process, it is not logically fallacious.

Woods (2007, p. 109) makes a distinction between the rhetorical and logical domain of *ad hominem* argument. Rhetorical *ad hominem* is "the heart and soul of slanging. Slanging is a rhetorical device, as old as the hills. Its objective is to expose, embarrass, ridicule, mock, calumniate or humiliate one's opponent, typically with the intent of rattling him dialectically." Woods emphasizes that slanging is not argument assessment; it has nothing to do with opponent's argument; it is not a reaction on his claim or proposition; and, therefore it is of no interest to logicians.

Woods refers to Hitchcock (2006) who claims that what is known as abusive *ad hominem* argument does not exist as a fallacy. It is either a legitimate argument relevant to the discussion or a pure diversionary tactic. Fallacy is usually defined as a mistake in reasoning, as an argument which looks like a real argument but is in fact deceptive. So, by making a difference between pure offensive talk and a mistake in reasoning, Hitchcock concludes that abusive *ad hominem* argument cannot be a fallacy.

> It can be a relevant attack on some aspect of an opponent's ethos that bears on the acceptability of her position. It can be purely diversionary, an attempt to divert attention from the substantive claim or argument of one's opponent. In the latter case, it is generally objectionable as a rhetorical strategy, but is not a kind of reasoning, and so not a mistake in reasoning. Hence, on the conception of fallacy with which we are working, it is not a fallacy.

Another perspective on *ad hominem* argument is provided by the pragma-dialectical approach to argumentation which treats fallacies as violations of discussion rules. The specific discussion rule that is violated with *ad hominem* argument is the freedom rule. The freedp, rule says that "no limitation whatsoever is imposed on the standpoints that may be brought forward, or equally on the persons that bring forward a standpoint or cast doubt on a standpoint" (van Eemeren et al.2009, p. 52). Unlike contemporary argumentation scholars who mostly treat *ad hominem* argument as a legitimate strategy in the right conditions, the pragma-dialectic approach always sees *ad hominem* argument as a fallacy. As a conclusion to a discussion on whether *ad hominem* argument is a fallacy, a legitimate argument, or in some cases pure diversionary tactic, it is important to emphasize one more time that each particular argument should be assessed considering the context, situation, audience, topic etc.

A helpful summary of critical questions and general problems concerning *ad hominem* argument is provided by Tindale (2007, p. 88–89):

1. An arguer concludes that a person's position is false on the basis of introducing material that questions the person's credibility. This is a case of concluding too much, since the most that can be shown is that the person's advocacy of the position is not enough to warrant believing it.

2. The features of the person's character to which the arguer draws attention are irrelevant to the position that person is advocating. This is a case of introducing irrelevant considerations.
3. In the context of a dialogue, an arguer attempts to prevent another party from advancing her view by attacking her in some way and not addressing her view. This is a case of ignoring the issue in favor of addressing the person instead.

In short, to answer the questions when, how, and why sometimes *ad hominem* arguments are considered a fallacy and sometimes a legitimate argument, it has to be said that "for some *ad hominem* arguments, the line between the cases where character or circumstances are relevant, and those in which they are not, is not always clear" (Yap, 2013, p. 103).

1.1 Classifying the Types of *Ad Hominem* Arguments

Logic textbooks define an *ad hominem* argument as a "fallacious attack in which the trust is directed, not at a conclusion, but at the person who asserts or defends it" (Copi and Cohen, 1986, p. 97). Copi and Cohen (1986, p. 97–98) also distinguish between two major forms of *ad hominem* arguments: abusive and circumstantial.

An abusive *ad hominem* argument is illustrated by a typical argument in politics: "To contend that proposals are bad or assertions false because they are proposed or asserted by 'radicals' (of the left or right) is a typical example of the fallacy abusive *ad hominem*. Abusive premises are irrelevant—but they may sometimes persuade by the psychological process of transference. The circumstantial *ad hominem* fallacy is: the irrelevant connection between the beliefs held and the circumstances of those holding it that gives rise to a mistake. An opponent ought to accept (or reject) some conclusion, it is argued fallaciously, merely because of that person's employment or nationality or other circumstances."

In addition to abusive and circumstantial *ad hominem* arguments, Tindale (2007, p. 94) describes a *tu* quoque *ad hominem* argument which is a subtype of circumstantial *ad hominem* and "shows inconsistency between what a person does and what he says, or what he said in the past and what he is proposing now." Tindale also writes about a specific type of *ad hominem* argument entitled guilt by association. Guilt by association represents an attack "based on real or alleged association that person has, weather the association is with another person, organization or way of thinking. The attack assumes that any 'guilt' that characterizes the other part of the association can be transferred to the person making the argument" (Tindale, 2007, p. 96).

Walton (2007, p. 168) writes about several types *ad hominem* arguments. Apart from direct or abusive and circumstantial, he describes a bias type of *ad hominem* argument "which is different from direct and circumstantial types and represents attack on the opponent credibility in which the proponent argues that the respondent is biased and therefore his arguments should not be taken as plausible. Bias of this sort can be shown by a number of indicators, such as having something to gain or being strongly committed to a viewpoint."

A bias *ad hominem* argument is similar to a situationally disqualifying argument and resembles a typical example from politics: "No matter what the politician says, because of his financial involvement, his argument is bound to be discredited. It may seem to follow then, that in this kind of case, the *ad hominem* argument is fallacious, because it leaves the politician no further room to argue" (Krabbe and Walton 1993, p. 82). Such arguments are often dialectically strong and rhetorically effective.

Similar to what Tindale calls Guilt by association, Walton (2007, p. 68) describes poisoning the well *ad hominem* in which "the proponent alleges that the opponent is strongly committed to some position in a rigid and dogmatic way. It is concluded that he can never be trusted to judge an argument on its merits, in an open-minded way, and will always push on his preferred position."

2 Analysis of *Ad Hominem* Arguments in Croatian Political Discourse

Corpora for the analysis were based on Croatian Parliamentary debate during the period of one year (from May 2012 until May 2013). Debates are available on the official web site of Croatian Parliament (http://itv.sabor.hr/video/) and include discussions on various topics (e.g., economic issues and budget cuts, laws on violence prevention, science and education, social issues etc.).

The main goal of this analysis was to determine which type of *ad hominem* argument appears most frequently, to examine every specific case considering the context and situation, and to determine whether it is a legitimate argument or a fallacy. The analysis also differentiated real fallacies (i.e., errors in argumentation) from pure insults which serve as rhetorical strategies in political speeches.

Zarefsky (2008, p. 318) writes about the characteristics of political argumentation with its lack of time limits, no clear ending for discussion, a heterogeneous audience, and open access: "Political argumentation is about gaining and using power, about collective decision-making for the public good, about mobilizing individuals in pursuit of common goals, about giving effective voice to shared hopes and fears."

One of the specifics of political argumentation is the importance of so called *ethotic arguments*. Persuasiveness of political speech is closely connected to a speaker's ethos. We tend to have more trust in people who are known to be honest, credible, people of good moral qualities and expertise. As Aristotle (1991, p. 38) explains in his *Rhetoric*: "There is persuasion through the character whenever the speech is spoken in such a way as to make the speaker worthy of credence; for we believe fair-minded people to a greater extent and more quickly [than we do others] on all subjects in general and completely so in cases where there is not exact knowledge but room for doubt."

It can be concluded that when a speaker is known by good character, high expertise, and admirable reputation, it will enhance the plausibility of the argument he or she advocates especially in political argumentation. Therefore, undermining a speaker's ethos is often a way to gain advantage in political discourse, especially in election campaigns. Thus, the *ad hominem* argument has crucial reasons for being a frequently occurring fallacy.

Walton (2007, p. 161) writes: "The *ad hominem*, or personal attack, argument is now highly familiar in politics, especially in the use of negative campaign tactics in elections." In short, *ad hominem* is based on drawing attention to the credibility of the speaker claiming he or she is not credible: that is, he or she is of a bad character, is biased, is not an expert, etc. If a person is not credible, his argument should not be taken as plausible.

3 Results and Discussion

3.1 *Ad Hominem* Argument as a Fallacy

A very common type of fallacious *ad hominem* argument in political discourse is what Krabbe and Walton (1993) call a *situationally disqualifying ad hominem* attack. The typical example is: a proponent (political representative of opposition in Parliament) criticizes the government for bad economic decisions, poor results in the investment policy, etc. The opponent responds with: When your party was leading the country you left nothing but debts. We are now forced to clean up after you. One even more typical response is: You had your chance when you were in power. Now, let us do our job.

This situation emerges when a politician is discredited just by belonging to a party which was previously in power. It is worth mentioning that when a party is affected by scandals, it gives opponents a good reason to criticize it. Furthermore, a bad political party reputation is used to discredit any argument form a party member. In Croatian political discourse, the strongest opposition party gained a bad reputation while its former president was in jail accused of corruption. Therefore, their criticism on the policy of a current government is disqualified due to the fact that they belong to a particular party.

A specific characteristic of this situationally disqualifying *ad hominem* is that it is always fallacious because it does not leave room for the speakers to defend themselves. For instance, when someone's expertise is in question (whether or not he or she is a qualified, educated, experienced, etc.), one can always defend himself or herself by presenting a proof of expertise. When a situationally disqualifying *ad hominem* discussion reaches its end, a politician is disqualified from any further arguing and his or her arguments are not taken into account.

Additionally, a specific type of *ad hominem* which frequently appears in Croatian political discourse is the poisoning the well type. Walton (2007, p. 163) describes it in this way: "In this type of attack, the proponent alleges that the opponent is strongly committed to some position in a rigid and dogmatic way. It is concluded that he can never be trusted to judge an argument on its merits, in an open-minded way, and will always push instead for the side of his preferred position."

The Left-wing political party in Croatia is frequently connected to the Communist Party of former Yugoslavia, and therefore even today is "accused" of being "closed-minded" and "poisoned" by the totalitarian regime and communist ideology. This is a source for the poisoning the well *ad hominem* argument, especially when social and ideological issues are discussed in Parliament. However, even the discussions on budget or education have raised ideological differences between right-wing and left-wing parties. For example, a current government (left-wing party representatives) proposes budget cuts in the Croatian Army which includes discharging the military chaplains. In their explanation, opposition representatives respond: Your actions are driven by the hatred toward the Catholic Church. You are driven by Christian phobia. What is next? Persecutions, imprisonment, and killings of priests and bishops like in 1945? A combination of an *ad hominem* argument and a slippery slope argument is a reaction to argumentation on budget cuts in the military. Similarly, during a heated discussion in Parliament on the issue of introducing sexual education as a subject in Croatian schools, left wing representatives were accused of working against Catholic heritage by introducing in elementary schools topics on homosexuals which once again signals hatred toward the Catholic Church and the love for atheism and communism.

3.2   *Ad Hominem* as Legitimate Argument

Argumentation theorists generally agree that *ad hominem* argument can be a legitimate rebuttal of argument from authority. Walton (2007: 191) writes:

> A personal attack can be a reasonable criticism of an arguer's position by showing that the concessions or commitments of that arguer are inconsistent with the propositions asserted in his argument. Some might say that such an attack is, or can be, specious because it misses the real point of looking to the external evidence and instead, concentrates on the internal relationships within the arguer's position.

For instance, if a claim is defended by an argument from authority, when claiming that a particular economic strategy is going to show results next year according to the Minister of Economy or that a particular law is going to help attract investors according to a professor of law, revealing the lack of competence and expertise of the Minister of Economy or law professor constitutes a legitimate, relevant argument. Results of the analysis of Croatian political discourse have shown that only several examples of legitimate *ad hominem* arguments appear.

When presenting the reconstruction of the Croatian Electricity Company (the largest state company) the President of the company argued that solutions presented are best based on his experience and knowledge. Response to that argument was that it reminded the public of several of his business failures.

Two of the companies he ran went bankrupt. Interestingly, his response to the criticism was: Let us be civil and let us not get personal. Rarely does anyone react to personal criticism, so it is a surprise when it happened at the wrong moment. In this case, the arguer's businesses experience, competence, and expertise are not personal but professional issues.

Another example might be seen as being ambiguous. During the discussion on the topic of sexual education in Croatian schools, one of the representatives declared: "You have always been more close to the thinking of agnostics and atheists." Of course, criticism continues with examples which put the person addressed in a position closer to atheists. This would be irrelevant if any other representative was in question, but it becomes relevant when directed to a former priest—an independent representative in Parliament. In this case, it is irrelevant for the topic of the discussion but is relevant for the credibility of the representative in general. This illustrates that even if the fallacious attack is recognized as an irrelevant piece of information, it may nevertheless detract from the credibility of the agent under attack. Yap (2012:98) writes: "The way in which it may do so is a result of unconscious bias. And the implication is that there may be certain illegitimate moves an agent can make in the course of a critical discussion which may, even if retracted, render it very difficult to return to an equitable discussion."

3.3 Abusive *ad hominem* Argument as a Rhetorical Strategy in Political Discourse

Humiliating and discrediting a political opponent is the most frequent rhetorical strategy in Croatian political discourse. Using abusive *ad hominem* arguments and using irrelevant attack on the character or competence of the opponent surface in cases when competence and character have nothing to do with the issue in question. The best example can be seen in the treatment of the former Prime Minister who was often a target of such irrelevant attacks. As an illustration, a Parliament representative says: I did not ask my question in English Prime Minister, so I am surprised that you did not understand me. How can an average person live on a minimum salary? The representative is referring to the Prime Minister's poor knowledge of the English language which was publicly demonstrated during her conversation with foreign tourists. The representative is using her lack of foreign language competence to humiliate her. The discussion was on social issues and governmental unemployment policy. Her language skills had nothing to do with issues discussed. In corpora which was analyzed, many such diversion tactics were used by the current Prime Minister and the main goal was to avoid difficult questions and to distract the opponent and public in general. An opponent asks a question: What are the results of your economic strategies? The Prime Minister answers: You have been preparing this question for four months and you are still not able to read it? Where have you been over the last four months while we were working? When was the last time you were sitting here in the Parliament? By using abusive *ad hominem*, the Prime Minister is avoiding the answer and humiliates the person who asked the question. If there was a discussion on increasing salaries or benefits for the Parliament representatives, his remarks might be important and relevant. In a discussion of the results of economic policies, they are irrelevant. There are many more examples of similar tactics the Prime Minister uses for humiliating a person: namely, a person asks a question and then the Prime Minister ignores the question itself. For example, the Prime Minister might sarcastically say: Please concentrate and read the proposal again if you are an educated man. Why let them write questions for you which you don't even understand or which I have been explaining for two hours and you still don't get it?

The analysis showed that abusive *ad hominem* arguments are not fallacies but diversionary tactics. They are not mistakes in reasoning but pure insults which are logically irrelevant to the argument or the claim itself. In that respect they are sometimes rhetorically effective but have nothing to do with arguments or argumentation. As Hitchcock (2006:3) writes: "The purely abusive *ad hominem* is either a relevant attack on the opponent's ethos in a rhetorical context or a diversionary tactic that does not involve reasoning and so is not a mistake in reasoning."

4   Conclusion

The traditional concept of *ad hominem* argument as fallacious and irrelevant attacks on the character of the speaker raises two questions. First, whether *ad hominem* can in some situations serve as relevant and legitimate arguments or whether fallacious *ad hominem* arguments exist at all. This paper tried to answer those questions and illustrate possible answers with examples from political discourse. *Ad hominem* arguments are frequent fallacies in political dis-

      © Frank & Timme   Verlag für wissenschaftliche Literatur

course because political opponents often try to diminish and degrade the ethos of their rivals. The credibility of a politician is a strong persuasive means. Govier (1993:94) defined credibility as "his or her worthiness to be believed. Normative credibility depends on a person's sincerity, honesty, and reliability. A person is normatively credible if and only if he or she is honest and is in an appropriate position to be a believable asserter of the sort of claim made." Besides credibility, an important characteristic of a politician is trustworthiness which, based on Govier (1993:94), depends on integrity, character, motivation and competence. It can be concluded that when we have reasonable doubts concerning a politician's motivation, competence, integrity, and character, we can use *ad hominem* argument in a legitimate way. However, it has to be emphasized that every particular case has to be analyzed and assessed separately taking context and situation into account. Based on several examples in Croatian political discourse, it can be concluded that abusive *ad hominem* arguments are not fallacies because they are neither argument assessments nor refutations. Rather, they are pure diversionary tactics. Trudy Govier (1995: 172) sums up the standard conception of a fallacy in the logical tradition as follows: "By definition, a fallacy is a mistake in reasoning, a mistake which occurs with some frequency in real arguments and which is characteristically deceptive." Based on the alternative view covered in this study, examples of abusive *ad hominem* arguments are not fallacies but pure slanging as a rhetorical device.

An analysis of Croatian political discourse covered in this study showed that the most frequent fallacious *ad hominem* arguments are the bias *ad hominem* and the poisoning the well arguments. To enhance the understanding of argumentation in political discourse, the final goal of this study was to make a distinction between fallacious *ad hominem* argument, legitimate *ad hominem* argument, and pure slanging as a rhetorical tactic. The author's intention was to contribute to increasing consciousness about the importance of argumentation skills in Parliamentary debate and to augmenting the culture of communication in political discourse.

References

Aristotle (1991). *On Rhetoric: A Theory of Civic Discourse* (translated George A. Kennedy). New York: Oxford University Press.

Brinton, A. (1995). "The *Ad hominem*" In: H.V. Hansen & R.C. Pinto (Eds.). *Fallacies: Classical and Contemporary Readings*. University Park; PA: Penn State University Press. 214

Copi, I.M. & Cohen, C. (1998). *Introduction to Logic*. Tenth Ed. Upper Saddle River, NJ: Prentice Hall.

Eemeren, van F.H., and Houtlosser, P. (2006). "Strategic maneuvering: A synthetic recapitulation". *Argumentation* 20: 381–392.

Govier, T. (1993). "When logic meets politics: Testimony, distrust, and rhetorical disadvantage". *Informal Logic* XV (2): 93–104.

Govier, T. (1995). "Reply to Massey". In: H.V. Hansen & R.C. Pinto (Eds.). *Fallacies: Classical and Contemporary Readings*. University Park; PA: Penn State University Press. 172–180.

Hitchcock, D. (2006). *Why there is no argumentum* ad hominem *fallacy.* http://www.humanities.mcmaster.ca/~hitchckd/adhominemissa.htm (30.06. 2013.)

Hoaglund, J. (1981). "Argumentum *Ad hominem*: Aut Bonum aut Malum?" *Informal Logic* 4, 7–9.

Johnson, R., Blair, A. (2006). *Logical Self-defense*. New York: International Debate Education Association.

Johnstone, H. (1952). "Philosophy and Argumentum *Ad hominem.*" *Journal of Philosophy* 49: 489–498.

Krabbe, E., Walton, D. (1993). "It's All Very Well for You to Talk! Situationally Disqualifying *Ad hominem* Attacks". *Informal Logic* XY.2, Spring: 79–91.

Mizrahi, M. (2010). "Take My Advice—I Am Not Following It: *Ad hominem* Arguments as Legitimate Rebuttals to Appeals to Authority". *Informal Logic*, Vol. 30, No. 4: 435–456.

Mackenzie, P.T. (1980). "*Ad hominem* and Ad Verecundiam". *Informal Logic* 3: 9–11.

Salmon, M.H. (2007). *Introduction to Logic and Critical Thinking*. Fifth Ed. Belmont, CA: Thomson Wadsworth.

Tindale, Ch. (2007). *Fallacies and Argument Appraisal*. Cambridge: Cambridge University Press

Walton, D. (2002). *Legal Argumentation and Evidence*. Pennsylvania: Pennsylvania State University Press.

Walton, D. (2006). "*Ad hominem* Argument". In *Encyclopedia of Rhetoric*. Ed. Thomas O. Sloane. Oxford University Press. The Midnight University.

Walton, D. (2007). *Media Argumentation: Dialectic, Persuasion and Rhetoric*, Cambridge: Cambridge University Press.

Walton, D. (2008). *Informal Logic A Pragmatic Approach*. 2nd ed. New York: Cambridge University Press.

Woods, J. (2007). "Lightening up on the *Ad hominem*". *Informal Logic* Vol. 27, No. 1: 109–134.

Yap, A. (2013) "*Ad hominem* Fallacies, Bias, and Testimony". *Argumentation*, Volume 27, 2: 97–109

Zarefsky, D. (2008). "Strategic Maneuvering in Political Argumentation". *Argumentation*, 22: 317–330.

Dr. Panagiotes Kontonasios, National and Kapodistrian University of Athens

From *Democratia* (δημοκρατια) to *Res Publica*: Adaptation and Evolution of Classical Rhetoric

Abstract: The study examines the adaptation and evolution of classical rhetoric. Its main purpose is to explore how Roman rhetoric emerges and enriches Ancient Greek rhetoric. Stressed here are the particular characteristics of the polity of the res publica. Also addressed is the fact that free rhetoric dominated in the early Roman polity before Rome turned to militarism. Covered in the research are Greek deliberative oratory, Roman justice and eloquence, demonstrative Roman oratory, Cicero's contional rhetoric, Greek influence from the Stoics, the Peripatetics, and the Epicureans in Roman oratory. The study concludes by linking Isocrates with the politically and culturally stabilizing possibility of a European "constitution" in modern Europe.

1 Introduction

The aim of this study is to explore the role of *democratia* (δημοκρατία) in Athens and the *res publica* of Rome in shaping rhetoric in these two city-states. Within this context, Roman rhetoric emerges as the continuity of Greek, enriching it especially thanks to the particular characteristics of the type of polity the *res publica* was from which the former emanates. The particular importance of what retrospectively might be called the "constitution" of each of these ancient democracies (in both the general course of achieving the policy objectives they set themselves and in the development of rhetorical theory and practice that followed their promotion) has been noted since antiquity (literary sources n. 1–3). In this study, I highlight the elements that led to the initial success along with the ultimate failure of the Athenian democracy and to the impressive results of the Roman *res publica*. The impressive results of the *res republica*, however, did not prevent the final fall of this culture as well. One goal here is to show their repositories to rhetoric in modern democracies. Since the democratic character of the Roman *res publica* is being disputed by many scholars, it is obvious that free rhetoric dominated in this polity before it turned into militarism. Remarks on the comparison follow.

2   Greek Deliberative Oratory

Although in Greek culture the political act was linked to political discourse since the Homeric epics (literary source n. 4), this linkage increased after the Persian Wars. The democracy of Athens was the vehicle that advanced this political tactic. The same constitution, however, in combination with the Spartan one, has been projected by Herodotus as the leading cause of the success of the Greeks in their apparently unequal struggle against the Persians (490–479 BC) (literary source n. 5). The more democratic and liberal nature of the Athenian democracy, in contrast to the more conservativism and inflexibility of Sparta, led to an outward-looking foreign policy with the ultimate objective of the union of the Greek and Mediterranean world in general under the leadership of Athens (literary sources 6 and 7).

In this context, the political power that could be offered by the Athenian *demos* raised vertically the demand for primarily deliberative rhetoric and hence for the other classes of it insofar as they were relevant to the actual political activity. Especially after the reforms of Ephialtes in 462 BC, who subtracted the political powers of the Parliament of the Supreme Court (Ἄρειος Πάγος) and transformed the constitution to pure democracy (ἄκρατον δημοκρατίαν), the scope of the application of rhetoric in public life grew even more: thereby opening the way for the sophists who promised to teach with a view to benefit all concerned with the art of persuasion and not exclusively the aristocrats (literary source n. 8).

The ablest orator of the time was Pericles himself, the leader of the Athenian democracy. That Pericles was the ablest orator is evidenced by the orations, especially the famous epitaph, that Thucydides has quoted (although not without his own intervention) in his history.[1]

It seems that the initial optimism about the effects of the substantial elimination of the Supreme Court, which at least Aeschylus did not share from the

---

1   Th. 1.140–144; 2.35–46; 2.60–64; for his method in composing the speeches in his history, see 1.22.

beginning (literary source n. 9), did not emerge from wise calculation. After Pericles, the phenomenon of populism appears in Athens: the base, the practices, and the devastating consequences of which writers like Thucydides and Plato commented (literary sources n. 10 and 11). Isocrates, Demosthenes and Aristotle also pointed out the serious problems caused in the Athenian state by this tactic, which foreshadows its decline (literary sources n. 12–15). It is, in short, the pernicious practice of πρὸς χάριν/ἡδονὴν δημηγορεῖν (*indulging rhetoric*).

That the sincere critics of the way the Athenian democracy worked were substantially right has been demonstrated clearly by the history of this State: defeat in the Peloponnesian War and loss of political sovereignty until about the middle of the 4th century BC. In this period, the domination of the Greeks of the North (namely, the Macedonians) who had no democracy led inevitably to the decline of deliberative oratory. The rise of Rome, which occurred rapidly, transferred the decision-making centers to Roman civic bodies: the People's Assemblies, the Senate, and the Magistrates—especially the Consuls.

3   The Roman Backround

3.1   Forensic Orations

The way justice was awarded in Rome[2] contributed decisively to the cultivation of eloquence. Every Roman citizen could bring to a court of justice anyone else, regardless of social status.[3] The judicial system, however, was based on patron-client relationship, the former delivering the speech in favor of the latter before the court or the popular assembly. The Judges, in the former case, were juries from the senatorial and/or equestrian orders under the chairmanship of the *praetor*. The meetings took place in the *forum Romanum*, where typically a large crowd, the *corona*, watched and affected, by its reactions, the outcome of the cases and were therefore taken seriously by the orator.[4] This, of course, was an absolute necessity for the trials before the people. From the

---

2   Millar (1998) 41: "Around them, as was essential to both the public character of the occasion and the nature of the oratory that needed to be deployed, was a shifting crowd (*corona*) of spectators, whose reactions played a vital part in the course of the case." For a full discussion, see Alexander (1990); cf. idem (2006) 236–55.

3   David (2006) 427.

4   Cic. *Brut.* 290; cf. Alexander (2007) 104–5.

mid-second century BC, since the institution of *quaestiones perpetuae* (i.e., the permanent criminal courts) met publicly, forensic oratory in Rome evolved and acquired great political power.[5]

3.2   Demonstrative Orations

Demonstrative oratory[6] was supported in Roman funeral speeches, the *laudationes funebres*, for men or even women of ambitious families, and some evidence-speeches on the character of important persons without specific rhetorical demands. In a best case scenario, according to Cicero, this class could be used only for the training of the orator, as to make him effective in the other two classes, the forensic and the deliberative.[7] Nevertheless, an eminent Roman with such an oration could demonstrate publicly his generation and its prominent members, even if it was only one such member, thereby earning the admiration and favor of the people towards him[8] and passing the political message (especially to the youth) that virtue, which coincides with bravery (*virtus*), is something that the Romans never forget.[9]

3.3   Deliberative Orations

The *genus deliberativum* in Rome had necessarily, due to its constitution, two main application areas: the Senatus and the *contiones*[10] (literary source n. 16)—a term that, depending on the context, meant "an informal public meeting called by an office holder, a speech delivered at such a meeting, or the actual crowd attending it".[11] The presentation of the differences between these two civic bodies of the *res publica* is not the subject of this treatise. What, however, challenges us here is to identify the *eloquentia popularis*, to demonstrate its real role in the *res publica* and thus the nature of this polity, which others, the majority, declared aristocratic or oligarchic and the minority declared almost

....

5   David (2006) 422 and 426–7.

6   For a full discussion, see Rees (2007).

7   Cic. *Orat.* 37.

8   Suet. *Jul.* 6; cf. Millar (1984) 10; idem (1989) 149; idem (1998) 75; Hölkeskamp (2000) 218.

9   Plb. 6.52.11–54. 3.

10   David (2006) 422–6.

11   Millar (1995) 111.

democratic.[12] In particular, rhetoric of the *contiones* will help us to understand further the role of this specific audience in the *res publica*. This audience is characterized as special not in the sense that it was popular but in the sense of its different role in the system of government compared to that of the Greek, eminently the Athenian, crowd—which essentially gave birth to rhetorical theory.

In this sense, the Senate was also a special audience, as it was a political body with a particular function. The difference, however, is obvious: the Senate is not disputed by anyone as a state institution which was crucial to the operation of the government. On the contrary, its role has made many scholars characterize the system of government as being purely aristocratic or oligarchic. Not quite the same for the *contio*: most scholars underestimate its role and consider it rather formal than substantial, arguing that orators before it did nothing other than pretending.[13] For a serious democratic process to operate, according to this logic, not even a simple discussion can be made.

4   Greek Influence

We have to look for the beginning of the thread, as already pointed out, in Athens and not without good reason. Cicero very clearly notes it in his *Brutus*. According to him, the orator, the ideal *orator*, first began his course in the historical process in this very town (literary source 17). Thus Roman rhetoric is officially presented as the continuation of Greek rhetoric. The reason vivid Greek rhetoric became in essence a simple lesson at the various Greek schools was purely political: the absence of independent political action in a state with democratic governance had led to decline the means to achieve political objectives, namely rhetoric (literary source 18).

This observation is crucial for the history of rhetoric, which essentially starts from Athens and continues in Rome, where there was already a relevant background due to the nature of the Roman constitution[14] (literary source 19). The overall evolution of Roman rhetoric before and after its very fruitful con-

12   For the relevant discussion, see Hölkeskamp (2010) 1–11.

13   13Morstein-Marx (2004) 241–78; according to the writer, the speakers from the *rostra* (i.e., the platform in the *forum* decorated with the warships' rams captured during the victory at Antium in 338 BC) supported the interests of the ruling class.

14   Culpepper Stroup (2007) 23.

tact with Greek rhetoric, from the perspective of Cicero, absolutely documents the importance of rhetoric in the operation of the *res publica* before the latter acquired the universality, which in turn emerges precisely as a natural consequence of this operating mode of Roman polity, as illustrated by the comment of Polybius in literary source n. 2 we saw above.

Therefore, the Greek influence, made possible because of the *res publica*, is inevitable for Rome, which finds in this very influence those cultural elements that make it a particular state in conjunction with its own merits. Within these contexts, since the mid-second century BC, the Greek embassies to Rome have given excellent examples of senatorial oratory. The speeches of these ambassadors were translated for many decades into Latin[15]. However, from 81 BC, according to Valerius Maximus[16], the speeches began to be read out directly in Greek. Historically, this is a very important fact. At about the same time, during the mid-second century BC, in Rome the "Circle of Scipio" was created and included Tiberius Gracchus, Mucius Scaeola, and Polybius. Polybius was a hostage in Rome under the influence of the Stoic philosopher Panaetios.[17] From the Circle of Scipio emerged Roman *humanitas* based on philosophy, rhetoric, and grammar.[18] From this point on, we are talking about the beginning of the forcible entrance of Greek rhetoric in Rome with huge political implications for the very operation of the *res publica*. For Cicero, this can be explained very well by the fact of the expansion of Roman rule. Roman rule created the right conditions for the cultivation of rhetoric and great interest in it in the more dynamic part of Roman society: namely, the youth of the Roman ruling class (literary source n. 20), just as it happened gradually in the case of Athens after its victories in the Persian Wars and the spread of its hegemony. Of course, the application of rhetoric in political practice also requires common points among the polities of these two ancient cities and puts in a precarious position those who argue that Rome was merely a form of oligarchy.

There was another, though, very serious aspect of Greek influence in Roman intellectual life in general and especially in the rhetoric expressed by Greek philosophical schools. Romans who could afford them attended them with zeal, and without necessarily being aristocrats, mainly from the last pre-

---

15   Gel. 6.14.9.

16   V. Max. 2.2.3.

17   Long (1990²) 335.

18   Albrecht (2000³) 552.

Christian century onward. For my thoughts on this issue, I defer once again to Cicero.

4.1   The Stoics

For Cicero, oratory based on Stoic rhetorical theory is inappropriate for convincing a popular audience, partly because it is profound and artful and partly because of the lack of style suitable to such an audience: that is, a style with digressions, loose and varied (literary source n. 21). In contrast, the style of the Stoics is better suited to dialectic than rhetoric. Hence, it is more useful argumentative accuracy than analysis. Since its style is so short and dense, a popular audience is not able to attend to it.

This, however, did not deter a Stoic, L. Aelius Stilon (*Lucius Aelius Stilo*), from writting speeches for others. Stilon had no ambition to be an orator.[19] A noteworthy example of a Stoic orator was *Quintus Aelius Tubero*, praetor of 123 BC. He had the characteristics of an implacable opponent of G. Gracchus. He possessed politically important qualities but he had a rough, uncultivated, and wild verbal style.[20] The Stoics of Rome then were not effective orators, with the sole exception of Cato the Younger, who excelled both in *sententia senatoria* and in *contiones*. Thus, Brutus in the homonymous Ciceronian treatise characterizes his eloquence as supreme.[21] Especially before the Senate, the Stoic characteristics of Cato's rhetoric are particularly evident.

4.2   The Academics and the Peripatetics

In his comments on the Academy and the Peripatetic school, Cicero notes that these two philosophical schools, especially the latter[22], are more appropriate than others for the education of the orator, if he were to rely solely on a particular school. Regretfully, the style these schools cultivated was too free and loose, elements that exceed the tolerable limits for trials and for a popular audience (literary source 22). As for the relationship between these two schools of philosophy addressing the education of the orator, Cicero believes

....

19   Cic. *Brut.* 206.

20   Cic. *Brut.* 117.

21   Cic. *Brut.* 118.

22   Cic. *Brut.* 119.

that no one should expect that he will be an orator by studying in any single school. Yet, he emphasizes that it is impossible for anyone to become an orator without them. The model orator here is Demosthenes. While Demosthenes appears to have an academic philosophical education, he was above all an orator thanks to the style of his orations. In short, the style of his orations was more suitable for rhetoric than for philosophy.

4.3   The Epicureans

Epicurean philosophy was regarded generally as unfit for rhetoric by Cicero. As a fine example of an Epicurean orator, Cicero presents *Titus Albucius*. *Titus Albucius* lived around the late second century BC. He studied Greek so intensely, and particularly the Epicurean culture, that he could be considered a true Greek.[23] His orations, though, are of little value. Because Epicurean philosophy, as is also evidenced by the Greek case, did not favor one's participation in politics and eloquence (literary source n. 23).

5   Deliberative Oratory in Rome: Ἀγὼν λόγων *in the Senate*

In the Senate, there used to take place a full *ἀγὼν λόγων* (that is, a confrontation of antithetical orations[24]). These orations were peculiar because of the special nature of this civic institution of the *res publica*. Subsequently, it is not surprising that there were orators skilled only in this kind of rhetoric and not necessarily in another. The main feature of this rhetoric, as can be reasonably understood, is brevity. The existence of many speakers, time pressure, and the highly, in many cases, educated senators necessarily and strictly limited the speaker thematically. Thus, senatorial oratory suggests the kind of oratory we find in the Royal Council of Xerxes, as presented by Herodotus, rather than that before the Athenian *demos*. An example of senatorial oratory can be found in Sallust[25]; it pertains to the discussion that took place in the Senate on the fate of the arrested conspirators in the case of Catiline (*Lucius Sergius Cati-*

---

23 Cic. *Brut.* 131.

24 For a comprehensive discussion, see Ramsey (2007) 122–35; cf. Millar (1984) 15–6; Dyck (2008) 12–3. For the meaning of the phrase *ἀγὼν λόγων*, cf. Romilly (1988) 180 and 215–7.

25 Sal. *Cat.* 51–2.

lina). Although there were more than two speakers, Sallust quotes only the orations of Caesar (*Gaius Iulius Caesar*) and Cato the Younger (*Marcus Porcius Cato Uticensis*), as the most representative of two opposing proposals. In both these orations, we find the same individual rhetorical questions seen, however, from different angles.

These two orations have the characteristics of a contradiction (ἀντιλογία) as we know it from Thucydides: the second oration achieves a complete reversal, step by step, of the positions taken by the orator in the first one.[26] Their differences with the contradictions included in Thucydides' history are determined by the different target audiences. Ergo, the structure of the above orations is adapted to the time pressure and to the necessity of the orators' thematic limitation. For these reasons there is virtually no *exordium* and *peroratio*, in the classic sense of the terms, in either oration. Rather, we have short introductions and recommendations respectively. Almost all of the content of the two orations is dedicated to argumentation, and the main effort of the orators is to focus on rebuttal. The rhetorical issues used by both speakers, as already mentioned, are common and revolve around philosophy, history, and especially the *mos maiorum*—as opposed to the "demoralization" which presumably occurs in the speakers' era. Politically, these three elements are of great importance. Especially the last point seems to have had a decisive impact on the minds of the senators and to have shaped their final decision according to Cato's proposal. To the extent that Cato managed to harmonize his speech with this element, he also managed to secure a positive vote of the Senate for his proposal.[27] In terms of its success, his oration, contrary to the oration of Caesar, utilizes the element of πάθος (*the rousing of emotions*), yet not excessively. Avoiding accentuation of passion is certainly due to an audience that relied mainly on logic to decide. Nonetheless, it seems that without the touch of passion as well, things would prove difficult for the orator in *sententia senatoria*.

---

26 For the characteristics of this kind of rhetorical confrontation in Thucydides' history, see Romilly (1988) 179–238.

27 Sal. *Cat.* 53.

5.1   Ἀγὼν λόγων in the *Contio*

In the contio, in which all Roman citizens and whoever else was in the *forum*[28] could be involved, often a true confrontation of antithetical orations was conducted, especially in cases of legal proposals (*rogationes*), usually by the tribune of the plebs, who had the power to convene (*potestas contionandi*) this kind of assembly.[29] In the beginning of this procedure, the proposer (*auctor*) read the law and then delivered a speech to support it—or vice versa. As the chairman of the assembly, the proposer of the law had the exclusive right to designate who else would speak in the *contio* and in what order. Usually, however, he called persons who supported and others who opposed the law so that the public would be informed comprehensively about it. But if the specific magistrate omitted to present, in a reasonable degree, the opposite view, anyone else with *potestas contionandi* could convene additional *contiones* to propound his position to the audience. Of course, the supporters of the *rogatio* could act similarly.[30] At the end of the procedure, there was a vote in the *comitia centuriata* or in the *comitia tributa*.[31] Of course, only the citizens voted at this time.

There was an opportunity for the orators to have a real confrontation which the *contiones* provided mainly in legislative initiatives, and the assembly was generally suitable for political struggles waged before the people by the Roman politicians on all current issues. In short, the *contio* was a real rhetorical school, especially for younger orators, as Cicero informs us (literary source n. 24).

5.2   Cicero's Contional Rhetoric and Oratory

My basic thesis is that democratic political speeches before the crowd, as Cicero's *contiones* were, involve a largely democratic polity basis. However, its final image, as revealed by the specific speeches, directly or indirectly, must be formed only after thorough research: research that strive to highlight the causes that Cicero regarded as critical to the decline of the paternal republic. Par-

....

28   Taylor (1966) 62; Thompson (1978) 23–7. Women also could attend a *contio* or even deliver a speech there on very special occasions though; see Culhman (2004) 156; App. *BC* 4.32–3.

29   Pina Polo (1995) 205–6.

30   Pina Polo (1995) 207–8

31   For these two assemblies of *populus Romanus*, see Taylor (1966) 6–7 and 59–106; Brennan (2004) 62; North (2006) 261–3.

ticular emphasis is placed on populism as an independent factor which shocks and ultimately overthrows a democratic constitution and transforms it into totalitarianism.

The detailed discussion of this subject leads to conclusions that confirm my initial thesis. Consequently, Roman rhetorical theory (developed by Cicero in full form, emanating from the kind of oratory the *res publica* as a peculiar political system required, and being enriched by the achievements of corresponding Greek) concerns itself eminently with oratory before the crowd. This finding brings us already to a democratic basis for government: the ground in which that kind of oratory took place. Because of the coexistence of primarily deliberative oratory before the Senate, Roman rhetorical theory introduces a transverse incision in already existing Greek theory, reciprocating somehow the enrichment it received from the latter. The constant dialectic of oratory with a humanist and practical political philosophy, at the level we see it in Cicero, is the most important element that constitutes the renewal of classical rhetoric, as we knew it from the Greeks.

This renewal, nevertheless, was made possible partly thanks to the type of polity of the *res publica* and partly because of the dominant political position of Rome. Rome was, after Athens and on a much larger scale, the second major power in the Mediterranean in which free oratory was honored.

Subsequently, the historical valuation of Roman deliberative oratory by Cicero himself takes place on the basis of two trends: two trends whose collision course is identified clearly from the era of Gracchi onwards.[32] The first trend is prone to demagogy, which varies from a once true but often hypocritical interest in the problems of the people to a tendency toward hegemonic self-concentration—a power that violates what we might retrospectively call "the Constitution of the *res publica*". The second trend, which essentially existed since the time of Tarquinius's overthrow, is pro-constitutional and aims to maintain the status of the *res publica* (i.e., the distinct roles of the people, the Senate and the magistrates in it) and its manifest democratic base, as the offices, which were open to all citizens, and to the laws of the state (i.e., almost the whole of the political power eminating from the universal right to vote).

The fullest expression of the second trend in Roman deliberative oratory is Cicero's *contiones*. The key elements of this kind of oratory, which according to Cicero is the true *eloquentia popularis*, are: the strong theoretical back-

....

32 It seems that this is exactly the key point in the treatise *Brutus*.

ground on which it is built, the deep philosophical education of the orator and, most importantly, the orator's faith in the constitutional form of the *res publica*. Consequently, the oratory that promotes this idea does not allow itself the divisive phraseology that opposes one political body to another one, such as the people against the Senate or vice versa. Yet, this oratory is directed against individual persons or groups that threaten the constitutional order. So, through his contiones, Cicero does not try to tie the people to the chariot of the Senate. Rather, Cicero addresses one of the three factors, a factor whose role is crucial for the proper operation and adjustment of the paternal polity to the current political developments. The *contiones* addressed the real master of the political life of the *res publica*, namely the *populus Romanus*. The *populous Romanus* was the bearer of the democratic and liberal ethos and generated from the idea of *libertas*, the strength of individual rights, social mobility, and democratic oratory.

Cicero's *contiones* clearly show that the demagogues (the *populares*) systematically denounced the Senate, championed ostensibly the popular interests, were regarded as hypocrite politicians, and were possessed of undemocratic attitudes. Moreover, it was them who actually abolished the position of the Senate and the people in the *res publica*, decomposed it, and eventually transmogrified it into militarism.

Both Cicero's contional oratory and rhetoric present the Roman *res publica* as the stopover of the development of democracy between ancient Athenian and modern parliamentary democracies. The role of the Senate was the key element which worked as a safety valve between the demagogues and the people, the lack of which in the Athenian δημοκρατίαν made Isocrates complain. The contribution of this political system to history has, therefore, colossal ramifications. The Roman political system spawned a model constitution. The constitution united democratically the best elements of other polities and provided the conditions for the greatest inner peace within freedom. What followed was a reasonable expectation that by the necessary strengthening and deepening of institutions and individual rights, there would be a parallel reinforcement of true democratic consciousness and per capita cultivation of the citizens. Freedom could not be degraded to an arbitrariness that would endanger the structure of the constitution by the independent corrosive factor of populism.

The rapid spread of the modern parliamentary democracy, elsewhere with more or less success noted in our time, shows that this type of government is the most effective political vehicle for humanity to meet the challenges of the future. Parliamentary democracy accords better than any other alternative to empower citizens to feel jointly responsible for shaping the future. If Cicero saw current developments, he would surely feel significantly vindicated for his political struggle, a struggle which made him truly a martyr of democracy.

6 Conclusion

In sum, it seems that political oratory and rhetoric are meaningful only in dynamic democracies. Through rhetorical means, democracies must maintain citizen vigilance in order to enhance basic principles and institutions to keep their citizens safe from external and internal hazards. Demagogy is seen by Cicero as the most dangerous to democracy. In today's world, the real European integration could and should be promoted through the democratic principles of rhetoric in order to isolate from the continental body the risk of modern demagogy, a demagogy heavily responsible currently for creating the political crisis primarily and the economic crisis secondarily. Consequently, it seems obvious that the most powerful weapon of modern Europe to combat any risk of endangering democracy would, and hopefully will be, the establishment of a single European Constitution, especially if we are to believe Isocrates (literary source n. 25).

Literary Sources

1) *ἔστι γὰρ ψυχὴ πόλεως οὐδὲν ἕτερον ἢ πολιτεία, τοσαύτην ἔχουσα δύναμιν ὅσην περ ἐν σώματι φρόνησις. αὕτη γάρ ἐστιν ἡ βουλευομένη περὶ ἁπάντων, καὶ τὰ μὲν ἀγαθὰ διαφυλάττουσα, τὰς δὲ συμφορὰς διαφεύγουσα. ταύτῃ καὶ τοὺς νόμους καὶ τοὺς ῥήτορας καὶ τοὺς ἰδιώτας ἀναγκαῖόν ἐστιν ὁμοιοῦσθαι, καὶ πράττειν οὕτως ἑκάστους οἵαν περ ἂν ταύτην ἔχωσιν.*

Isoc. VII. 14

[For the soul of a state is nothing else than its polity, having as much power over it as does the mind over the body; for it is this which deliberates upon all questions, seeking to preserve what is good and to ward off what is disastrous; and it is this which of necessity assimilates to its own nature the laws, the public orators and the private citizens; and all the members of the state must fare well or ill according to the kind of polity under which they live.]

Trans. George Norlin, Ph.D., LL.D. Cambridge, MA, Harvard University Press; London, William Heinemann Ltd. 1980.

2) *τὴν δὴ τοιαύτην, ὥσπερ εἶπον, κυρίαν ἐποίησαν τῆς εὐταξίας ἐπιμελεῖσθαι, ἢ τοὺς μὲν οἰομένους ἐνταῦθα βελτίστους ἄνδρας γίγνεσθαι, παρ᾽ οἷς οἱ νόμοι μετὰ πλείστης ἀκριβείας κείμενοι τυγχάνουσιν, ἀγνοεῖν ἐνόμιζεν· οὐδὲν γὰρ ἂν κωλύειν ὁμοίους ἅπαντας εἶναι τοὺς Ἕλληνας ἕνεκά γε τοῦ ῥᾴδιον εἶναι τὰ γράμματα λαβεῖν παρ᾽ ἀλλήλων.*

Isoc. VII. 39

[Such, then, as I have described, was the nature of the Council which our forefathers charged with the supervision of moral discipline—a council which considered that those who believed that the best citizens are produced in a state where the laws are prescribed with the greatest exactness were blind to the truth; for in that case there would be no reason why all of the Hellenes should not be on the same level, at any rate in so far as it is easy to borrow written codes from each other.]

3) *μεγίστην δ᾽ αἰτίαν ἡγητέον ἐν ἅπαντι πράγματι καὶ πρὸς ἐπιτυχίαν καὶ τοὐναντίον τὴν τῆς πολιτείας σύστασιν.*

Plb. 6.2.9

[As the most important reason for success and failure, one should consider the *composition* of the constitution.]

  © Frank & Timme   Verlag für wissenschaftliche Literatur

4) *… μύθων τε ῥητῆρ᾽ ἔμεναι πρηκτῆρά τε ἔργων.*

Hom. Il. I 443

[You have to be both an effective orator and fighter.]

5) *Ἀθηναῖοι δὲ πρὸς μὲν Ἀλέξανδρον ὑπεκρίναντο τάδε. ʿκαὶ αὐτοὶ τοῦτό γε ἐπιστάμεθα ὅτι πολλαπλησίη ἐστὶ τῷ Μήδῳ δύναμις ἤ περ ἡμῖν, ὥστε οὐδὲν δέει τοῦτό γε ὀνειδίζειν. ἀλλ᾽ ὅμως ἐλευθερίης γλιχόμενοι ἀμυνεύμεθα οὕτω ὅκως ἂν καὶ δυνώμεθα.…᾽*

Hdt. 8.143.1

[But, to Alexander, the Athenians replied as follows: "We know of ourselves that the power of the Mede is many times greater than ours. There is no need to taunt us with that. Nevertheless, in our zeal for freedom we will defend ourselves to the best of our ability…."]

English translation by A. D. Godley. Cambridge. Harvard University Press. 1920. – cf. idem 7.135.3.

6) *…καὶ ἄλλους οὐκέτι ὕστερον ἐξέπεμψαν οἱ Λακεδαιμόνιοι, φοβούμενοι μὴ σφίσιν οἱ ἐξιόντες χείρους γίγνωνται, ὅπερ καὶ ἐν τῷ Παυσανίᾳ ἐνεῖδον, ἀπαλλαξείοντες δὲ καὶ τοῦ Μηδικοῦ πολέμου καὶ τοὺς Ἀθηναίους νομίζοντες ἱκανοὺς ἐξηγεῖσθαι καὶ σφίσιν ἐν τῷ τότε παρόντι ἐπιτηδείους.*

Thuc. 1.95.7

[…and the Lacedaemonians did not send out any to succeed them. They feared for those who went out a deterioration similar to that observable in Pausanias; besides, they desired to be rid of the Median war, and were satisfied of the competency of the Athenians for the position, and of their friendship at the time towards themselves.]

Thucydides. The Peloponnesian War. London, J. M. Dent; New York, E. P. Dutton. 1910.

7) *ἐπλεύσαμεν ἐς Σικελίαν πρῶτον μέν, εἰ δυναίμεθα, Σικελιώτας καταστρεψόμενοι, μετὰ δ᾽ ἐκείνους αὖθις καὶ Ἰταλιώτας, ἔπειτα καὶ τῆς Καρχηδονίων ἀρχῆς καὶ αὐτῶν ἀποπειράσοντες. εἰ δὲ προχωρήσειε ταῦτα ἢ πάντα ἢ καὶ τὰ πλείω, ἤδη τῇ Πελοποννήσῳ ἐμέλλομεν ἐπιχειρήσειν, κομίσαντες ξύμπασαν μὲν τὴν ἐκεῖθεν προσγενομένην δύναμιν τῶν Ἑλλήνων, πολλοὺς δὲ βαρβάρους μισθωσάμενοι καὶ Ἴβηρας καὶ ἄλλους τῶν ἐκεῖ ὁμολογουμένως νῦν βαρβάρων μαχιμωτάτους, τριήρεις τε πρὸς ταῖς ἡμετέραις πολλὰς ναυπηγησάμενοι, ἐχούσης τῆς Ἰταλίας ξύλα ἄφθονα, αἷς τὴν Πελοπόννησον πέριξ πολιορκοῦντες καὶ τῷ πεζῷ ἅμα ἐκ γῆς ἐφορμαῖς τῶν*

πόλεων τὰς μὲν βίᾳ λαβόντες, τὰς δ' ἐντειχισάμενοι, ῥᾳδίως ἠλπίζομεν
καταπολεμήσειν καὶ μετὰ ταῦτα καὶ τοῦ ξύμπαντος Ἑλληνικοῦ ἄρξειν.

Thuc. 6.90.2–3

[We sailed to Sicily first to conquer, if possible, the Siceliots, and after them the Italiots also, and finally to assail the empire and city of Carthage. [3] In the event of all or most of these schemes succeeding, we were then to attack Peloponnese, bringing with us the entire force of the Hellenes lately acquired in those parts, and taking a number of barbarians into our pay, such as the Iberians and others in those countries, confessedly the most warlike known, and building numerous galleys in addition to those which we had already, timber being plentiful in Italy; and with this fleet blockading Peloponnese from the sea and assailing it with our armies by land, taking some of the cities by storm, drawing works of circumvallation round others, we hoped without difficulty to effect its reduction, and after this to rule the whole of the Hellenic name.]

8) *παρὰ δ' ἐμὲ ἀφικόμενος μαθήσεται οὐ περὶ ἄλλου του ἢ περὶ οὗ ἥκει. τὸ δὲ μάθημά*
ἐστιν εὐβουλία περὶ τῶν οἰκείων, ὅπως ἂν ἄριστα τὴν αὑτοῦ οἰκίαν διοικοῖ, καὶ περὶ
τῶν τῆς πόλεως, ὅπως τὰ τῆς πόλεως δυνατώτατος ἂν εἴη καὶ πράττειν καὶ λέγειν.

Plat. *Prot.* 318e–319a

[Whereas, if he applies to me, he will learn precisely and solely that for which he has come. That learning consists of good judgement in his own affairs, showing how best to order his own home; and in the affairs of his city, showing how he may have most influence on public affairs both in speech and in action.]

Translated by W.R.M. Lamb. Cambridge, MA, Harvard University Press; London, William Heinemann Ltd. 1967.

9) *τοιόνδε τοι ταρβοῦντες ἐνδίκως σέβας*   700
 ἔρυμά τε χώρας καὶ πόλεως σωτήριον
 ἔχοιτ' ἄν, οἷον οὔτις ἀνθρώπων ἔχει,
 οὔτ' ἐν Σκύθῃσιν οὔτε Πέλοπος ἐν τόποις.
 κερδῶν ἄθικτον τοῦτο βουλευτήριον,
 αἰδοῖον, ὀξύθυμον, εὑδόντων ὕπερ   705
 ἐγρηγορὸς φρούρημα γῆς καθίσταμαι.

A. *Eu.* 700–6

[Stand in just awe of such majesty, and you will have a defense for your land and salvation of your city, such as no man has, either among the Scythians or in Pelops'

      © Frank & Timme   Verlag für wissenschaftliche Literatur

realm. I establish this tribunal, untouched by greed, worthy of reverence, quick to anger, awake on behalf of those who sleep, a guardian of the land.]

English translation by Herbert Weir Smyth, Ph. D. in two volumes. 2. Eumenides. Herbert Weir Smyth, Ph. D. Cambridge, MA. Harvard University Press. 1926.

10) οἱ δὲ ὕστερον ἴσοι μᾶλλον αὐτοὶ πρὸς ἀλλήλους ὄντες καὶ ὀρεγόμενοι τοῦ πρῶτος ἕκαστος γίγνεσθαι ἐτράποντο καθ᾽ ἡδονὰς τῷ δήμῳ καὶ τὰ πράγματα ἐνδιδόναι.

Thuc. 2.65.10

[With his (Pericles') successors it was different. More on a level with one another, and each grasping at supremacy, they ended by committing even the conduct of state affairs to the whims of the multitude.]

11) ΣΩ. ἔλεγές τοι νυνδὴ ὅτι καὶ περὶ τοῦ ὑγιεινοῦ τοῦ ἰατροῦ πιθανώτερος ἔσται ὁ ῥήτωρ.
ΓΟ. καὶ γὰρ ἔλεγον, ἔν γε ὄχλῳ.
ΣΟ. οὐκοῦν τὸ ἐν ὄχλῳ τοῦτό ἐστιν, ἐν τοῖς μὴ εἰδόσιν; οὐ γὰρ δήπου ἔν γε τοῖς εἰδόσι τοῦ ἰατροῦ πιθανώτερος ἔσται.
ΓΟ. ἀληθῆ λέγεις.

Plat. *Gorg.* 459a 1–6.

[Socrates: You were saying just now, you know, that even in the matter of health, the orator will be more convincing than the doctor.
Gorgias: Yes, indeed, I was—meaning, to the crowd.
Socrates: "To the crowd" means "to the ignorant?" For surely, to those who know, he will not be more convincing than the doctor.
Gorgias: You are right.]

12) οἱ γὰρ κατ᾽ ἐκεῖνον τὸν χρόνον τὴν πόλιν διοικοῦντες κατεστήσαντο πολιτείαν οὐκ ὀνόματι μὲν τῷ κοινοτάτῳ καὶ πραοτάτῳ προσαγορευομένην, ἐπὶ δὲ τῶν πράξεων οὐ τοιαύτην τοῖς ἐντυγχάνουσι φαινομένην, οὐδ᾽ ἣ τοῦτον τὸν τρόπον ἐπαίδευε τοὺς πολίτας ὥσθ᾽ ἡγεῖσθαι τὴν μὲν ἀκολασίαν δημοκρατίαν, τὴν δὲ παρανομίαν ἐλευθερίαν, τὴν δὲ παρρησίαν ἰσονομίαν, τὴν δ᾽ ἐξουσίαν τοῦ πάντα ποιεῖν εὐδαιμονίαν, ἀλλὰ μισοῦσα καὶ κολάζουσα τοὺς τοιούτους βελτίους καὶ σωφρονεστέρους ἅπαντας τοὺς πολίτας ἐποίησεν.

Ἰσοκ. VII. 20

[For those who directed the state in the time of Solon and Cleisthenes did not establish a polity which in name merely was hailed as the most impartial and the mildest of governments, while in practice showing itself the opposite to those who lived un-

der it, nor one which trained the citizens in such fashion that they looked upon in-
solence as democracy, lawlessness as liberty, impudence of speech as equality, and
licence to do what they pleased as happiness, but rather a polity which detested and
punished such men and by so doing made all the citizens better and wiser.]

13) τὴν δὲ κατὰ τὴν ἀξίαν ἕκαστον τιμῶσαν καὶ κολάζουσαν προῃροῦντο, καὶ διὰ ταύτης
ᾤκουν τὴν πόλιν, οὐκ ἐξ ἁπάντων τὰς ἀρχὰς κληροῦντες, ἀλλὰ τοὺς βελτίστους καὶ
τοὺς ἱκανωτάτους ἐφ᾽ ἕκαστον τῶν ἔργων προκρίνοντες. τοιούτους γὰρ ἤλπιζον
ἔσεσθαι καὶ τοὺς ἄλλους, οἷοί περ ἂν ὦσιν οἱ τῶν πραγμάτων ἐπιστατοῦντες.

Ἰσοκ. VII. 22

[And preferring rather that which rewards and punishes every man according to his
deserts, they governed the city on this principle, not filling the offices by lot from all
the citizens, but selecting the best and the ablest for each function of the state; for
they believed that the rest of the people would reflect the character of those who
were placed in charge of their affairs.]

14) πέπεισμαι γὰρ ἐξ ὧν παρὼν καὶ ἀκούων σύνοιδα, τὰ πλείω τῶν πραγμάτων ἡμᾶς
ἐκπεφευγέναι τῷ μὴ βούλεσθαι τὰ δέοντα ποιεῖν ἢ τῷ μὴ συνιέναι. ἀξιῶ δ᾽ ὑμᾶς, ἂν
μετὰ παρρησίας ποιῶμαι τοὺς λόγους, ὑπομένειν, τοῦτο θεωροῦντας, εἰ τἀληθῆ λέγω,
καὶ διὰ τοῦτο, ἵνα τὰ λοιπὰ βελτίω γένηται· ὁρᾶτε γὰρ ὡς ἐκ τοῦ πρὸς χάριν
δημηγορεῖν ἐνίους εἰς πᾶν προελήλυθε μοχθηρίας τὰ παρόντα.

Dem. III. 3

[For what I have seen and heard convinces me that most of your chances have es-
caped us rather from a disinclination to do our duty than from a failure to understand it. I must ask you to bear with me if I speak frankly, considering only whether
I am speaking the truth, and speaking with the object that things may go better in
the future; for you see how the popularity-hunting of some of our orators has led us
into this desperate predicament.]

Demosthenes with an English translation by J. H. Vince, M.A. Cambridge, MA,
Harvard University Press; London, William Heinemann Ltd. 1930.

15) ἡ μὲν οὖν τῶν Ἀρεοπαγιτῶν βουλὴ τοῦτον τὸν τρόπον ἀπεστερήθη τῆς ἐπιμελείας.
μετὰ δὲ ταῦτα συνέβαινεν ἀνίεσθαι μᾶλλον τὴν πολιτείαν διὰ τοὺς προθύμως
δημαγωγοῦντας.

Arist. *Ath.* 26

    © Frank & Timme   **Verlag für wissenschaftliche Literatur**

[In this way, the Council of the Areopagites was deprived of the superintendence of affairs. After this, there came about an increased relaxation of the constitution, due to the eagerness of those who were the leaders of the people.]

Translated by H. Rackham. Cambridge, MA, Harvard University Press; London, William Heinemann Ltd. 1952.

16) *Alterum, quod remoto foro, contione, iudiciis, senatu statuisti oratorem in omni gene-re sermonis et humanitatis esse perfectum.*

Cic. de Orat. 1.35

[Secondly, your pronouncement that, even if we take no account of the forum, of popular assemblies, of the court of justice, or of the Senate-house, the orator is still complete over the whole range of speech and culture.]

Translated by E. W. Sutton, Harvard University Press: Cambridge, Massachusets, William Heinemann Ltd. 1959.

17) *In quam cum intueor, maxime mihi occurrunt, Attice, et quasi lucent Athenae tuae, qua in urbe primum se orator extulit primumque etiam monumentis et litteris oratio est coepta mandari.*

Cic. Brut. 26

[And, when I think of Greece, it is especially your Athens which comes to my mind, Atticus, and shines out like a beacon. It was there that the orator first made his appearance, and there first that oratory began to be consigned to written records.]

Translated by G. L. Hendrickson, Harvard University Press: Cambridge, Massachusets, William Heinemann Ltd. 1962.

18) *…illi {Graeci} nati in litteris ardentesque his studiis, otio vero diffluentes, non modo nihil acquisierint sed ne relictum quidem et traditum et suum conservaverint.*

Cic. de Orat. 3.131

[Whereas the Greeks, though born in a world of literature and enthusiasts for these studies, are yet demoralized by sloth and have not only made no further acquisitions but have not even preserved their own heritage that came down to them.]

19) *Videmus item paucis annis post reges exactos, cum plebes prope ripam Anionis ad tertium miliarium consedisseteumque montem, qui Sacer appellatus est, occupavisset,*

M. Valerium dictatorem dicendo sedavisse discordias eique ob eam rem honores amplissimos habitos et eum primum ob eam ipsam causam Maximum esse appellatum. Ne L. Valerium quidem Potitum arbitror non aliquid potuisse dicendo, qui post decemviralem invidiam plebem in patres incitatam legibus et contionibus suis mitigaverit.

Cic. Brut. 54

[We see again a few years after the expansion of the kings, when the plebeians had withdrawn to the third milestone near the Anio, and occupied the eminence which thereafter was called the Sacred Mount, that Marcus Valerius the dictator appeased their discord by his eloquence. For this success we learn that the most distinguished honours were conferred upon him, and that for the same reason he was the first to be called Maximus. Nor do I think that Lucius Valerius Potitus was without capacity as an orator, since by his laws and public harangues he succeeded in assuaging the passions of the common people against the patricians after the odium aroused by the rule of the decemvirs.]

20) *Nam posteaquam, imperio omnium gentium constituto, diuturnitas pacis otium confirmavit, nemo fere laudis cupidus adulescens non sibi ad dicendum studio omni enitendum putavit.*

Cic. de Orat. 1.14

[For as soon as our world-empire had been established and an enduring peace had assured us leisure, there was hardly a youth, athirst for fame, who did not deem it his duty to strive with might and main after eloquence.]

21) *…in Stoicis; quorum peracutum et artis plenum orationis genus scis tamen esse exile nec satis populari adsensioni accommodatum.*

Cic. Brut. 114

[…of the Stoics. Their style of oratory is acute and systematic, as you know, but meagre and not well suited to winning the assent of a popular audience.]

22) *…liberior et latior quam patitur consuetudo iudiciorum et fori.*

Cic. Brut. 120

[…too free and discursive for the usage of court and forum.]

23) *…minime aptum ad dicendum genus.*

Cic. Brut. 131

[…a creed ill-suited to public speaking.]

24) *Tum P. Sulpici in tribunatu cotidie contionantis totum genus dicendi penitus cogno-vimus.*

Cic. *Brut.* 306

[Publius Sulpicius was tribune at that time and addressed the people almost daily, so that I came to know his style thoroughly.]

25) *ἦν δὲ μεταβάλωμεν τὴν πολιτείαν, δῆλον ὅτι κατὰ τὸν αὐτὸν λόγον, οἷά περ ἦν τοῖς προγόνοις τὰ πράγματα, τοιαῦτ᾽ ἔσται καὶ περὶ ἡμᾶς· ἀνάγκη γὰρ ἐκ τῶν αὐτῶν πολιτευμάτων καὶ τὰς πράξεις ὁμοίας ἀεὶ καὶ παραπλησίας ἀποβαίνειν.*

Ἰσοκ. VII. 78

[But, if we effect a change of polity, it is evident by the same reasoning that such conditions of life as our ancestors enjoyed will come about for us also; for from the same political institutions, there must always spring like or similar ways of life.]

References

Albrecht, M. von (2000³). *Ιστορία της ρωμαϊκής λογοτεχνίας*, τόμ. 1, μετάφρ. Ε. Αρχοντοπούλου κ.ά., Ηράκλειο (in German: *Geschichte der Römischen Literatur*, I, München 1994²).

Alexander, M. C. (1990). *Trials in the Late Roman Republic, 149 BC to 50 BC*, Toronto.

Alexander, M. C. (2006). "Law in the Roman Republic", in Rosenstein, N., and Morstein-Marx, R. (eds.), 236–55.

Brennan, T. C. (2004). "Power and Process under the Republican 'Constitution'", in Flower H. I. ed., 31–65, Cambridge.

Culham, P. (2004). "Women in the Roman Republic", in Flower H. I. ed., 139–59, Cambridge.

Culpepper Stroup, S. (2007). "Greek Rhetoric Meets Rome: Expansion, Resistance, and Acculturation", in Dominik, W., and Hall, J. (eds.), 23–37, Blackwell.

David, J.-M. (2006). "Rhetoric and Public Life", trans. R. Morstein-Marx and R. Martz, in Rosenstein, N., and Morstein-Marx, R. (edd.), 421–38, Blackwell.

Dominik, W., and Hall, J. (edd.) (2007). *A Companion to Roman Rhetoric*, Blackwell.

Dyck, A. R. (ed.) (2008). *Cicero: Catilinarians*, Cambridge.

Flower, H. I. (ed.) (2004). *The Cambridge Companion to the Roman Republic*, Cambridge and New York.

Hölkeskamp, K.-J. (2000). "The Roman Republic: Government of the People, by the People, for the People?", review of Millar, F. (1998), *SCI* 19, 203–33.

Hölkeskamp, K.-J. (2010). *Reconstructing the Roman Republic: an ancient political culture and modern research*, trans. H. Heitmann-Gordon, Princeton, New Jersey.

Long, A. A. (1990²). *Η ελληνιστική φιλοσοφία: Στωικοί, Επικούρειοι, Σκεπτικοί*, μετάφρ. Στ. Δημόπουλος και Μ. Δραγώνα-Μονάχου, Αθήνα (in English: *Hellenistic Philosophy*, Duckworth).

Millar, F. (1984). "The Political Character of the Classical Roman Republic, 200–151 BC", *JRS* 74, 1–19.

Millar, F. (1989). "Political Power in Mid-*Republica*n Rome: Curia or Comitium?", *JRS* 79, 138–50.

Millar, F. (1995). "Popular Politics at Rome in the Late Republic", in *Leaders and Masses in the Roman World: Studies in Honor of Zvi Yavetz*. Malkin, I., and Rubinsohn, Z. W. (edd.), 91–113, Leiden, New York and Cologne.

Millar, F. (1998). *The Crowd in Rome in the Late Republic*, Ann Arbor.

Millar, F. (2002). *Roman Republic in Political Thought*, Hanover and London.

Morstein-Marx, R. (2004). *Mass Oratory and Political Power in the Late Roman Republic*, Cambridge.

North, J. (2006). "The Constitution of the Roman Republic", in Rosenstein N. and Morstein-Marx R. edd., 256–77, Blakwell.

Pina Polo, F. (1995). "Procedures and Functions of Civil and Military contiones in Rome", *Klio* 77, 203–16.

Ramsey, J. T. (2007). "Roman Senatorial Oratory", in Dominik W. and Hall J. eds., 122–35, Blackwell.

Rees, R. (2007). "Panegyric", in Dominik, W., and Hall, J. (eds.), 136–48, Blackwell.

Romilly, J. de (1988). *Ιστορία και λόγος στον Θουκυδίδη*, μετάφρ. Ε. Ι. Κακριδή, Αθήνα (in French: *Histoire et Raison chez Thucydide*, Paris, 1967).

Rosenstein, N., and Morstein-Marx, R. (edd.) (2006). *A Companion to the Roman Republic*, Blackwell.

Taylor, L. R. (1966). *Roman Voting Assemblies*, Ann Arbor.

Thompson, C. (1978). *To the Senate and to the People: Adaptation to the Senatorial and Popular Audiences in the Parallel Speeches of Cicero*, diss., Ohio State University.

Dr. Erik Bengtson, Uppsala University

The Concept of *Doxa* in the European Reinvention of Rhetoric

Abstract: Since the birth of rhetorical theory in ancient Greece the discussion of rhetoric has been intertwined with a discussion of knowledge. Hence, rhetoric has been situated in a struggle between doxa and episteme, where doxa is understood as belief or opinion and episteme is understood as true knowledge. In the American field of Speech/Communication, a reawakened discussion of rhetoric and knowledge has become known as the "Rhetoric as epistemic" debate. In the European reinvention of rhetoric, the subject did not, in the same way, take the form of a structured discipline, but instead grew as a research interest within other disciplines. This does not, however, mean that Europe lacks a modern, insightful and explicitly rhetorical discussion on the relationship between rhetoric and knowledge—the fact is quite the opposite. This study describes how the classical concept of doxa is used in the European reinvention of rhetoric. This is done through a comparative discussion of the different alignments of doxa developed by Roland Barthes, Pierre Bourdieu, and Martin Heidegger and developed further by Ruth Amossy, Mats Rosengren, and Robert Hariman. The comparison highlights central issues in the formation of a modern rhetorical view on knowledge: such as the relationship between a critical and a constructive view on doxa, the relationship between substance and appearance, and the relationship between structures of power and human agency. The concept of doxa is shown to be a fertile focal point for a transnational discussion of rhetoric and knowledge related to the classical rhetorical tradition as well as the relatively modern tradition of continental philosophy.

The birth of rhetorical theory in ancient Greece has been described as founded on a conflict between *doxa* and *episteme*, or between the opinion of rhetorical knowledge and the truths of philosophical knowledge.

This article describes how the concept of *doxa* has been used by Martin Heidegger, Roland Barthes and Pierre Bourdieu to formulate a view on knowledge—and also how these views have been further developed by subsequent and more explicitly rhetorical thinkers such as Robert Hariman, Ruth Amossy and Mats Rosengren.

The aim is not to deepen the understanding of any one of these highly individual thinkers, but to better formulate the foundations of their views and frame them as part of conceptual discussion with one another despite their historical distance. Through this process I hope to formulate an understanding of different alignments of the concept of *doxa* and present a modern discussion of rhetoric and knowledge rooted in the tradition of continental philosophy.

The discussion of *doxa* in the work of Heidegger is closely related to his search for the meaning of Being; in that context *doxa* is given a central role in explaining the human position. Heidegger's understanding of *doxa* has been linked to Husserl, but his explicit historical reference is to a pre-Socratic understanding of the concept. Heidegger does not ally himself with the early rhetorical theorists, but describes Plato and the sophists as equally to blame for the reduction of *doxa* to expression of opinion.

For Heidegger beings should not be understood as objects in themselves—instead Being lies in the aspects that are shown and comprehended. Truth (or *Aletheia*) for Heidegger is not correspondence between the spoken word and a reality—instead truth is a foundational happening when beings appear, when they come into Being by stepping out of concealment.

The concept of *doxa* for Heidegger means both the outward characteristics that someone shows and the esteem in which they are held by others; it is both "Aussehen" and "Ansehen". *Doxa* also carries more negative connotations, such as superficial appearance or unsupported opinion. This negative view is based on an idea about a false or distorted showing of aspects and a false apprehension of these aspects.

Heidegger states that *doxa* is false because it hides its mechanisms and presents itself as apparent. Heidegger also describes *doxa* and *aletheia* as different types of *logos*, where *logos* is not rational thinking but a combination of "discourse" and the process of "gathering" and "structuring".

Aletheia is when the process of gathering also becomes the process of revealing. *Doxa* on the other hand is understood as the discourse that conceals and covers-up Being. Heidegger states that the revealing discourse must turn away from all mere recitation. Doxa is the mindless repetition of that which is already accepted while *aletheia* is a creative language that reveals the essence of Being

It is clear that Heidegger despises both the blind fanaticism of epistemic truth and the ignorant masses, who in his own analogy passively accept what they are told like dogs. The ideal human position for Heidegger is the faculty to make decisions regarding beings based on awareness of the processes of concealment and unconcealment.

The writings of Heidegger presents a highly interesting setting for a philosophical conversation on *doxa*. From a rhetorical perspective his view lacks an idea of the active rhetoricist—for Heidegger the human position is primarily a hermeneutic position. His writings on *doxa* also lack an explicit theory of the socialization of knowledge. Even though his mentioning of collective identities such as Western *Dasein* or his statements about the influence of our prior line of sight, implies an awareness of the social aspect of Being, it is far from the emphasis on the social situation that characterize much of contemporary and ancient rhetorical theory.

In contrast, the starting point for Robert Hariman in his discussion of *doxa* is completely different from that of Heidegger. Hariman writes from within an American field of rhetorical studies, and his article on *doxa* should be understood as a part of the lively discussion in said field on the relevance of rhetoric and on the relationship between rhetoric and knowledge.

Hariman imports—but also transforms—Heidegger's perspective on *doxa*. He agrees with Heidegger that *doxa* is characterized by the concealing of its own mechanisms and that *aletheia* is a discourse that reveals these mechanisms—but the position of the critic described by Hariman is very different form the questioning *Dasein* described by Heidegger.

The main difference between their theories of *doxa* is the emphasis and lack of emphasis on the social dimension. Heidegger does not formulate a sociology of *doxa*, but presents *Dasein* as a hermeneutic position. Hariman, in contrast, emphasizes *doxa* as social and as related to power. Where Heidegger discusses how meaning is created through structuring Hariman specifies that this structuring process works through attributions of status, and specifically by a normative structuring related to the positions of center and margin that according to Hariman exist in every society.

This interpretation of the Heideggerian idea of creating meaning by gathering and structuring makes the approach of Hariman an interesting platform for the practice of rhetorical criticism, but it also makes it very different from the thought of Heidegger. When Hariman describes *doxa* as "intersubjective" this implies that the social arena is the constitutive field, but Heidegger's thinking could instead be interpreted as focused on the relationship between a human Dasein and other beings that are not necessarily human or at all capable of apprehension.

Harriman's *doxa* theory could be described as a rhetorical and sociological shift in relation to Heidegger. Hariman proposes that a rhetorical theory focused on status and power could be used to situate claims on being in social discourse. He also mentions the constitutive force of rhetoric—the possibility of going beyond hermeneutic interpretation and doing real work on *doxa* through reclassification.

Barthes uses the word *doxa*, but his explicit historical reference is to the Aristotelian concept of *endoxa*. The central move in Barthes' take on *doxa* is to adapt the Aristotelian concept and use it to understand contemporary mass culture. This use of the term is influenced by Flaubert's critic of bourgeois stupidity and a critic of ideology and mass communication influenced by Marx.

From classical rhetoric Barthes picks the idea of *doxa* as "public opinion", "the probable" and "ideas shared by the majority". *Doxa* is both the starting point of rhetorical argumentation and the judge who decides its effectiveness. "The probable" in Barthes interpretation is not at all concerned with statistical probability, but rather with widespread acceptability. It has been noted that Barthes description of *doxa* and his dichotomy between opinion and knowledge is more close to Plato's view—than the views of Aristotle which he claims to discuss. The Platonian understanding of *doxa* makes for an easier fit with modern mass culture—which, according to Barthes, is mainly concerned with stereotypes and widespread beliefs.

Barthes describes modern mass communication as a corrupted and diffuse version of ancient rhetoric. These two practices of language belong to different eras but they are linked together by their focus on *doxa*. Barthes is fascinated by rhetoric, but he is in search of something new—a linguistic practice that could replace rhetorical language and a theory that could replace rhetorical theory.

Central to Barthes' early writings is the close connection between language and *doxa*. *Doxa* is seen as a parasite on language, a metaphorical viral entity that is spread through the practice of symbolic communication. The focus of Barthes is not on the author behind the rhetoric—rather he tends to either describe language as the active force producing *doxa*—or *doxa* as the power, enforcing itself on language and individuals.

In his autobiography it becomes clear that Barthes views the struggle with *doxa* as a personal struggle—an individual fight against both the stupidity that lurks within himself and the cultural myths that enforce themselves on him through mass culture. The early Barthes put's the focus on dispelling rhetoric—the later Barthes instead focus on liberating the reader by making reading a play with meaning rather than a passive accepting of the dominant rhetoric.

In relation to Heidegger, Barthes share the negative assessment of *doxa*—and especially the understanding of it as both false and as mindless repetition. Their ideal of a liberating critical position is formulated differently but it is built on the same negative judgment of those who passively accept the *doxa* as presented.

Ruth Amossy describes two traditions of doxic thinking within French thought. The first tradition—where Barthes is a main figure, is a tradition of criticism in the footsteps of Plato. The second tradition constitute a constructive turn—where *doxa* is not condemned as stupid or manipulative but neutrally described as a fundamental part of human language. Amossy proposes that we should go back to the thinkers of the first tradition and explore how we could make use of their theories in a constructive way.

Compared to Barthes' approach, Amossy's view on *doxa* constitutes a shift in several ways. The valuation shifts from negative—to neutral or even positive. *Doxa* is described as a prerequisite for intersubjectivity and a source for communicative effectiveness. This shift also changes the nature of academic work on *doxa*—from a politically driven critique to a scientifically and linguistically oriented analysis of discourse.

Barthes has a focus on "the text", which is kept by Amossy, but the active rhetor gets a stronger position within her thought. *Doxa* becomes a tool that can be used in discourse.

The structuralist focus on ideology as a system from the early Barthes is abandoned by Amossy. Instead she allies herself with the later writings of Barthes, where he finds *doxa* in the fragments and refuse to put them in an integrated whole.

Amossy dismisses the ontological question on the essence of *doxa* and poses the pragmatic question on how to do things with *doxa*. Her point is that to understand *doxa* we must study how it is used in language, because it is given form through language.

In the thinking of Pierre Bourdieu the concept of *doxa* seems to include both a certain kind of knowledge and the order that produces this knowledge.

Doxa is the experience where the natural and the social world appears as self-evident, this happens through misrecognition of the limits of cognition. *Doxa*, according to Bourdieu, is a mechanism of concealment that tends to conserve the pre-existing power structure. *Doxa* is the universe of the truly undiscussed and undisputed; a realm that has to be understood in contrast to the realm of argumentation.

Seen in relation to Barthes and Amossy, Bourdieu shifts focus from the structure of language to the power of social relations. For Bourdieu mere semiotics is not enough, instead we must study the social conditions for the production and reception of messages. The power does not lie within language, but rather in the extra-linguistic mechanisms, structures and resources that empower it.

Both Barthes and Amossy tend to see *doxa* as that which is not said explicitly, but Bourdieu takes this a step further and claims that *doxa* shouldn't be understood as representation (or false representation) at all. The power of *doxa*, according to Bourdieu, lies within the accepted systems and mechanisms; it is the undiscussed which is often transferred directly through bodies, akin to the practical knowledge of the worker. Bourdieu describes it with an emphasis on the negative as "bodily submission, unconscious submission, which may indicate a lot of internalized tension, a lot of bodily suffering".

Both Bourdieu and Amossy ally themselves with Austin in focusing on speech as acts rather than on language as an object, but where Amossy seems to uphold the idea of an active rhetorician *using* language to achieve certain goals, Bourdieu questions the individual subject and describes our dispositions to act in certain ways as constituted by a social tradition. To follow Bourdieu in thinking about language and *doxa* is to consider the extra-linguistic social conditions and power structures—and to direct our gaze toward all that which is taken for granted—that which is never heard or said.

Bourdieu is critical of the dichotomy, which can be found in the Marxist tradition, between those who are aware and those who are not. The social world does not, according to him, revolve around the conscious/unconscious axis, but instead work through practices and mechanisms.

The thinking of Bourdieu is at the same time closely related to all the other theorists discussed, yet remains completely different. Perhaps its most problematic characteristic for this comparative study is that Bourdieu uses the term *doxa* to imply a stricter meaning that does not make distinctions along the same lines as any of his counter-theorists. The thinking of Bourdieu could thus function as a dialogic partner for any of the other thinkers, but to describe the other approaches with the terminology of Bourdieu *doxa* as has to be combined with other terms.

The starting point for Mats Rosengren's analysis of the term is a deconstruction of the dichotomy between *doxa* and *episteme*. His main idea, linked to Protagoras' *homo mensura*-statement, is that all knowledge is *doxa*—because all knowledge is human. Rosengren proposes that to better understand Protagoras notion of man as the measure of all things, we must acknowledge that *logos*, as both language and thought, is the tool that humans use when measuring the world. This move sidesteps the definition of the human being, but still emphasizes that humans are social beings and that our identities, worlds and practices as thinking and speaking beings are constantly overlapping and changing.

Rosengren's project is to formulate a theory of knowledge based on *doxa* rather than *episteme*. For him Rhetoric becomes a tool that can be used to study *doxa*, but not only from the position of the observer, it is instead a tool to actively manipulate *doxa* through displacements, adjustments and refigurations. *Doxa* is thus understood as in constant change and constant migration.

The concept of *doxa* in the writings of Rosengren is a broad term; it includes both the conscious opinions which are expressed through language and the unformulated fields of knowledge that we take for granted. He emphasizes the importance of language in structuring our sensations and perceptions and our very ability to perceive talk and think; but he also states that *doxa* is not only discursive, but includes all our abilities. As well as linguistically structured knowledge it includes emotional values and predispositions to act in certain ways in relation to different symbols and situations. *Doxa* also, according to Rosengren, includes the individual, social, historical and discursive situation and cannot be understood separate from power structures.

Rosengren combines a linguistic understanding of *doxa*, as the one Amossy makes, with an understanding of the extra-linguistic functions described by Bourdieu—and connects this to a philosophical discussion on what it means to be in the world.

When it comes to the potential for strategic human action Rosengren could be described as occupying the middle ground between the idea of an active rhetorician and an emphasis on the coercive force of tradition and social conditions. He stresses the importance of social conditioning, but describes the possibility of choices and the creation of alternative ways of acting from a starting position formed by the past.

To study *doxa* in the spirit of Rosengren is not just to study linguistics but to study the human position as a social and physical being placed in a world of traditions and structures, and to recognize that humans can create meaning and act through other means than the formulation of words.

This *discussion of doxa has merely scratched the surface of the complex and dynamic field of study,* but as I have argued this kind of comparative study exposes some important characteristics of the contemporary European rebirth of rhetorical study.

It exposes how the rhetorical theory of our days is a reformulation of a pluralistic rhetorical heritage to contemporary ends, within the existing traditions of academic thought.

This comparative approach also turns the limelight on important questions and conflicts that lie within any contemporary understanding of rhetorical knowledge. It raises questions such as whether the human position is socially determined or open to political activity, of whether rhetorical knowledge is something positive or negative, and it asks whether contemporary rhetorical theory focus on language and text—or perhaps include a broad understanding of what it is to be human, picked up from sociology and philosophy? Lastly, it poses the question of whether the scholar of rhetorical studies be an interpreter and revealer of rhetoric or an active *rhetorician* transforming our vocabulary and *doxa.*

It is clear that the different thinkers in this study approach the concept from different positions and with different purposes—but we still find common threads of meaning: including the idea of *doxa* as widespread beliefs, as something repeated, as concealment and as a knowledge constituted by our positioning as social beings, rather than through correspondence to a specific reality.

These common threads of meaning exemplify one of the beauties of contemporary rhetorical studies—that disparate and highly creative thinkers might be united in a common field, as it is their position as reformulators of a pluralistic rhetorical heritage that unites them and thus makes them suitable for comparison.

When looking at these six thinkers we can also see a general shift from the first generation to the second generation of thinkers; from Heidegger to Hariman, from Barthes to Amossy and from Bourdieu to Rosengren. This shift

constitutes a rhetorical turn in the way that the latter generation of thinkers
has a more positive view of *doxa* and how they emphasize the active *rhetorician* to a higher degree than their forerunners do. This shift confirms
Amossy's idea of a constructive turn within the study of *doxa*, even though the
thinkers studied here, with the exception of Barthes, are not included in her
own work.

References

Amossy, Ruth (2002). "Introduction to the Study of *Doxa*", *Poetics Today*, 23(3), 369–
394.

Amossy, Ruth (2002). "How to Do Things with *Doxa*: Toward an Analysis of Argumentation in Discourse", *Poetics Today*, 23(3), 465–487.

Barthes, Roland (1970). "L'ancienne rhétorique: Aide-mémoire", *Communications* 16,
172–229.

Barthes, Roland (1975). *Roland Barthes*. Paris: Seuil.

Bourdieu, Pierre (1972). *Esquisse d'une théorie de la pratique précédé de Trois études
d'ethnologie kabyle*, Genève, Droz.

Hariman, Robert (1986). "Status, marginality, and rhetorical theory", *Quarterly Journal
of Speech*, vol. 72, 38–54.

Heidegger, Martin (1953). *Einführung in die Metaphysik*. Tübingen: Niemeyer.

Rosengren, Mats (2002). *Doxologi: en essä om kunskap*. Åstorp: Rhetor.

Rosengren, Mats (2012). *Perception, Cave Art and Knowledge*, Palgrave MacMillan,
London.

Dr. Richard Fiordo, University of North Dakota

Richards' Non-Aristotelian "New" Rhetoric: Grounds for a Microscopic Rhetoric and a Macroscopic Hermeneutic

Abstract: Much commentary on Richards seems to miss the point of his creative theoretical endeavors in rhetoric, semantics, hermeneutics, and criticism. Attacks on Richards' output tend to work from a premise of groundless and foolish perfectionism toward which Richards never worked. Fortunately, supportive commentary shows Richards in the favorable light of rhetorical history in which he so richly deserves to be seen. As an imaginative wordsmith, Richards generated a new rhetoric deserving of increased conceptual praise. His development of a microscopic rhetoric is based on semantics and advances toward a macroscopic hermeneutic or general system of interpretation. Seeing rhetoric as the "study of misunderstanding and its remedies" and a "philosophic inquiry into how words work in discourse," Richards also established himself in general semantics. Overall, Richards' pivotal non-Aristotelian and anti-Aristotelian contributions to rhetoric and hermeneutic are presented. Featured in the study are his iconic notions in communication of a counterdiscursive orientation, a semantic triangle, remedies for misunderstanding, and comparison fields.

1   Overview

A minority of commentary on Ivor Armstrong Richards' works seem to fall short of the glory of God, academic excellence, and acceptable notions of the "new" rhetoric. Preoccupied with serving the scholarly critical function of the devil's advocate, much commentary on Richards fails to serve the function of the angel's advocate (Fiordo, 2011). Much of the destructive commentary rests on assumptions that are neither relevant nor germane to Richards' creative development of rhetorical, critical, and philological theories. The less reasonable and destructive commentary on Richards' works tends to erect a philosophical and ideological scenario that they assert Richards' should have perfected but failed to perfect. The logical groundlessness of those with the austere commentary embarrass those with the more reasonable or constructive commentary on Richards' works: that is, the commentary with little or no prejudicial expectations of a rhetorical entelechy operating in Richards' theorizing. To assume that Richards had a theoretical agenda based on a telic contract with his less reasonable commentators is, or approaches, absurdity. As a reconstructive rhetorical theorist and critic, Richards did his best to originate ideas he believed were worthy of his acumen at any given time. Yet, both the destructive and constructive commentary on Richards' thought (Hyman, 1948; Black, 1949; Nichols, 1963; Schiller, 1969; Hayakawa, 1970; Hayakawa, 1970; Enholm, 1976; Hardy, 1978; Needham, 1982; Russo, 1982; Watson, 1996; Browne, 2000; Korzybski, 2000; Foss, Foss, & Trapp, 2002; Griffin, 2009; Haslam, 2011) deserve the honor of being a part of a robust dialectic striving to remedy any misunderstanding pertaining to what Richards generated with respect to rhetoric.

Negative commentary on Richards charges him with the undermentioned: for being a rhetorical poseur who makes ostentatious claims that are unwarranted, for merely calling attention to the conspicuous reality that scientific discourse is not the only form of communication, for falling short of his grandiose ideal of cultural hygiene, for lowering himself to the simplistic teaching of English and reading in public schools, for failing to develop a truly efficient system of teaching that coordinates the skills of the teacher to instruct and the student to learn, for using vague and undefined terms in his theorizing, for excoriating traditional rhetoricians ignorantly and unjustifiably, for seldom providing evidence to support his claims, for being inconsistent and superficial and wordy in his theorizing and writing, for overstressing scientific ideas and symbolism in his notion of rhetoric and criticism, for fruitless to fraudulent shifting from his critical theories of rhetoric and meaning in his earlier years to a focus on basic English education, for disappointing the world of rhetoricians and critics by leaving no thorough or noteworthy critical work demonstrating his rhetorical and interpretative and critical principles to posterity, and for falling significantly short of developing a rhetorical theory with the magnitude of effect hoped for and desired by rhetorical scholars (Hyman, 1948; Black, 1949; Schiller, 1969; Fisher, 1971; Enholm, 1976; Hardy, 1978; Needham, 1982; Russo, 1982; Watson, 1996; Foss, Foss, & Trapp, 2002).

Positive commentary on Richards honors him with the succeeding: for leaving a visible and favorable footprint on rhetoric and criticism, for advancing terms useful to the discipline of communication (such as, tone and intention, tenor and vehicle, or emotive and referential language), for challenging obsolete assumptions (such as, meanings being in people rather than in words, words having only one meaning, and confusing a word for a thing), for promoting his novel and complementary paradigm of a microscopic rhetoric, for drawing from related disciplines to elaborate his views on rhetoric, for accenting the linkages among language and mind and empirical realities, for disseminating hermeneutic ideas on interpretative criteria to rhetorical and literary critics, for conceiving rhetoric as a means to diagnose and remedy social disorders (in contrast to teaching students of rhetoric how to score points in a debate), for striving to improve human communication and life by reducing verbal issues and focusing on substantive ones through education in general and the humanities in particular, for following his exploratory and creative scholarly tendencies to improve on a time-bound rhetorical tradition, for sharing ideas with science and philosophy and education to the betterment of rhetoric and criticism, for daring to improve on the delusion of rhetorical perfection traditional rhetoricians promulgated, for arguing that a new rhetoric can solve and resolve the problems discourse causes and enhance the interpretation of discourse so that misunderstandings can be minimized or abolished in human communication (Hyman, 1948; Nichols, 1963; Enholm, 1976; Hayakawa, 1972; Hardy, 1978; Russo, 1982; Watson, 1996; Browne, 2000; Korzybski, 2000; Foss, Foss, & Trapp, 2002).

As a creative and imaginative wordsmith rhetorical theorist, Richards generated a new and novel rhetoric. He created a perspective, if not a paradigm, that incorporated, and to a degree augmented, the related disciplines of semantics, semiotics, general semantics, sociolinguistics, psycholinguistics, stylistics, literary criticism, argumentation, and language learning—especially English. As a theoretician extraordinaire of a new semantic and microscopic rhetoric and hermeneutic, as mentioned above, Richards has been criticized for his theoretical shortcomings almost as much as appreciated for his theoretical contributions. The emphasis of some of his critics appears to be more on what he failed to explain to the academic world and how he fell short in his grand intentions in rhetorical studies more than what he actually delivered through his philosophical reflections on language studies. In this study, noting what his commentators declare are his theoretical shortcomings and accomplishments, we focus on his non-Aristotelian and anti-Aristotelian (both of which can be seen as his un-Aristotelian) orientation to rhetoric and hermeneutics (or interpreting discourse and communication) and stress his ideas that contribute positively to a complementary system of rhetoric and interpretation. Richards' linguistic work on teaching and learning English has implications that need to be reconsidered in light of computer technologies for intercultural communication.

Overall, this study respects Richards' anti-Aristotelian and non-Aristotelian contributions to rhetoric, hermeneutics, communication, semantics, general semantics, meaning, criticism, education, and societal transformation. Richards' new wordsmith slant on rhetoric shows that his un-Aristotelian microscopic approach to rhetoric can serve as a basis for developing a macroscopic hermeneutic. His innovative construction, knowingly and willingly or not, of a new rhetoric operates in relation to the non-Aristotelian system of general semantics and constitutes the central idea of this study. The study links the classical role of Hermes from Ancient Greek mythology to the rhetorical adjustment of communicators to messages and their interpretation. As the helpful to deceitful messenger of the gods, Hermes of Ancient Greek mythology may be the perfect icon for the rhetoric Richards espouses. And, the study demonstrates a system for interpreting words and symbols in diverse contexts.

2   Richards' Anti-Aristotelianism and Non-Aristotelianism

I.A. Richards has long been honored within the tradition and discipline of general semantics, a non-Aristotelian approach to language, symbolism, communication, and behavior (Hayakawa, 1990; Korzybski, 2000; Levinson, 2006). Richards' rhetoric and theory of meaning overlaps significantly with the non-Aristotelian approach language and symbols pursued in general semantics. While officially general semantics is a non-Aristotelian system, some general semantics writers assume more of an anti-Aristotelian attitude. Richards might be seen as vacillating between non-Aristotelian and anti-Aristotelian attitudes toward rhetoric. Exerting himself rhetorically to remedy misunderstanding, Richards also incorporates a critical un-Aristotelian hermeneutic into his rhetorical and critical systems (Richards, 1924, 1929, 1936, 1955; Ogden and Richards, 1946).

Long after Richards commented on the limitations of the ephemeral treatment of traditional rhetoric in academic circles, teachers of rhetoric until today still attempt to draw tight lines between so-called informative and persuasive speeches. Such teachers of rhetoric seem to live by a confused philosophy

      © Frank & Timme   Verlag für wissenschaftliche Literatur

of as if. In the case of teaching rhetoric, they teach as if Richards never wrote a critical word about rhetoric and instruction in it. Many have not had the pleasure of taking a course from Professor Kenneth Andersen of the University of Illinois – Urbana. Anderson (1972, 1974, & 1978) favored the concept of persuasion over the concept of communication when he argued that human interaction in general leaned toward persuasion with perhaps only trivial transactions in special contexts being predominantly, or even exclusively, communicative or informative.

In March of 2014, a long-time professor of spoken rhetoric with over-whelming traditionalist leanings informed us that a particular student's speech, by the fictional and arbitrary definitions of this particular instructor, was informative and not persuasive. A step into the traditional past Richards and Andersen critiqued is alive and imposing in the teaching of spoken rhetoric as demonstrated by this traditional instructor of rhetoric. The instructor's comments suggest a material line drawn in the sand of discourse—a line, of course, nowhere to be witnessed or measured. Even today, the traditional shortcomings Richards decried manifest themselves. Will the limited and marginally conscious contemporary traditionalist rhetorician ever be expand-ed? We will have to see how much rhetorical enlightenment surfaces among tradition bound rhetoricians. Maybe the progressive rhetorical theory of Rich-ards will allow traditionalist rhetoricians to see the bright blue sky of an un-Aristotelian rhetoric.

Beginning with Richards' non-Aristotelian perspective that is consistent with general semantics, Richards' anti-Aristotelian sentiments will also be reported. Note that although there is little reason to believe that Richards dis-liked Aristotle as a philosopher or as a person, he was likely frustrated by those who followed Aristotle with such an unscientific, unprogressive, and time-bound attitude. His animosity, in short, targeted mostly Aristotelians who followed Aristotle and never challenged Aristotle ideologically or theoretically in a fundamental manner. Simplistic and narrow-minded assumptions in the teaching of rhetoric today surface too frequently. As an amiable heretic, Rich-ards fortunately did not suffer the Inquisitional consequences of Giordano Bruno for voicing divergent views.

Along with the general semanticists, Richards abided by and contributed to the following content from general semantics. General semantics entails an empirical, commonsense, and scientific discipline that deals with language and symbols that offering deliverance from the world of illusion and self-delusion through a generalized scientific orientation to experience and life. In addition, general semantics entails a process-oriented and problem-solving system that helps people improve their evaluation and understanding of the world and consequently make more intelligent decisions. General semantics involves a perspective that teaches people how to deal efficiently with their capacity to abstract: that is, make selections or note highlights from the world of experience. Abstracting, or selecting from the world of observation, depends on many factors: for example, one's biological constitution, emotional temperament, intelligence, education, cultural and linguistic habits, et cetera (Korzybski, 2000; Kodish & Kodish, 2001; Fiordo, 2011a & 2011b; Hayakawa, 2013).

Insofar as Richards accepts the following list of general semantics concepts and views, he joins the non-Aristotelian zone of general semanticist in his formation of a new rhetoric. Richards and the general semanticists, for the most part, respect the following empirical scientific principles and premises: namely, a) that as many problems as possible should be solved through the scientific method; b) that a map represents a territory but is not the territory; c) that when a conflict occurs between a map and a territory, the territory should serve as the base for problem-solving; d) that words are like maps of territories; e) that accurate mental maps produce sane and healthy thinking and communicating while inaccurate mental maps produce "unsane" or insane and unhealthy thinking and communicating; f) that sane people depend more on the territory than on the map while "unsane" people depend more on the map than on the territory; g) that when used, the linking verb "is" should be treated with care and might best, when possible, be dropped in favor of active verbs; h) that we cannot know all there is to know about anything and we cannot say all there is to be said about something; i) that no two things are identical, technically speaking; j) that all things are in process; k) that the world and life are complex; l) that things change in degree constantly over time; m) that thinking in terms of degrees rather than in terms of either-or is preferred; n) that facts, inferences, and judgments are different and should be distinguished with care; o) that we have semantic reactions to words with some reactions being instantaneous and risky while other reactions being delayed and preferred; p) that humans are a time-binding form of life and consciousness that connects, for better or for worse, with former generations through religious, scientific, mathematical, musical, artistic, and other symbolic modes; and, q) that as humans, we can create and grow by treating the familiar as unfamiliar (Hayakawa, 1990; Korzyski, 2000; Levinson, 2002 & 2006; Fiordo, 2011a & 2011b).

However, Richards unites with some of the extreme positions in general semantics by entering the anti-Aristotelian zone. Richards saw rhetoric in his time around 1920 as sunken to abhorrently impoverished levels. Subsequently, he objected to the traditional view of rhetoric abused at that time in diverse academies. He thought rhetoric in devolved classical form would be better off jettisoned than used. His inclination was to reject Aristotle as well as Whately. He thought both were irrelevant to how rhetoric functioned in modern times and how a new and improved rhetoric should function. To Richards, rhetoric as a "philosophic discipline aiming at mastery of the fundamental laws of the use of language" (Richards, 1936, p. 7) should replace an Aristotelian rhetoric of persuasion, especially as traditionally mistreated as "theory of the battle of words…dominated by the combative impulse" (p. 24).

What rhetoric should be, according to Richards, is the "study of misunderstanding and its remedies" (p. 3) and a "philosophic inquiry into how words work in discourse" (p. 8). Richards pooh-poohed the reductionist study of rhetoric as a collection of Aristotelian elocutionary rules about how to speak and write effectively: for example, be clear, respect conventional usage, and avoid ambiguity. Rhetoric should not be about learning a bunch of rules. Like Charles Morris and others (Fiordo, 1977; Foss & Foss, 2003), Richards paints persuasion as merely one of many rhetorical aims. Exposition, he maintains, is one of many other goals of rhetoric. Narrowing rhetoric to persuasion, but one function, discourages scholars from studying the larger problem of how language works and communication fails. Discourse has many functions, and many combined functions. Persuasion and exposition are only two of them. Others include at least acculturation and argumentation (Foss & Griffin, 1995; Fiordo, 2011a; DeVito, 2012).

In his construction of a new rhetoric, Richards attempts to explain how to measure communication losses, how effective communication differs from ineffective communication, and how outmoded and fallacious assumptions about and attitudes toward words and how they operate in human thought and interaction weaken or destroy communication (Richards, 1936; Foss, Foss, & Trapp, 2002). He argues that three conditions have to be present to actuate a new rhetoric. First, the challengeable presumptive premises of rhetorical theory largely derived from Aristotelian renditions of rhetoric should be tested and reevaluated. The innovative rhetorical goal Richards has is to transcend the rhetorical assumptions of Aristotle and the Aristotelians and try to determine how discourse actually operates over how discourse ought to operate (Morris, 1970; Fiordo, 1977) according to traditional rhetorical theorists (Richards, 1936).

Richards seems to be anticipating the qualitative method of Grounded Theory. His traditionalist critique of the rhetorical theories of the Aristotelians might suggest to some a version of a method consistent with Grounded Theory—that is, a method of inductive reasoning derived from carefully observing the phenomenal world. The results of the research method of Grounded Theory "emerge through consideration and analysis of the data." Grounded Theory starts with the data and develops "theories based on the data (i.e., grounded in the data)" (Patten, 2007, p. 159; Mertens, 2009). To evolve a new rhetoric, research must be performed to "provide the observations and conclusions on which researchers can induce theory": that is, "develop theories that explain events they have observed." The theory has to be "grounded on observations." Being evolutionary, theories from the grounded method usually develop "during the process of making observations." The theory is then "regularly revised (i.e., evolves) as new observations warrant" (p. 27).

Second, Richards maintains that rhetorical studies should begin microscopically with the analysis of words. His focus on words distinguishes his counterdiscursive approach to rhetorical studies from the approach of traditional Aristotelian scholars, Aristotelian rhetoricians focusing on the broad sweeps of language used in speeches, essays, and other lengthy verbal works. In scrutinizing how words operate in communication, Richards believes smaller messages can be developed into interminable lengths of discourse to some end or ends (Richards, 1936; Foss, Foss, & Trapp, 2002).

Third, Richards expects a new rhetoric to have a starring, not a cameo, epistemic role in interdisciplinary studies. Rhetoric should not be seen as being merely decorative, as having no substance, as being epistemologically marginalized, or as attaining relevance only in relation to other studies. Rhetoric can and should provide a sound educational core to curricula in general. As the "systematic study of the inherent and necessary opportunities for misunderstanding which language offers" (Richards, 1955, p. 74), rhetoric can center curricula. For example, with a new rhetoric having semantic roots, important conceptual terms like being and cause can have, across subject areas, fluctuating meanings resulting in misinterpretations. Ironically yet beneficially, misinterpretations in one subject area can elucidate misinterpretations in other subject areas. Problems in one area can shed light on problems in other areas. Richards admonished that since identifiable interpretative problems surface in most, if not all, subject areas, an inquiry into motifs of problematic meaning might serve as an integrating instructional principle (Richards, 1955; Foss, Foss, & Trapp, 2002). In sum, Richards' new rhetoric would begin with words and go to whatever lengths language might take its users and abusers.

3   Richards' Hermeneutic

Richards' comments on misinterpretation serve as a ground for understanding how his non-Aristotelian microscopic semantic view of rhetorical discourse can inspire a macroscopic hermeneutic—or, a theory of verbal and nonverbal "text interpretation, broadly speaking" (Fiordo, 2013, p. 93). As language users interpret discourse, they can work from the hermeneutic premise of predictable patterns of meaning and misunderstanding being present across diverse areas of study. Subsequently, to identify understanding and misunderstanding provides a unifying educational theme across various studies. To seek out that which is understood and misunderstood is to seek out potential and actual communication breakdowns.

Understanding is not a taken-for-granted accomplishment; rather, it is something to be proven continuously. The proving in Richards' plan begins at the semantic level, progresses through sentences and paragraphs, and advances to discourse at the broadest implementation of language: speeches, essays, books, and so forth. As an amiable heretic (Watson, 1996), Richards' seems to have embodied the mythos of Hermes' role in hermeneutics—the Greek god who served multiple purposes in sending and interpreting legitimate messages as well as in fabricating, distorting, and misinterpreting messages that he judged circumstantially to be necessary. Those who trusted in Hermes petitioned him for "restful sleep, robust dreams, safe passage for travelers crossing boundaries, traveling on roads, and passing between doorways." Hermes was approached as a "deity of good luck and gain—whether the gain was honest or dishonest." Serving as a "possible link between the rational and irrational in delivering messages," Hermes reigned over "discord, absurdity, and chaos as well as tempered reason" (Fiordo, 2013, p. 93). Mediating between the "gods and between the gods, and human beings," Hermes escorted "souls to the underworld after death" (pp. 93–94).

Among his many depictions, Hermes was portrayed as the "inventor of language and music." In his multiple and seemingly contradictory roles as "an interpreter, a liar, a thief, and a deceiver," Hermes had to comprehend "multifarious dimensions and meanings to accomplish his hermeneutic ends through any means necessary: kindness and honesty or cruelty and dishonesty." Treating the Greeks of antiquity as if their views of words and messages hold true today, which they do for a number of people, words become inspirited with the "power to reveal and conceal (i.e., to lead to truth or falsehood)."

Words and messages also have ambiguity, a quality Hermes celebrated by watching communicators wrestle with the trials and tribulations of trying to reduce uncertainty caused by ambiguity. When dilemmas emerged from verbal conflicts, those faithful to Hermes might appeal to him for verbal interpretations. In interpreting the words, Hermes might use subterfuge. In a way, one of the premises Hermes likely worked from is that some people "overestimate the value of the truth." Since confusion and uncertainty commonly accompany messages, the Ancient Greek hermeneutic method could dispel the madness by divining the "truth or falsehood of a statement and thereby attain a sane rendition." The ways of Hermes can be implemented to determine, "one way or another as well as by any means necessary," a sane and rational interpretation of an instance of rhetorical discourse when there are "hermeneutic needs" (p. 94).

Specifically, Richards might help communicators remedy misunderstanding through any number of non-Aristotelian and anti-Aristotelian ideas and techniques he developed for interpretative purposes. He provided terminological screens (Burke, 1966) through which to read, decode, decipher, or interpret discourse (Richards, 1924, 1929, 1936, 1938, 1942, 1955, 1960, & 1970; Ogden & Richards, 1923). A selection of Richards' un-Aristotelian hermeneutic contributions, explained succinctly for illustrative and didactic purposes, follows: a) his counterdiscursive orientation, b) his semantic triangle, c) his remedies for misunderstanding, and d) his comparison fields in communication.

4   Counterdiscursive Orientation

Richards' counterdiscursive orientation toward non-Aristotelian and anti-Aristotelian rhetoric and hermeneutics involves countering institutionalized ways of thinking and discoursing. In the case of Richards' new microscopic rhetoric and macroscopic hermeneutic, a family of compound words beginning with "counter" may come into play to explicate and justify Richards' theorizing attempts to undo centuries of traditionalist Aristotelian rhetorical supremacy. In plain English, ideologically, he is rebellious. Richards goes against the flow and challenges that which is taken for granted. To unseat Aristotelian rhetorical hegemony, Richards struggles through various counters to provide the scholarly world with a perspective other than, and even opposed to, that of the Aristotelians. In other words, to replace and oppose the traditional Aristotelian rhetoricians, Richards proffered his microscopic new rhetoric as a counteraction, counterargument, counterbalance, counterclaim, counterexample, counterforce, countermand, countermeasure, countermove, counteroffensive, counteroffer, counterplot, counterpoint, and counterproposal. He exerted tremendous talent, energy, and commitment to initiate a dialog to update and advance the centuries of Aristotelian hegemony in rhetorical theory. His counterdiscursive orientation allows a rhetorical and critical theorist on a holy or heretical mission to begin to change the presumptuous changeless Aristotelian rhetoricians. His counterdiscursive orientation solidified his will to go against the wind, go up the down staircase, and fight the uphill battle to knock out, or at least daze, a really beatable foe in the form of his worthy opponents—the rhetorical traditionalists.

5 Semantic Triangle

As entitled by Odgen and Richards (1946), the semantic triangle, due to its extensive discussion by Ogden and Richards and numerous communication theorists, is merely sketched here. The non-traditionalist un-Aristotelian semantic triangle involves three operating factors that create meaning: the symbol, the reference or thought, and the referent of the object of the reference or thought. The symbol is placed to the left of an equilateral triangle at the base. The referent is to the right of the triangle at the base. At the apex of the triangle is the thought or reference. The line between the symbol and reference or thought is solid and symbolizes a direct relationship. The line between the reference or thought and referent is solid and symbolizes a frequently direct relationship. The line between the symbol and the referent is dotted and symbolizes a usually indirect relationship.

The symbol refers to the word or sign that elicits the referent through the cognitive operations of the reference or thought. The referent signifies the object perceived that generates the cognitive operations stored in memory and experience. The reference or thought points to recollections through memory, experience, and contexts. Ordinarily, an arbitrary and indirect relationship exists between the symbol and the referent of the object of the reference or thought. In the symbol-referent relationship, the symbol merely stands for the referent. No necessary or causal relationship prevails. While onomatopoeic utterances strive to be direct, a cow "mooing" in English has alternative onomatopoeic sounds in other languages. Between the symbol and the reference, a direct or indirect relationship exists. Between the reference or thought and the referent, a direct, even causal, relationship exists. When communicators think about an object immediately present to them like the Eiffel Tower while standing in front of it in Paris, the relationship is direct. When communicators think about an object not immediately present like the Coliseum in Rome while standing in front of the Castle in Heidelberg, the relationship is indirect.

Again, the semantic triangle usually has a base of dots symbolizing ordinarily a non-causal relationship between the symbol and the referent. With the sides of the triangle moving upward from the symbol to the reference or thought and moving downward from the reference of thought to the referent, both are solid lines. For example, the symbol or word "horse" stands for the empirical referent of a hoofed quadruped cowpokes ride while the word may symbolize to the thought or frame of reference of an interpreter an animal he or she fears or likes. As a communication tool, the semantic triangle has a utility in opposing Richard's proper meaning superstition or the bogus notion of a single and proper meaning residing in a word rather than in those who use the word. A familiar illustration in general semantics may clarify Richards' proper meaning superstition. When Gardener Alpha declares to a Gardener Omega that there is a dog in a yard of the estate she has to enter to cultivate the garden, Gardener Omega may ask what kind of a dog it is to determine the dog's danger to either of them. When the Gardner Alpha says it is a Pekingese versus an Akita, the size and potential danger of the dog becomes clear through the specificity of the symbol used as the referent.

6   Remedies for Misunderstanding

Only two non-Aristotelian and anti-Aristotelian remedies for correcting misunderstanding from Richards will be sketched here: literary context and specialized quotation marks. To reduce misunderstanding, communicators can contextualize. Words occur in explicit or implicit literary, literate, or verbal contexts: phrases, sentences, paragraphs, compositions, and beyond. The context for words being used or misused involves an interdependency of words in sentences and broader forms of discourse. When interpreting words, communicators who contextualize, as Richards suggests, can rightfully be thought of as contextualizers. To reduce or abrogate misunderstanding, contextualizing is one predictably reliable path. Words makes sense and have meaning in relations to other words situationally. To judge the meaning of words accurately, context must be observed. Context functions like a Rosetta Stone in interpreting the intended meaning of words. Contextualizers may have an advantage in correctly interpreting the source's attitude toward various factors in the communication situation. Contextualization varies as well with whether the discourse is at the scientific or referential end of the discourse continuum where meanings may fluctuate but slightly or at the poetic or emotive end of the discourse continuum where meanings may fluctuate highly (Richards, 1936 & 1970; Foss, Foss, & Trapp, 2002).

Richards' specialized quotation marks, adopted and expanded systematically in general semanticists (Hayakawa, 1990; Kodish & Kodish, 2001; Levinson, 2006; Fiordo, 2011c), constitute his attempt to remedy problems pertaining to misunderstanding in general and verbal misunderstanding in particular. In general semantics, commonly used specialized markings include indexing (horse1 is not horse2), dating (The Dalai Lama1950 is not the Dalai Lama 1990), and special sense quotation marks (The "savior" from Metz arrived) (Hayakawa, 1990). Any number of specialized metalinguistic marks can be added to the general semantics list. Thanks to computer technology, metalinguistic markers of words or sentences can take the form of different colors or print styles (Fiordo, 2011c). Not naïve, Richards' grasp of the limited potential of his remedial devices is clear. His hermeneutic remedies do not guarantee totally effective communication. As regards specialized quotation marks, Richards endorsed the utility of these metalinguistic devices to "better keep track of the uses we are making of our words" (Richards, 1955, p. 29). For example, the special quotations marks of w…w indicate that a word per se is intended: in effect, the w…w marks stand for "the word." Thus, "wDaow in Mandarin has no unequivocal English" (Richards, 1960). In sum, although his remedies for misunderstanding are not foolproof or infallible, they constitute possible antidotes for the misconstruing of meaning (Foss, Foss, & Trapp, 2002).

7   Comparison Fields

Comparison fields in human communication are the last non-Aristotelian and anti-Aristotelilan hermeneutic term from Richards that is discussed here. The important factor in Richards' comparison fields entails communicators requiring for effective communication *"an exceptional fund of common experience"* (Richards, 1924, p. 178). Richards' model of communication noted a message source or generator who encoded meaning through words a message receiver or interpreter decodes. The message receiver interprets the words in light of past experiences. When the experiences of the message generator and message interpreter have a sufficient quantity and quality of shared experience, effective communication may likely result. Noise refers to any factor or dynamic that disturbs, trouble, obstructs, obscures, interposes, or destroys the meaning—especially the intended meaning—of a message. Almost any factor can function as noise: slurred speech, unreadable handwriting, unfamiliar diction, confounding syntactic formations, unintelligible dialects, and so on.

As the comparative fields of the communicators' experiences and contexts escalate significantly, the likelihood of communication establishing a commonage shrinks. Similarity between the experiences and contexts of the message sources and message interpreters is critical to Richards' theory of meaningful and effective communication (Ogden & Richards, 1946). Successful communicators need not have identical experiences and contexts, for such an expectation is groundless. The use of similar symbols interpreted similarly is what Richards offers as a key to decreasing or purging misunderstanding and increasing understanding (Richards, 1955). As different individuals with divergent experiences from diverse contexts, communicators may attach assorted meanings to the same words (Foss, Foss, & Trapp, 2002). Mindful awareness of words must be respected to augment our opportunities to be understood. In short, the similar fields of experience, contexts, and symbols lead toward a meeting of the minds of the communicators: that is, when the thoughts or references of the communicators are similar.

8 Conclusion

Richards' indisputably and indubitably envisions and formulates a new rhetoric and critical hermeneutic that depart from traditional perspectives in being un-Aristotelian. In this study, one goal was to demonstrate how Richards' new wordsmith rhetoric functions in a rhetorical context that is counterdiscursive to traditionalist renditions of rhetoric. Richards theorizes as a rebel with a humane cause: the remedy of misunderstanding in human communication and the betterment of human life as a result. The study closes with a brief account and illustration of Richards' non-Aristotelian and anti-Aristotelian hermeneutic.

References

Andersen, K. E. (1972). *Introduction to communication theory and practice.* Menlo Park, CA: Cummings.

Andersen, K. E. (1978). *Persuasion: Theory and practice.* Boston: Allyn and Baco.

Andersen, K. (1974). *Lecture heard and interview with Dr. Kenneth Andersen on "Communication and Persuasion," Professor of Speech Communication, University of Illinois – Urbana,* Urbana, Illinois.

Black, M. (1949). *Language and philosophy: Studies in method.* Ithaca, NY: Cornell University.

Browne, S. H. (2000). "I. A. Richards (1893–1079)". In *Twentieth-Century Rhetorics and Rhetoricians: Critical Studies and Sources,* edited by Michael G. Moran and Michelle Ballif. CT: Greenwood, 304–312.

Burke, K. (1966). *Language as symbolic action: Essays on life, literature, and method.* Berkeley: University of California Press.

DeVito, J.A. (2012). *The essential elements of public speaking,* 4th ed. New York: Allyn & Bacon.

Enholm, D. K. (1976). "Rhetoric as an instrument for understanding and improving human relations". *Southern Speech Communication Journal,* 41, 223–236.

Fiordo, R. (1977). *Charles Morris and the criticism of discourse.* Bloomington: Indiana University.

Fiordo, R. (2011a). *Arguing in a loud whisper: A civil approach to dispute resolution.* Saarbrucken, Germany: VDM.

Fiordo, R. (2011b). "Contributions to general semantics from Charles Morris: An abstraction". *ETC: A Review of General Semantics,* 68, 156–178.

Fiordo, R. (2011c). "The Extensional Orientation, Hegemony, and General Semantics". *ETC: A Review of General Semantics* 68: 321–361.

Fiordo, R. (2013). "Midlevel abstracting: An underserved zone of general semantics". *ETC: A Review of General Semantics*, 70, 82–110.

Fisher, B. A. (1971). "I. A. Richards Context of Language: An overlooked contribution to rhetorico-communication theory". *Western Speech*, 35, 104–111.

Foss, S.K., & Foss, K.A. (2003). *Inviting transformation: Presentational speaking for a changing world*, 2nd ed. Prospect Heights, IL: Waveland.

Foss, S.K., Foss, K.A., & Trapp, R. (2002). *Contemporary perspective on rhetoric*, 3rd ed. Prospect Heights, IL: Waveland Press.

Foss, S.K., & Griffin, C.L. (1995). "Beyond persuasion: A proposal for an invitational rhetoric". *Communication Monographs*, 62, 2–18.

Griffin, E. (2009). *Communication: A first look at communication theory*, 7th ed. Boston: McGraw-Hill Higher Education.

Hardy, W.G. (1978). *Language, thoughts, and experience: A tapestry of the dimensions of meaning*. Baltimore: University Park Press.

Haslam, G. W. with Haslam, J. E. (2011). *In thought and action: The enigmatic life of S.I. Hayakawa*. Lincoln, NB: University of Nebraska.

Hayakawa, S.I. (1990). *Language in thought and action*, 5th ed. San Diego: Harcourt.

Hayakawa, S.I. (1970). *Personal Interview with Professor Hayakawa at San Francisco State College, San Francisco, CA*.

Hayakawa, S. I. (2013). "75th Anniversary reprint – Semantics, general semantics: An attempt at definition". *ETC: A Review of General Semantics*, 70, 202–208.

Hyman, S. E. (1948). *The armed vision: A study in the methods of modern literary criticism*. New York: Alfred A. Knopf.

Kodish, S.P., & Kodish, B.I. (2001). *Drive yourself sane: Using the uncommon sense of general semantics*, rev. 2nd ed. Pasadena, CA: Extensional.

Korzybski, A. (2000). *Science and sanity: An introduction to non-Aristotelian systems and general semantics*. Brooklyn, NY: Institute of General Semantics.

Levinson, M.H. (2002). *Practical fairy tales for everyday life*. New York: iUniverse.

Levinson, M. H. (2006). *Sensible thinking for turbulent times*. New York: iUniverse.

Mertens, D. M. (2009). *Transformative research and evaluation*. London: The Guilford Press.

Morris, C. (1970). *Signification and significance: A study of the relations of signs and values*. Cambridge, MA: The MIT Press.

Needham, J. (1982). *The completest mode: I. A. Richards and the continuity of English literary criticism*. Edinburgh, Scotland: Edinburgh University.

Nichols, M. H. (1963). *Rhetoric and criticism*. Baton Rouge: Louisiana State University.

Ogden, C.K., & Richards, I.A. (1946). *The meaning of meaning*. New York: Harcourt, Brace & World.

Patten, M.L. (2007). *Understanding research methods: An overview of the essentials*, 6th ed. Glendale, CA: Pyrczak Publishing.

Richards, I.A. (1942). *How to read a page: A course in efficient reading with an Introduction to a Hundred Great Words*. New York: W.W. Norton.

Richards, I.A. (1938). *Interpretation in teaching*. New York: Harcourt, Brace.

Richards, I.A. (1970). *Poetries and sciences*. UK: Routledge and Kegan Paul.

Richards, I.A. (1929). *Practical criticism: A study of literary judgment*. London: Kegan Paul, Trench, Trubner.

Richards, I.A. (1924). *Principles of literary criticism*. London: Kegan Paul, Trench, Trubner.

Richards, I.A., (1936). *The philosophy of rhetoric*. London: Cambridge.

Richards, I.A. (1960). *So much nearer: Essays toward a world English*. New York: Harcourt, Brace and World.

Richards, I.A. (1955). *Speculative instruments*. Chicago: University of Chicago.

Russo, J.P. (1982). "I.A. Richards in retrospect". *Critical Inquiry*, 8, 743–760.

Schiller, J. P. (1969). *I.A. Richards theory of literature*. New Haven, CT: Yale University.

Watson, G. (1996). "The amiable heretic: I. A. Richards 1893–1979". *Sewanee Review*, 54 (April–June), 248–262.

Dr. Brandon Inabinet, Furman University

Stoic Influence in a Ciceronian Rhetorical Tradition: Kant, Arendt, and Perelman's "Rule of Justice"

Abstract: In a world where persuasion still allows people to identify around religious and nationalist symbols other than an almighty reason (λόγος), Cicero's mediation of Stoic rhetoric showed productive ways to "inform and moderate political ambition ... [and] elevate and temper international competition" (Pangle 1998, 261–2). Cicero's sophistic cosmopolitan ethic, based in Isocrates, Aristotle, and the Stoics, created a political theory of communities ethically oriented toward cooperation, while acknowledging divisions. For Cicero, sapientia et eloquentia unites all on a deep philosophical level of truth and aesthetics, giving new life to a place for shared, universal speech coupled with individual capacity for distinction and virtue. All are equal and worthy of enacting rhetorical judgment; yet, some would rise through distinction (of birth, experience, and education) to speak well and attain virtue through speech. In this study, I read Kant, Arendt, and Perelman as modern theorists in this European tradition of mediating Stoic ethics and rhetoric (perhaps unintentionally), each with a different approach: first viewing Kant's hostility to rhetoric but rich recovery of Stoic universalism; Arendt's usage of the term "action" and turn toward pluralism as the basis of speech; and Perelman's "rule of justice" (sometimes understood as the Universal Audience concept) to escape from the relativism that comes with equating ethical philosophy with adherence from a particular audience. I conclude that a sophisticated ethical theory of rhetoric today can learn from all these recuperations but must yet recapture embodied and practical theories of Cicero to adequately deal with the present cultural strife in Europe and abroad. Moreover, these practices must not only take into account current discourse across borders, but, given environmental concerns as well, must also anticipate intergenerational audiences.

Rhetoric, as a European tradition traced to Athens, contains several continuous propositions: an argument for the contingent nature of truth based in human communication, for speech pedagogy as central to good, transparent governance, and for improved situational awareness and judgment as cultivation of self. This essay will carve out a particular rhetorical tradition among these, vital to contemporary European identity and global liberalism. This tradition, inherited from Athens through Cicero and the Stoics advanced by Chaïm Perelman and Hannah Arendt in the mid-twentieth century, is crucial because it gives the most coherent ideology against illiberal and totalitarian politics, through rhetorical judgment.

Perelman and Arendt rarely cite Cicero as their primary influence, often calling out Aristotle rather than the Isocratean-Ciceronian tradition. One can imagine this has to do with the preeminence of serious thought devoted to philosophy instead of rhetoric in modern European universities. By following the Isocratean-Ciceronian tradition into the work of Perelman and Arendt, this essay traces the development of rhetorical judgment against twentieth-century totalitarian horrors. This tradition of thought creates an anti-foundational, pluralist natural rights theory, with human action borne of diversity and aware the aesthetic, contextual nature of justice; yet, at the same time it still allows a place for limited and provisional unity and a higher sense of glory and equity. In short, in provides the basis for liberal cosmopolitanism that undergirds European Union identity against nationalist and authoritarian detractors. By recovering this thread of rhetoric, we might build a stronger sympathy for liberalism beyond mere tolerance.

The first section of this analysis will review Cicero's reception of Stoicism and his subtle absorption of Greek rhetorical theory from Isocrates. The second section will then uncover Perelman and Arendt's negotiations of this theory in the context of modernity. The conclusion will review the two moves and argue to center contemporary rhetorical studies around this vital humanist tradition, and extend it into post-humanist grounds for the demands of global and environmental social justice today.

1   Cicero & the Stoics: Rhetorical Justice

Stoic thought had a significant impact on the European history of rhetoric. Only recently have these influences gained much notice. Catherine Atherton's 1988 essay gave early coverage to the Stoic handling of the distinction between rhetoric and dialectic made by Cicero. More recently Lois Agnew's book (2008) looked at how Stoic ideas of propriety might have influenced eighteenth century rhetorics of taste and eloquence. And then a special issue of *Advances in the History of Rhetoric* surveyed various statements and receptions of Stoic thought from Roman antiquity to contemporary cosmopolitanism (O'Gorman, 2010).

Most ideas about Stoicism generally, but especially about Stoic rhetoric, come through Cicero, whose works preserve the fragments and ideas by generations of Stoic philosophers. As anyone knows who has read Cicero, though, it is not easy to categorize him as a Stoic (Glucker, 1988). He borrowed, and in some cases, nearly copied wholesale many of their ideas; yet, at the end of the day, he also owed much to Plato and the Academics, Aristotle, Isocrates, and even occasionally the Epicureans. But especially on the topic of justice, Cicero was chiefly Stoic.

In *De Legibus,* Cicero argued that shared law commands individual obedience through the internalization of duties. For the Stoics, accentuated by Cicero, this shared sense of law had a great deal to do with speech and common language (*Logos),* which gives meaning to certain things as praiseworthy (*De Leg.* I.17). For Cicero, what really mattered was that individuals could "firmly fix" and "fully develop" this capacity as part of their nature as intelligent beings. (*De Leg.* I.6.18–19) Cicero added that this capacity, whether developed or not, helped form a unity of humankind that is the benchmark of justice. In fact, Cicero formed the bedrock of Perelman's "judicial analogy," also called the "Rule of Justice," when he wrote that:

There is no difference in kind between man and man; for if there were, one definition could not be applicable to all men; and indeed reason, which alone raises us above the level of the beasts and enables us to draw inferences, to prove and disprove, to discuss and solve problems, and to come to conclusions, is certainly common to us all, and, though varying in what it learns, at least in the capacity to learn it is invariable. For the same things are invariably perceived by the senses, and those things which stimulate the senses, stimulate them in the same way in all men; and those rudimentary beginnings of intelligence to which I have referred, which are imprinted on our minds, are imprinted on all minds alike; and speech, the mind's interpreter, though differing in the choice of words, agrees in the sentiments expressed. (*De Leg.* I.10.30)

While we all might speak in different languages and have different contexts for such speech, certain maneuvers of making meaning (definition, metaphor, synecdoche, metonymy, among others) implant an inherent capacity to make distinctions, praise and blame, and so forth. Thus, even in very different cultural milieus, as Cicero noticed of the Roman-conquered lands, a basic human analogy allows for argumentative mechanisms across all people. Because of this, very similar and thus shareable laws, principles, and moral dictates emerge.

Cicero added to the Stoic ideas about justice by thoroughly finessing the basis of speech, or rhetoric (*Eloquentia*), in ways that Stoics had not. Stoics had left the project incomplete, to Cicero, by simply conflating the dialectical and rhetorical modes of speech put forward by Plato, essentially saying that all speech was a unity revealing man's capacity to reason. To pull this off in practice, they often spoke in terse syllogisms and philosophical absolutes in public life (Atherton, 1988). Cicero rejected this style (Cic. *De or.* 3.65), even as he agreed that the Platonic binary between dialectic and rhetoric was fallacious. He instead theorized rhetoric by focusing on a robust diversity of speech modes that could ground naturalness, distinction, and universality. Because it was natural to speak passionately and broadly, and because this demonstrated our capacities of reason most fully, eloquence and wisdom united were the gateway to then imagine and institute shared judgment for universal truth, laws, and justice.

It is of course unlikely that Cicero was really intending to tout plurality in the way we moderns think of equality or multicultural respect. In many of his works, he mocks the idea, highlighting the position of masculinity and elite Greco-Roman thought above all others. Still, in *De Legibus*, Cicero emphasizes that justice and law are not static things "out there," but develop from speech, as the basis of thought and language, across individuals. In upholding the Stoic ideas as worthy of tweaking toward robust oratory, he began a path toward speech as a centerpiece of human nature, and thus, human duties and justice.

Speech, for Cicero, was natural because it was common and embodied (Cic. *De or.* 1.114), and not even the most learned orators or philosophers should deviate too far from natural styles (Cic. *De or.* 1.12). As a faculty of judgment, the capability of speech takes in an understanding of the full range of human nature (Cic. *De or.* 1.53; 1.124–25), in contexts organic to that particular community (Cic. *De or.* 1.307–308). Speeches themselves are composed and arranged organically (Cic. *De or.* 1.310–1.325). Rhetoric, as embodied speech, reflected human nature at its finest and an organic community from which such excellence sprung. Stoics, on the other hand, had gone astray in positing a universal reason without stressing public oratory as a vital and culturally contingent part of such speech. Cicero begins an emphasis on plurality and diversity out of a universal, natural rights ethic—even if his focus was more on supreme excellence of the good man, rather than on fostering tolerant pluralism or diversity.

Out of Stoic work, though, it is possible to glean such a focus. Stoics emphasized that choosing rightly or wrongly depended upon a person's nature and their material environment. The excellence of no two persons was exactly the same, because the familiarization process by which each person had come to access their material surroundings varied. In *De Oratore*, Antonius and Crassus are praised for their dissimilar forms of thought and eloquence. Distinction from different aspects education, the relative types of training, regional differences, and specific civic duties all work together for better political action.

Finally, rather than radical incommensurability or diversity, as we sometimes see in postmodern theory, Cicero used the naturalness and distinctiveness of *eloquentia* to argue for unity. Quoting Eleatic philosophy, *De Oratore* calls wisdom and eloquence the basis of an underlying unity of the universe, "bound together by a single, natural force and harmony. For there is nothing in the world, of whatever sort, that can either exist on its own if it is severed from all other things, or that can be dispensed with by the other things if they are to preserve their own force and eternal existence" (Cic. *De or.* 3.20). Cicero utilized synecdoche and metaphor to suggest basic and ultimate coherence amid the chaos of language and difference.

Because of this complex view of unity and diversity, Cicero formed the bedrock for much in the way of contemporary natural rights and democratic theory. Cicero made situational wisdom and taste the centerpiece of this system, as each particular judgment of appropriateness (*decorum*, Cic. *Or.* 69–71) gave meaning to the larger system of a universal ethic. This ability to connect the particular with the universal should be available to all, in the Ciceronian system, but of course historically this sense was best captured by the upper classes. Cicero himself was quite elitist, but he was also Stoic, focusing on the striving toward decorous judgment, and putting forward a model in the *orator perfectus* … at the same time, admitting this model could never be fully achieved even by the rich and powerful (Cic. *De or.* 1.6–16, 94) and that all free men could emulate it (leaving out, of course, women and other social categories).

With the decline of civic republicanism as a coherent philosophy in the rise of modern democracy, there also arose the question of the masses: can thousands or even millions be prudent? Perhaps, but prudence became an economic and docile private quality (mapped onto femininity in the modern era), not one of courageous judgment, in order to sustain political power among the few (Hariman, 2004). In the realm of theory, this shift occurred as well. Immanuel Kant, the person most responsible for reviving the Stoic-Ciceronian of a universal ethic for politics, reduced the orator to the philosophical thought-project of the legislator: the imagined space of making rules for all despite one's modern subject position. Prudence needed to be rational and abstract to be political; otherwise, politics was the domain of either coercion or manners.

Yet there were counter-impulses by those slightly more attuned to rhetoric apart from rationality. Giambattista Vico, a Ciceronian humanist, tried to tease the two apart in theorizing *sensus communes* separate from the rational sciences, acknowledging that the former was still incredibly important for political action in the domain of rhetorical influence. Thinkers in the British tradition, such as Anthony Ashley Cooper, Third Earl of Shaftesbury, Thomas Reid, Adam Smith, Lord Kames, George Campbell, Hugh Blair, and Richard Whatley, reframed classical rhetoric in modern terms of epistemology and psychology, attempting to return to rhetorical judgment. Yet Lois Agnew argues the failure of eighteenth-century British treatises was their focus on lifting common men to be sophisticated and polite (As Agnew, 2008, 16). Emotional control and entrance into society dominated over any coherent theory of action. All of these useful projects contribute to a notion of "civility," of civic and economic management, and of reasonableness. But only in the mid-twentieth century did the recuperation happen at an ultimate level of truth and action in politics. Totalitarian regimes thrived when they oriented polite, 'civil,' and 'prudent' (quieted) subjects, who put their economic or national improvement as their ultimate concern. Rationality, as defined in modern terms, could lead to ultimate destruction or demands for purity, rather than messy compromise and dissent.

In 1958, at least five significant works in rhetorical studies (as understood today) emerged from the presses touting contextual thinking, ancient rhetoric, pluralist political action and justice as answers to modernity's ills (Frank, 2011). Totalitarian regimes, genocide, and war framed political communication in early twentieth-century Europe, so these authors looked for alternatives in argumentation and rhetoric.

Two of these authors, Chaïm Perelman and Hannah Arendt, were resisters to the Nazis, and after the war, used their writings to dislodge the thought that made totalitarianism possible. Their rhetorical theories explicitly tried to bridge the *vita contemplativa* with the *vita activa* by foregrounding lived argumentation as natural human activities, amidst pluralism and agonism (Frank and Bolduc, 2004). Both modified the Stoic-Cicero rhetorical justice traced above, for modern times, differing only in the way they characterized and framed their contribution. Perelman and Olbrechts-Tyteca read Cicero's rhetorical ideas, reporting the experience as a "revelation" (Frank and Bolduc, 2011, 76). Arendt's vision of a new republican theory based on the "political genius of Rome" (*The Human Condition,* 195) came throughout her writings, but explicitly shifted to Cicero's works in her *Lectures on Kant's Political Philosophy* (63).

These modern theories hold up nature and natural speech acts without talking about essences or ideals, especially as to avoid promoting particular bloodline and ethnicity, or by extension, gender, class, and other identifiers. Rather, both take from Kant one particular part of naturalness that Cicero had given him—free will. Perelman started not from a rational grounding for these rights, but from a theory of natural speech as reason-giving (see Mootz, 2010). He argued that humans produce language and meaning that cohere with recognized ways of thinking and speaking; and he assigns to both the status of reasonable thought (Perelman 1979, 113). Moreover, the capacity to think deeply is not reserved to philosophers. Instead, he follows Cicero and the Stoics (without saying so) to see dialectic and rhetoric as parts of the same reasoning system: all humans can imagine universals through multiple modes of speech. There is no clear boundary between the philosopher and the uneducated; both appeal to the universal audience of all reasonable people from time to time in values they imagine timeless or global, even if the philosopher does it more as part of her profession. But as a philosopher, Perelman did not want to say these were mere generalizations or just unfounded abstractions. Humans also have the capacity to assent or not, without arbitrary coercion, through Perelman's idea of *adherence*. 'Rationality' comes from argumentative apparatuses, that is, from the process of making good reasons.

Arendt's system recuperated this natural autonomy, with an even stronger negotiation of Kant in place of a focus on argumentation. Arendt, following Martin Heidegger and Karl Jaspers' phenomenology, theorized that humans have a natural capacity for being with others in the world of labor, work, and action, and that the latter is uniquely important to define our lives as a way to guarantee plurality and the space for shared action. Rather than focus on speech alone, Arendt highlighted the communal settings that allow human flourishing in ways not determined or expected.

For Arendt, this creation of communal space was natural, but only insofar as it was a decision of the free will to enter them and do something unique that contributes to the life of the larger communities ("Truth and Politics," 263). The rise of technologies that allow for mass society and totalitarianism, she viewed as an "unnatural growth" (*Human Condition*, 47) against the natural political condition—a cancer on good thought and action.

She joins Perelman in a departure from any totalizing claim about mankind's natural state as philosophical rationality or pre-given rights. Rather, she focuses her attention on thought, speech, and action, as common capacities (*On Revolution*). She also imports Cicero wholesale into her work when she says there exists in humanists a "faculty of judgment and taste which is beyond the coercion which each speciality imposes upon us." (*Lectures*, 225). This insistence on irreducible humanity through the faculty of rhetorical judgment spans two millennia.

So both Arendt and Perelman return to political action as natural capacity, even as they are not as bold as Cicero about the uniquely human qualities of robust oratory or the most excellent forms of speech. Rather, with Kant's influence, and in light of early twentieth-century history, they looked for a more humble basis for political thought and action in basic rhetorical capabilities. Language and political action became the paradigmatic human act, within which the entire range of human thought and communication occur.

This centering on something other than pure rationality takes us back to something almost pre-modern. By not reducing "natural" down to philosophically pure attributes, the two theorists also included at least some human diversity, just as Cicero had theorized. This also restored something bolder than

Kant's "abstract character," as the focus is not on an individual's rationality, but bodies, capacities, and technologies of communication in community. As Perelman wrote, "In all fields … pluralism is the rule." (Perelman, 1982, 160) This entails an acknowledgement of diversity as a precondition for successful argumentation. Although values are socially constructed, they are produced by discourse in such a way as to allow for some values that straddle multiple cultures.

Perelman harnessed diversity and the pluralism of values into adherence by the universal audience, a way to provisionally and temporarily overcome differences. In a world where particular identities could be the *telos*, Perelman instead suggested the tendency of better discourse—discourse motivated to stand the test of time—to speak to a universal audience: an imagined set of ideal audience members who embody the plurality and reasoning-faculty of humans world-over and over time.

Perelman refocused Cicero's interest in the perfect orator toward a priority on audience, ensuring we turn our eyes from ourselves to others. This creates a problem, as it lacks a significant reason to argue internal to the self. For Cicero, it was the way to demonstrate innate virtue and greatness for the great orator, naturally built to lead, act dutifully, and deserving of rights. In a modern era, Perelman offered very little reason to act politically, when values are so plural and contested. This makes some sense, as Perelman was mostly interested in the realm of professional legal argument, which presupposed institutions requiring participation.

Arendt, alternatively, used the term "enlarged mentality" to argue for diversity, following Kant's "impartial spectator" position, to imagine the position of others—not to "feel sentimentally" like them (which Arendt finds impossible), but to use reasoning power to think in another's space as one encounters a plurality of viewpoint and identities in political practice. This results in a kind of "universal interdependence" ("Truth and Politics," 242), as an internalization and externalization of Cicero's political performance. To feel as others, there must be others, and they must be encountered and understood. This is not instrumental rationality, but rather, the kinds of discourse that share a range of human experiences in myths, stories, and personal narratives (Trish Roberts-Miller, 589). Arendt famously adapted Kant's theory of aesthetic judgment (where he situates taste and decorum) for political decision-making, so that decorum is not limited to art or high society, but is the inherent, situational reasoning capacity of living with others and being able to think representatively in terms of preferences.

Still, the cultivation of those aesthetic preferences up toward higher a universal interdependence is not mandated and clearly falls apart, especially in view of efficient technologies that lead to mass alienation. Arendt recuperates the Ciceronian quest for fame and glory through public display as the means to save public action. That personal desire, bolstered by historians and poets in a good culture, create the conditions for future political action.

Perelman, as a secular Jew living in Belgium after the Holocaust, gestured more toward a ultimate value of "equity," a kind of supreme virtue that demands assent even when formal systems of justice are tested (*Justice*, 31). Following Cicero, he suggested that this is not done through careful rational institutions, but rather through the judicial analogy of seeing people as similar, as well as the qualities of compassion and care that cannot easily be subsumed into logical judgment systems, but often get expressed in transcendent ethics of religion or human rights.

This "rule of justice" allows that, by simple analogy between persons ("the equal treatment of beings who are essentially alike" *Justice*, 23) or situations ("essentially similar situations be treated in the same manner," *Justice*, 83) being alike, certain rights, obligations, or capacities are due to be protected, maintained or nurtured. In another sense, the rule of justice also provides that arguments "capable of convincing in a specific situation will appear to be convincing in a similar or analogous situation," thus protecting argument against arbitrary or extremely relative judgments (Perelman and Olbrechts-Tyteca 1969, 464). Perelman's "rule of justice" is open-ended, but not entirely relativistic because it does not equate truth with adherence from particular audiences, but instead with a form of universal duty compatible with and drawn from Cicero's *De Legibus*.

In short, both Arendt and Perelman rewrote Ciceronian inheritances of Stoic humanism in modern terms. Justice was enlarged beyond the abstract legal question into every type of justification for argumentation. The actual practices of argument themselves became the "natural" grounding for them, without the foundation of a religious or transcendent external to the activity of arguing, given that those led to the nation or particular god as supreme. Public renown (for Arendt) or equity through argumentation (for Perelman) continued to buttress against the complete unreasonableness that modern illiberalism and totalitarianism represent. Perelman and Arendt go further than Cicero in studying the systems of language and public action that would allow far more access of participation than Cicero might have ever imagined.

3   Conclusion

Perelman and Arendt both pushed Cicero's premodern vision of the virtuous civic orator to a postmodern anti-foundational theory of argumentative action. New possibilities of destruction, of liberal democracy, and of scientific awareness called for adjustment of the Stoic-Ciceronian tradition. These twentieth century theorists gave contingent, rhetorical bases for "natural" spaces and capabilities. Duties and rights, from the Stoic-Ciceronian bridge of dialectic and rhetoric, of *vita contemplativa* and *vita activa*, provided pathways to a humanist understanding for rhetoric, 2400 years later.

The focus on distinction for personal improvement and distinctiveness as an asset of robust controversy shows a related change. In the modern uptake, the authors privilege plurality in a more egalitarian sense, even if the natural basis for these egalitarian expectations can be read in Cicero's elitist works. Instead of starting from "universal natural rights" that are premised on a perfect ideal, God-given, or primary and external to constructed meaning systems, Arendt and Perelman posit argumentative practice itself as reason to construct agreements to protect further capacities for debate, plurality, and good judgment.

In this tradition, all humans are capable of enacting justice, and are thus equal and worthy in deserving of rights and access to public reason-giving. Recent focus on the rhetoric of human rights (Lyon and Olson) could be aided by acknowledging this lineage for judgment and human rights theory. Similarly, works on rhetorical judgment (Beiner, 1984; 2011) can do more with Cicero's rhetorical theory (rather than Aristotelian categories), as this better links with Stoic cosmopolitanism and natural rights theory that ground much of contemporary liberal cosmopolitan thought.

Most significantly, all of these ideas about the value of rhetorical judgment as a means to justice need to be placed within post-humanist framing. The threat of totalitarian power is less likely to emerge from the modernist ideology of comprehending a complete or final truth today, but instead from internalized fundamentalisms that react to a slow realization that man is weak in the face of genocide and environmental degregation, instability of the nation-state from global digital networks, or economic insecurity caused by unmanaged cash flows to the world's richest. In this context, we can take the projects forward: making the universal audience intergenerational and framed within a natural, environmental habitat; considering action in digital and physical contexts, as technologies extend us toward anonymous thought and data collection; and thinking across cultural boundaries outside of self-interested, short-term economic concerns. In other words, rhetoricians need to think beyond classic political contexts and theorize the recuperation of Cicero's humanistic ideal of rhetorical judgment when individuals feel helpless to massive systems beyond individual human control.

As Plutarch captured the Stoic sentiment, this will require living as "one way of life and order," like a herd grazing together nurtured by a common law [η σύννομος αγέλη συντρεφομένη νόμω κοινώ, *De Fortuna Alexandri*, 329a–b]. It will require seeing unity through connectedness and shared capacities, without assuming a universal direction or goal. As humans come to reimagine their place in the world order they continually re-create, rhetorical scholars have a leading role to play in building on this important rhetorical tradition of shared Stoic-Ciceronian rhetorical judgment in the face of illiberal threats.

References

Agnew, Lois Peters (2008). *Outward, Visible Propriety: Stoic Philosophy and Eighteenth-Century British Rhetorics*. Columbia: University of South Carolina Press.

Arendt, Hannah (1958). *The Human Condition*. University of Chicago Press.

Arendt, Hannah (1989). *Lectures on Kant's Political Philosophy*. University of Chicago Press.

Arendt, Hannah (1963). *On Revolution*. New York: Viking Press.

Arendt, Hannah (1963). "Truth and Politics". In *Between Past and Future*, 227–264. New York: Viking Press.

Atherton, Catherine (1993). "Hand over Fist: The Failure of Stoic Rhetoric." *Classical Quarterly* 38, no. 2: 392–427.

Beiner, Ronald (1984). *Political Judgment*. University of Chicago Press.

Beiner, Ronald, and Nedelsky, Jennifer (2001). *Judgment, Imagination, and Politics: Themes from Kant and Arendt*. Lanham, MD: Rowman & Littlefield Publishers.

Cicero, Marcus T. (1991). *Cicero: On Duties*, trans. M. T. Griffin and E.M. Atkins. New York: Cambridge University Press. Cited parenthetically as De Officiis.

Cicero, Marcus T. (2001). *Cicero: On Moral Ends*, trans. Julia Annas and Raphael Woolf. New York: Cambridge University. Cited parenthetically as De Finebus Bonorum et Malorum.

Cicero, Marcus T. (1999). *Cicero: On the Commonwealth and On the Laws*, trans. James E. G. Zetzel. New York: Cambridge University. Cited parenthetically as *De Legibus*.

Cicero, Marcus T. (2001). Cicero: *On the Ideal Orator*, trans. James M. May and Jakob Wisse. New York: Oxford University Press. Cited parenthetically as De Oratore.

Cicero, Marcus T. (1939). *Cicero: Brutus, Orator*, trans. G. L. Hendrickson and H.M. Hubbell. Cambridge, MA: Harvard University Press. Cited parenthetically as Orator.

Frank, David (2011). "1958 and the Rhetorical Turn in 20th-Century Thought." *The Review of Communication*. Vol. 11, no. 4 (October): 239–252.

Frank, David, and Bolduc, Michelle (2004). "From Vita Contemplativa to Vita Activa: Chaïm Perelman and Lucie Olbrechts-Tyteca's Rhetorical Turn." *Advances in the History of Rhetoric*. Vol. 7, no. 1: 65–86.

Frank, David, and Bolduc, Michelle (2011). "Lucie Olbrechts-Tyteca's New Rhetoric." In *The Promise of Reason: Studies in The New Rhetoric*. Edited by John T. Gage, 55–80. Carbondale: Southern Illinois University Press.

Glucker, John (1988). "Cicero's Philosophical Affiliations." In *The Question of "Eclecticism," Studies in Later Greek Philosophy*, ed. John M. Dillon and A.A. Long, 34–69. Berkeley, CA: University California Press.

Hariman, Robert (ed.) (2004). *Prudence: Classical Virtue, Postmodern Practice*. University Park: Penn State Press.

Lyon, Arabella, and Olson, Lester C. (eds.) (2011). "Human Rights Rhetoric: Traditions of Testifying and Witnessing". In Rhetoric Society Quarterly 41.3 (2011), 203–212.

May, James M. and Jakob Wisse. 2001. "Introduction." In *Cicero: On the Ideal Orator*. New York: Oxford University Press, 3–55.

Mootz, Francis (2010). "Perelman's Theory of Argumentation and Natural Law." *Philosophy and Rhetoric*. Vol. 43, No. 4: 383–402.

Nauert, Charles G. (2006). *Humanism and the Culture of Renaissance Europe*, 2nd ed., Cambridge: Cambridge University Press. (Chapters 4, 5, and 7 discuss Erasmus and Erasmian humanism.)

O'Gorman, Ned (2011). "Stoic Rhetoric: Prospects of a Problematic." *Advances in the History of Rhetoric*, Vol. 11. No. 1: 1–14.

Perelman, Chaïm (1980). *Justice, Law, and Argument: Essays on Moral and Legal Reasoning*. Trans. William Kluback et al. Boston: Reidel.

Perelman, Chaïm (1963). *The Idea of Justice and the Problem of Argument*. Trans. John Petrie. London: Routledge.

Perelman, Chaïm, and Olbrechts-Tyteca, Lucie (1969). *The New Rhetoric: A Treatise on Argumentation*. Trans. John Wilkinson and Purcell Weaver. Notre Dame, IN: University of Notre Dame Press.

Plutarch. *De Fortuna Alexandri*. Translated by Frank Cole Babbitt. Loeb Classical. Library, Vol. IV: 379-487. Harvard University Press. Available online at

<http://penelope.uchicago.edu/Thayer/E/Roman/Texts/Plutarch/Moralia/Fortuna_
Alexandri*/1.html>.
Roberts-Miller, Patricia (2002). "Fighting without Hatred: Hannah Arendt's Agonistic
Rhetoric." *JAC: A Journal of composition Theory* (formerly, *Journal of Advanced
composition*). Vol. 22, no. 3: 585–601.
Vico, Giambattista (1988). *On the Most Ancient Wisdom of the Italians.* Trans. L.M.
Palmer. London: Cornell University Press. Originally published 1710.
Vico, Giambattista (1968). *The New Science of Giambattista Vico, (1744).* Trans. Thomas
G. Bergin and Max H. Fixch. Ithaca: Cornell University Press.

Dr. Mark Longaker, University of Texas at Austin

Rhetorical Toleration:
John Locke on Ethics and Fallacy Theory

Abstract: John Locke deserves his reputation as a foremost if not the first theorist of the "ad" tradition of argumentative fallacy. Analysis of his public debates about religious toleration reveals that Locke ethically objected to one particular ad hominem fallacy (the guilt-by association argument) while tolerating other arguably fallacious arguments (both ex concessis and ad hominem) because the guilt-by-association threatened a tolerant republic of letters. This analysis enriches our understanding of the rhetorical approach to fallacy analysis, the ad hominem fallacy, and the importance of rhetorical norms in shaping tolerant public culture both in Locke's day and our own.

On the issue of tolerance, three questions immediately and generally arise: (1) What constitutes tolerance? (2) Who is tolerant? (3) Where does tolerance come from? Each question can only be addressed in a specific circumstance. Regarding the first, for instance, we might argue that the 21st century Western standard requires toleration of people, while the 18th-century standard required toleration of ideas.[1] In different eras, different practices of toleration lead to different forms of tolerance. The second question, likewise, requires close historical-intellectual inquiry. Recent scholarly debates about particular figures, such as Pierre Bayle, reveal, that the same person's writings can seem to promote both radical and moderate tolerance.[2] The third question, of course, requires the most creative historical thinking. It is always tempting to assume that arguments in favor or against tolerance principally constitute its shape, but ideas no more incite politics than spoken lyrics move bodies to dance.

....

1   Wendy Brown, *Regulating Aversion: Tolerance in the Age of Identity and Empire* (Princeton: Princeton University Press, 2006), 32–46.

2   For a review of the debate about whether Bayle was a radical or moderate advocate of toleration, see John Coffey, "Milton, Locke, and the New History of Toleration," *Modern Intellectual History* 5.3 (2008): 619–632.

During the British Enlightenment, for instance, we might argue that tolerance came into being through legislative happenings, such as the such as the lapsing of the Licensing Act (1695), or through demographic changes, such as the division of England into multiple religious sects.[3] Or we might investigate more mundane developments such as tolerationist societies, which followed certain behavioral norms; manners of keeping record; and means of distributing information. Writing letters, keeping commonplace books, exchanging information in journals—all of these quotidian activities added up to a culture of tolerance.[4] Wendy Brown has recently argued that tolerance is an "historically protean element of liberal governance," a technology with many facets and forms. Her Foucauldian analysis—"[c]omprehending tolerance in terms of power as productive force"—captures something that historians have long noticed about the virtue's manifestation in the 17th and 18th centuries.[5] Tolerance has limits, depends upon institutions, changes over time, and creates political subjects. To answer the third question, to examine mundane tolerant activities, to document everyday practices of toleration, can help us to answer the first two questions, for without understanding where tolerance comes from, we will be unable to determine who is genuinely tolerant or what constitutes genuine tolerance. To put this another way: The ethic of tolerance and the tolerant individual can only be understood by investigating the historical practices of toleration.

This article proposes just such an investigation. In order to understand John Locke as a tolerant political philosopher, we should pore over an often-overlooked facet of his work: his argumentative theory and practice. Recent historical work on tolerance in early Enlightenment England emphasizes the importance given to discursive norms among those actively seeking to create a tolerant republic of letters. John Marshall, echoing contemporary rhetorical theorists, demonstrates that norms of toleration added up to an "ethos of conversation."[6] Of course, as Aristotle was fond of pointing out, moral virtue arises

<hr>

3   Roy Porter, *The Creation of the Modern World: The Untold Story of the British Enlightenment* (New York: Norton, 2000), 108.

4   John Marshall, *John Locke, Toleration, and Early Enlightenment Culture: Religious Intolerance and Arguments for Religious Toleration in Early Modern and "Early Enlightenment" Europe* (Cambridge: Cambridge University Press, 2006), ch. 16.

5   *Regulating Aversion*, 10–11.

6   John Locke, *Toleration, and Early Enlightenment Culture*, 513. For contemporary rhetorical theorists discussing the importance of mundane discursive norms in any rhetorical culture, see Thomas Farrell, *Norms of Rhetorical Culture* (New Haven: Yale University Press, 1993), especially

from habit, not intellectual disposition.[7] A tolerant ethos depends less upon arguments about conversation and more upon conversational practices. Investigating such discursive norms should begin with argumentative forms and participants' conversational habits, not arguments about how to argue. Of course, the meta-discursive arguments deserve some attention as the critical philosopher often reflects upon her own practices.

In order to understand John Locke as someone who advanced tolerance by practicing and philosophically defending argumentative toleration, I look at his theory of fallacy alongside his own practices of argumentation in three late 17th-/early 18th-century debates, all touching on religion (one in particular on toleration). When philosophically theorizing an ideally tolerant discourse Locke seemed to favor a republic of letters characterized by arguments appealing to rational deduction and empirical observation (not audience presupposition, intellectual authority, or cultural commonplace). His argumentative practice, however, reveals that he regularly launched proofs not housed in the rational empiricist's arsenal. To be more specific, Locke regularly argued *ad hominem* to undercut his interlocutors' credibility. But he also regularly objected to one specific form of argumentation *ad hominem*: guilt-by-association. This argumentative form earned his scorn not because it interrupted the search for truth but rather because it corroded tolerance in the republic of letters. Locke objected to the guilt-by-association *ad hominem* on ethical, not philosophical, grounds.

Understanding Locke's willing entertainment and use of various argumentative forms allows us to see what discursive practices he thought appropriate to the ideally tolerant republic of letters. Below, I pursue such an understanding by reviewing Locke's philosophical writing on argumentative fallacy; by analyzing his use of "fallacious" argumentative forms; by analyzing his willing entertainment and rebuttal of similar argumentative forms; and by discussing his consistent objections to guilt-by-association arguments. Based on these analyses, I conclude that Locke enforced few argumentative restrictions in the tolerant republic of letters. Though his philosophical, meta-discursive writings suggest that he would only approve of empirical induction and rational deduction, his own arguments reveal that he permitted and practiced a much wider

---

the introduction and ch. 1; and Gerard Hauser's *Vernacular Voices: The Rhetoric of Publics and Public Spaces* (Columbia: University of South Carolina Press, 1999), especially ch. 1 and ch. 3.

7   *Nichomachean Ethics* 1103a33–b25.

range of argumentation. In fact, he only consistently objected to one argumentative form, which could interrupt the toleration of ideas.

When we examine Locke's argumentative practices in light of his commitment to a tolerant conversational ethos, we get a different picture of Locke the tolerationist. Surely, in his philosophical writings, Locke advocated a moderate toleration, but in his arguments (and his arguments about argument), he advanced a more radical ethos, a tolerance of all ideas regardless of their associated identities. Surely, this ethos of tolerance arose out of the local discursive practices. Locke likely did not imagine (and certainly never voiced a belief) that he would promote a radical Enlightenment ethos, tolerating all ideas and bracketing all identities. But he nonetheless engaged and defended practices of toleration that invoked just such an ethical ideal. In Locke's case, and arguably in many others, the ethical ideal came from the local practices. The three questions that began this article, due to their order, imply a hierarchy: the ethical ideal on top, the participants in second place, and the local practices of least importance. If the argument below about John Locke, argumentative fallacy, and toleration has any merit, then the order of these questions must be reversed: First, we should understand the local practices in any culture of toleration; then we must determine who engages these practices and for what specific reasons; finally, based on our knowledge of local practices and interested actors, we can see how specific actions yield ethical ideals. The ethic of tolerance comes from the habits of toleration. Seeing Locke's writings as local discursive practices that contributed to a broader culture and ethos of toleration changes our understanding of the man and the ethic.

1   How Locke Argued about Argumentation

Judging by the *Essay Concerning Human Understanding* (1690), we might conclude that John Locke desired a republic of letters where people argue *ad rem* (to the thing). Following Francis Bacon's Royal Society acolytes, Locke often adulated appeals to empirical observation over other forms of argumentative proof.[8]

---

8   Francis Bacon wanted people to study *res non verba*, things not words, defining the "first distemper of learning" thus: "when men study words and not matter." *The Advancement of Learning*, ed. Stephen Jay Gould (New York: Modern Library, 2001), 26. The Royal Society, particularly Thomas Spratt, asserted that the "mind of Man is a Glass, which is able to represent to itself, all the Works of Nature," The History of the Royal Society of London, for the Improving of Natural Knowledge (London: 1667), 97. Spratt particularly derided the classical topical system of invention and scho-

He labored to separate words from things, to elevate *res* by advancing the empirical sciences, and to denigrate *verba* by assaulting classical rhetorical education. In the Essay, he proposed that "truth" be found in the "consideration of things themselves" (WJL 1.74).[9] Similarly, in *Some Thoughts Concerning Education* (1693), he insisted that "Truth is to be found and supported by a mature and due consideration of things themselves, and not by artificial terms and ways of arguing" (WJL 8.178). Such ruminations led him to praise simple terms that reference impressions (i.e. simple ideas) (WJL 1.77–80). As he explained, "the names of simple ideas are, of all others, the least liable to mistakes" (WJL 2.18). Furthermore, he upheld "demonstration" as the best argumentative proof with the "highest degree of probability" since demonstration adduces "a man's constant and never-failing experience in like cases" (WJL 2.233).

Of course, the paragraph above misses some important elements in Locke's argumentative theory. After praising demonstration, he quickly conceded that it could not answer all questions. In fact, he worried that natural philosophy, limited to the narrow terrain of empirical observation, could never be a science and must therefore fail to address the central concern for all humanity: "morality [...] the proper science and the business of mankind in general" WJL 2.216). In the moral sciences, he suggested that people exercise "judgment" in addition to "knowledge," deductive reasoning in addition to inductive exploration. Judgment involves steady discursive labor through the degrees of probability, "signifying a proposition, for which there be arguments or proofs, to make them pass, or be received for true" (WJL 2.216). Through the exercise of reason (and without the interruption of scholastic syllogistic disputation), we can compare ideas premised upon observation and testimony in order to determine their (dis)agreement (WJL 2.233–2.262). Based on such passages from the *Essay*, previous scholars have drawn two principal conclusions. First, Locke's epistemology and communicative theory shifted the British intellectual tradition away from rhetorical "argumentation" and towards empirical "demonstration," a shift that would continue throughout the British

<hr>

lastic disputation exercises, Ibid, 90 and 18. Locke was a member of the Royal Society in its early days, so it is difficult to say that he did not follow their lead. He initially began writing the Essay at the request of five or six Royal Society friends after a conversation that led to great disagreement and confusion.

9   All references to Locke's works come from the Twelfth Edition of *The Works of John Locke* (London: C. and J. Rivington, 1824), 9 vols. The references themselves appear parenthetically as Works of John Locke (WJL), followed by the volume and page numbers. This reference, for instance is to volume 1, page 74.

Enlightenment.[10] Second, Locke's work shifted fallacy theory towards the "*ad*" tradition, an effort at cataloguing and critiquing everything that is not argumentation *ad rem* (to the thing) or *ad judicium* (to the judgment).[11] Both conclusions offer a convincingly clean picture of what Locke would expect in the tolerant republic of letters. Disputants should engage one another on the terrain of verifiable evidence and valid reasoning, bracketing any appeals to circumstance, authority, or character.

Doubtless, Locke's own writings on the fallacies lend further support to this characterization of his ideally tolerant republic of letters. Every fallacy that he identified in the *Essay* results from an appeal to something other than rational deduction or empirical induction. The *argumentum ad ignorantiam* appeals to ignorance; *the argumentum ad verecundiam* appeals blindly to authority; and the *argumentum ad hominem* appeals to the audience's untested assumptions. Only the argumentum *ad judicium* "brings true instruction with it" because such a contention "must come from proofs and arguments [...] from the nature of things themselves, and not from my shame-facedness, ignorance, or error" (WJL 2.261). However, tidy this portrait may seem, it contains fuzzy lines, for Locke did not forcefully condemn *argumentum ad hominem*. He simply labeled it one of "four sorts of arguments, that men, in their reasoning with others make use of to prevail on their assent" (WJL 2.260). Of all four "sorts of arguments," the *ad hominem* gets the briefest treatment, a short two sentences neither vituperative: "A third way is to press a man with conse-

....

10   For more on the contemporary distinction between "argumentation" and "demonstration," as well as the Enlightenment origin of this distinction, see Chaim Perelman and Lucie Olbrechts-Tyteca's *The New Rhetoric: A Treatise on Argumentation*, trans. John Wilkinson and Purcell Weaver (Notre Dame: University of Notre Dame Press, 1969). 13–17. For more on the part played by British empirical science in the shift from argumentation towards demonstration, and particularly for more on Locke's role in this shift, see Wilbur Samuel Howell's *Eighteenth-Century British Logic and Rhetoric* (Princeton: Princeton University Press, 1971), 268–297.

11   C.L. Hamblin contends that Locke initiated the "ad" tradition of fallacy categorization, though he worked in a longer tradition of anti-Aristotelians including Petra Ramus, Rudolphus Agricola, and Francis Bacon. Fallacies (London: Methuen and Company, 1971), 136–163. Locke's attention to the truth of premises and the validity of deduction places him squarely in the epistemic and alethic traditions of fallacy theory, an effort out of step with present-day approaches to the fallacies that emphasize dialogic forms and audience presuppositions. See Hamblin, Ibid, 231–234. For present-day approaches to argumentation that emphasizes dialogic forms, see Douglas Walton's *A Pragmatic Theory of Fallacy* (Tuscaloosa: University of Alabama Press, 1995) and Frans H. van Eemeren and Rob Grootendorst's *A Systematic Theory of Argumentation: The Pragma-Dialectical Approach* (Cambridge: Cambridge University Press, 2004). For efforts at approaching argumentation with an emphasis on audience presupposition, see the discussions of argumentation *ad hominem* in Chaim Perelman's and Lucie Olbrecht's Tyteca's *The New Rhetoric: A Treatise on Argumentation*, 110–114, and Henry Johnstone's article "Philosophy and Argumentum *ad hominem*," *Journal of Philosophy* 49.15(1952): 489–498.

        © Frank & Timme   Verlag für wissenschaftliche Literatur

quences drawn from his own principles or concessions. This is already known under the name of *argumentum ad homimen*" (WJL 2.260). C.L. Hamblin's diagnosis, now more than forty years old, remains apt—Locke did not "clearly condemn" the argumentum ad hominem. He deemed it "less than perfect," yet nevertheless potentially allowable "in practical politics."[12]

Following Hamblin's suggestion, in an effort to resolve Locke's ambivalence about argumentative fallacy and in a further effort to understand his desired tolerant republic of letters, we should turn to his participation "in practical politics," particularly to the extended public debates that he engaged during the latter years of his life. In these debates, Locke regularly entertained and deployed various forms of *ad hominem* argumentation, including the effort to press an interlocutor with "consequences of his own principles or concessions" (what is nowadays typically called *argumentum ex concessis*). Of course, critiquing and then practicing argumentation *ad hominem* could result from a failure to play by his own rules. In the fray of public discourse, many an argumentative moralist tosses principles aside. But when we regard Locke's other advice about argumentation and his own argumentative practices, we see no such inconsistency.

For an example of Locke's dogged consistency, we might consider his dedication to definition by "clear" terms that reference "simple" ideas. In the *Essay*, Locke regularly advised his readers to carefully define their terms by annexing "simple," "clear," and "distinct" ideas to their words (WJL 2.46). He defined his own terms in this fashion. When discussing "liberty," for instance, he insisted upon tying the abstract term to a clear idea of a particular experience: "having the power of doing, or forebearing to do, according as the mind shall choose or direct" (WJL 1.226). If he was consistent in his efforts to promote and to practice definition, then it seems reasonable that he would similarly be consistent elsewhere. He would not wholly condemn argumentation *ad hominem* and then deploy it. His ambivalence about the *ad hominem*, his regular use of the form, and his consistency on other matters of argumentation suggest that he did not object to argumentation *ad hominem*, though he may have harbored reservations about its use.

Locke's own allowance of *ad hominem* argumentation makes his approach to argumentative fallacy more pragmatic-sophistic than rational-empirical. Argumentation *ad hominem* may not be as reliable or as probable as argumentation

------

12 *Fallacies*, 161.

ad judicium, but it remains a constructive way to persuade an audience without warping their rational judgment or corroding their ethical foundation.[13]

2   How Locke Argued

Up until this point, I have conflated a variety of argumentative forms under the general heading of argumentation *ad hominem*. For the purposes of a more detailed analysis of Locke's practical arguments, I prefer to follow contemporary argumentation theorists who separate *ad hominem* argumentation from argumentation *ex concessis*, and then subdivide *ad hominem* argumentation into two categories, one of which can be even further taxonomized.[14] (See figure 1).

Fig. 1: Taxonomy of Argumentative Fallacies that Locke Used and Condemned

FALLACIES

I. *EX CONCESSIS* (used)
II. *AD HOMINEM*

       Circumstantial: Inconsistent Commitment (used)

       Abusive: a) Guilt by Association (condemned)

                        b) Poisoning the well (used)

....

13   My use of the term "constructive" borrows heavily from Christopher Tindale, who contends that a sophistic approach to argumentative fallacy will attend to an argument's ability to "tap into [...the audience's] general fund of knowledge concerning the customs of their society, their community, and how they know people generally to behave." *Reason's Dark Champions: Constructive Strategies of Sophistic Argument* (Columbia: University of South Carolina Press, 2010), 82. A fallacy, therefore, is something that is not constructive, that does not tap into or advance a society's principles of behavior, its ethical norms, or its stores of common knowledge. If Locke's ideal society is a republic of citizens who tolerate ideas, then any argumentative form leading to ideological intolerance is not constructive. Everything else, including many forms of argumentation *ad hominem*, are fair game.

14   Frans H. van Eemeren and Rob Grootendorst note that many have opted to emphasize argumentation *ex concessis* when discussing the *ad hominem*, including: the late 19th-century logician Richard Whately, the mid 20th-century rhetorical theorists Chaim Perelman and Henry Johnstone, and late 20th-century informal logicians E. M. Barth and J.L. Martens. "The History of the Argumentum *Ad hominem* Since the Seventeenth Century," in *Empirical Logic and Public Debate: Essays in Honour of Else M. Barth*, eds. Erik C.W. Krabbe, Renée José Dalitz, and Pier A Smit (Atlanta: Rodop, 1993), 49–68. Recently, Douglas Walton has separated arguments from commitment (*ex concessis* arguments) from *ad hominem* arguments (which include both poisoning-the-well and circumstantial arguments). See his "Argumentation Schemes and Historical Origins of the Circumstantial *Ad hominem* Argument," *Argumentation* 18 (2004): 359–368. For this analysis, in an effort at understanding the rhetorical fallacyin Locke's work, it is illuminating to discuss all three, even though argumentation *ex concessis* has significant formal differences that should remove it from the category of *ad hominem* argumentation.

The *argumentum ex concessis* draws conclusions from an opponent's concessions and is therefore primarily (though informally) logical. (Locke labeled what I call argumentation *ex concessis* argumentation *ad hominem*). The *argumentum ad hominem* assaults an opponent's person or character and is therefore a strictly ethotic argument, a claim undercutting credibility. An abusive *ad hominem* avers that we should not afford assent since the argument stems from an untrustworthy source. A circumstantial *ad hominem* presents inconsistency in order to contend that a speaker does not deserve trust, since s/he does not really believe what s/he is saying.

Below are examples of Locke using three argumentative forms: poisoning the well, inconsistent commitment, and argumentation *ex concessis*. The first two sets of examples are taken from a series of pamphlets that he wrote to engage the arguments of John Edwards and Bishop Edward Stillingfleet who had respectively questioned *The Reasonableness of Christianity* (1695) and the *Essay Concerning Human Understanding* (1690). The third set of examples is taken from a series of pamphlets that Locke wrote to defend his *Letter Concerning Toleration* (1689). For the time being, in an effort at demonstrating that Locke's ideally tolerant republic of letters could feature a range of argumentative tactics beyond argumentation *ad judicium*, I will focus on the arguments' formal qualities divorced of context. Each analysis is presented below in the fashion of contemporary informal logicians, first abstractly demonstrating the argumentative form, then translating Locke's argument into that form by way of paraphrase, and then giving the natural-language presentation of the argument (an extended quote from Locke's writings) to demonstrate how he used the form.

Group 1: Poisoning-the-Well Arguments against John Edwards

The Form:
For every argument A in dialogue D, person a is biased.
Person a's bias is a failure to take part honestly in a type of dialogue D that a is a part of.
Therefore, a is a bad person.
Therefore, a should not be given as much credibility as it would have without the bias.[15]

....

15 Douglas Walton, Ad hominem *Arguments* (Tuscaloosa: University of Alabama Press, 1998), 230–233.

Examples from Locke's Writing:

Formal Paraphrase: For every claim that he is honestly exchanging ideas and seeking truth, Edwards is biased towards his own orthodoxies. Edwards's orthodoxy is a failure to take part honestly in the free and open exchange of ideas or the search for truth. Therefore, Edwards is a rigid ideologue. Therefore Edwards should not be given the credibility he would deserve if unbiased.

Locke's Natural Language:

(1a) Mr. Edwards, who is entrenched in orthodoxy, and so is safe in matters of faith almost as infallibility itself, is yet as apt to err as others in matters of fact. (WJL 6.171)

(1b) It being not, it seems, a creed-maker's [Edwards's] business to convince men's understanding by reason; but to impose on their belief by authority; or, where that is wanting, by falsehood and bawling. (WJL 6.401)

Group 2: Inconsistent-Commitment Arguments against John Edwards and Edward Stillingfleet

The Form:
a advocates argument A, which has proposition A as its conclusion.
a has carried out an action or a set of actions that imply that a is committed to ~A (the opposite, or negation of A).
Therefore, a is a bad person.
Therefore, a's argument A should not be accepted.[16]

Examples from Locke's Writing:

Formal Paraphrase: Edwards advocates the true church, which imports a belief in the seriousness of the subject. Edwards has discoursed in a rude and hysterical manner that implies that he does not take his sub-

---

16 Douglas Walton, Ad hominem *Arguments*, 218–219.

ject seriously. Therefore, Edwards is an untrustworthy person. Therefore, Edwards's argument that he wants to advance the true form of Christianity should not be accepted.

Locke's Natural Language:

(2a) Mr. Edwards's ill language [...] is his way and strength in management of a controversy; and therefore requires a little more consideration in this disputant, than otherwise it would deserve. (WJL 6.184)

(2b) Those who, like Mr. Edwards, dare to publish inventions of their own, for matters of fact, deserve a name so abhorred, that it finds not room in civil conversation [...] There are two ways of making a book unanswerable. The one is by clearness, strength, and fairness of argumentation [...] Another way to make a book unanswerable, is to lay stress on matters of fact foreign to the question, as well as to truth; and to stuff it with scurrility and fiction. (WJL 6.192–193)

(2c) The rest of what he [Edwards] calls "Reflections on Mr. Bold's 'sermon'" being nothing but either rude and misbecoming language of him; or pitiful childish application to him, to change his persuasion at the creed-maker's [Edwards's] entreaty, and to give up the truth he hath owned, in courtesy to this doughty combatant; shows the ability of the man. (WJL 6.395)

Formal Paraphrase: Stillingfleet advocates an open dialogue about religious matters in order to pursue truth. Stillingfleet has used language in ways that imply he is not committed to rigorous pursuit of truth in religious matters. Therefore, Stillingfleet is not a trustworthy person. Therefore, Stillingfleet's arguments about religion should not be trusted.

Locke's Natural Language:

(2d) Your lordship's name in writing is established above control, and therefore it will be ill-breeding in one, who barely reads what you write, not to take every thing for perfect in its kind, which your lordship says. Clearness, and force, and consistence, are to be presumed always, whatever your lordship's words be: and there is no other remedy for an answerer, who finds it difficult any where to come at your meaning or argument, but to make his excuse for it, in laying the particulars before the reader, that he may be judge where the fault lies; especially where any matter of fact is contested, deductions from the rise are often necessary, which cannot be made in few words, nor without several repetitions; an inconvenience possibly fitter to be endured, than that your lordship, in the run of your learned notions, should be shackled with the ordinary and strict rules of language; and, in the delivery of your sublimer speculations, be tied down to the mean and contemptible rudiments of grammar: though your being above these, and freed from servile observance in the use of trivial particles, whereon the connexion of discourse chiefly depends cannot but cause great difficulties to the reader. (WJL3.257)

(2e) I find your lordship, in these two or three paragraphs, to use the word certainty in so uncertain a sense. (WJL 3.283)

(2f) My lord, relative definitions of terms [such as Stillingfleet's definition of "nature"] that are not relative, usually do no more than lead us in a circuit to the same place from whence we set out, and there leave us in the same ignorance we were in at first. (WJL 6.432)

Group 3: *Ex concessis* Arguments against Jonas Proast in Locke's *Defense of Locke's Letter Concerning Toleration*

The Form: a is committed to proposition A (generally, or in virtue of what s/he said in the past).
a is committed to proposition ~A, which is the conclusion of the argument that a presently advocates.
Therefore, a's argument should not be accepted.[17]

---

17 Walton explores this form in Ad hominem *Arguments*, 220–221; and "Argumentation Schemes and Historical Origins," 365–366.

Examples:

Formal Paraphrase: Proast is committed to toleration outside of England to allow for the free discussion and dissemination of true (Anglican) religion, yet Proast is also committed to using force to promote true (Anglican) religion in England; therefore, Proast's commitment to the spread of true religion should not be accepted.

Locke's Natural Language:

(3a) But if you allow such a toleration useful in other countries, you must find something very peculiar in the air, that it makes it less useful to truth in England; and it will savour of much partiality, and be too absurd, I fear, for you to own, that toleration will be advantageous to true religion all the world over, except only in this island. (WJL 5.65)

Formal Paraphrase: Proast is committed to having everyone thoroughly examine his/her religious beliefs, yet Proast would only have the magistrate require such examination of dissenters (not Anglicans); therefore, Proast's commitment to the promotion of true (Anglican) religion by examination of faith should not be accepted.

Locke's Natural Language:

(3b) [I]f you would propose that all those who are ignorant, careless, and negligent in examining, should be punished, you would have little to say in this question of toleration. For if the laws of the state were made, as they ought to be, equal to all the subjects without distinction of men of different professions in religion; and the faults to be amended by punishments, were impartially punished, in all who are guilty of them; this would immediately produce a perfect toleration, or show the uselessness of force in matters of religion. (WJL 5.131–2)

Of course, the above examples could warrant nothing more than a claim that Locke threw his argumentative principles aside in the heat of controversy. But two bits of evidence suggest otherwise. First, as mentioned above. Locke painstakingly struggled to practice what he preached. He suggested using simple terms to reference simple ideas, and he himself used such simple terms. He also insisted that, in moments of potential referential ambiguity, the speaker should define terms clearly and carefully (WJL 2.48). The debate with Stillingfleet can be characterized as an extended effort by Locke to define what he meant by "substance," "nature," and "person" when composing the *Essay*. During the last two rounds of this debate Stillingfleet defined "person" as "a complete intelligent Substance"[18]; and Locke insisted that his own definition of personal identity as presented in the *Essay* likewise divorced the principle of consciousness from the material body (WJL 3.330). Second, Locke regularly entertained Edwards's, Stillinfleet's, and Proast's *ad hominem* as well as *ex concessis* arguments. He refuted such arguments based upon their evidence or their inferential structure. He treated *ad hominem* and *ex concessis* arguments as if they were potentially valid.

3   How Locke (The Philosopher) Argued About Argumentation

In order to further explore my claim that Locke entertained *ad hominem* and *ex concessis* arguments, I must discuss the historical, intellectual, and religious context of Locke's debates with Edwards and Stillingfleet. As every historian of the era knows, there is no talking about Enlightenment toleration without extensively discussing religion, politics, and war.

Locke himself was notoriously quiet about his own religious affiliations. He wrote the *Essay* as well as his other works in an ostensible effort to advance knowledge without running afoul of the Church of England. He had seen religious differences result in a range of difficult and violent events, including a civil war; a bloody interregnum; a tense restoration; and a "glorious," though nonetheless tenuous, revolution. Locke drafted the *Letter Concerning Toleration* during the Restoration, a period punctuated regularly by sectarian violence. Though Charles II may have been more tolerant than his Parliament (and though he did not persecute Catholics with Oliver Cromwell's zeal), his quarter-century reign featured numerous state-led efforts to suppress non-

---

18   *The Bishop of Worcester's Answer to Mr. Locke's Second Letter; Wherein his Notions of Ideas is Prov'd to be Inconsistent with itself and with Articles of the Christian Faith* (London: J.H. for Henry Mortlock, 1698), 175.

conformity of any stripe. Having survived the interregnum violence advancing Puritanism, Anglicans under Charles II concluded that uniform belief in the state church would best maintain national peace. Parliamentary acts, such as the Quaker Act of 1662, persecuted specific sects. Public officials collected and jailed dissenters. Citizens gathered in mobs to assault people of non-Anglican faiths. Locke along with numerous Whig parliamentarians reached out to nonconformists to end such Anglican cruelties.[19] For consorting with Whig tolerationists, he found himself under investigation, so he fled to Rotterdam, where he wrote the most widely circulated (and anonymously printed) draft of the *Letter* and the first draft of the *Essay*. Shortly after returning to England, he wrote and anonymously published *The Reasonableness of Christianity*. This last work incited John Edwards's argumentative furor. Jonas Proast objected to the *Letter*, and Bishop Stillingfleet took issue with the *Essay*.

Voltaire's comment about the Stillingfleet controversy pithily summarizes all three debates: Three theologians "jousted with Locke and [… were] defeated, for [… their] reasoning was that of a rector and Locke argued as a philosopher, aware of the strength and weakness of human intelligence, and as one who used weapons whose temper he understood."[20] Thirty years after the last debate ended, Voltaire, the anglophile, positively evaluated Locke's performance, but the victory was not clear-cut at the end of the 17th century. Certainly, Locke argued as a philosopher, putting into practice much of the advice about public debate that he distributed in his *Essay*. He argued *ad judicium*, occasionally indulging a few words *ad hominem* or even an *ex concessis*. Attending to his arguments *ad judicium* reveals how a philosopher should argue. Notably, the philosopher consistently entertained and rebutted arguments *ad hominem* and *ex concessis* through argumentation *ad judicium* and *ad rem*.

4   The Locke-Edwards Debate

John Edwards sought publicly to reveal and revile all heresies and heretics. Like many other 17th century Calvinists, Edwards regularly drew anti-Trinitarian (and therefore heretical) conclusions based on premises asserted in

---

19   For a full review of Restoration-era intolerance, see John Marshall's *John Locke, Toleration, and Early Enlightenment Culture*, ch. 3.

20   *Philosophical Letters, or, Letters Regarding the English Nation*, ed. and intro. John Leigh, trans. Prudence L. Steiner (Cambridge: Hackett, 2007), 43.

ostensibly Trinitarian works. In short, Edwards argued *ex concessis* in order to accuse people of Socinianism (a belief system denying the coeval existence of three unique figures in the Godhead). Edwards based these arguments upon premises that people publicly adopted.[21]

In *Some Thoughts Concerning the Several Causes and Occasions of Atheism* (1695), Edwards applied this argumentative tack to Locke's *Reasonableness of Christianity*, contending that the work promoted Unitarian (anti-Trinitarian) ideas and therefore deserved to be grouped among other heretical writings including those that promoted the "very Socian Doctrine itself" which possessed an "Atheistick Tang."[22] Edwards also lumped Locke into a motley crowd including genuine Christians (Socinians), deists (quasi-Christians whose beliefs may have derived some support from Socinian theology), and radical secularists (whose beliefs contradicted Locke's own rational Christianity as well as Socinian dogma). By any reasonable measure, Edwards's charge appears wrongheaded, but not completely unfounded. Locke had charted a perilous middle course between systematic, mathematical reasoning (often allied with the secularism of Renée Descartes and Benedictus de Spinoza) and Christianity (often the province of conservative thinkers who decried all Enlightenment thought, deist, rational, moderate, or radical). Latitudinarian efforts at formulating a rational Christianity spurred many philosophically conservative Christian thinkers, like Edwards, to accusations of heresy. Locke was no radical philosophe, nor was he a public Socinian. And even if he were one of these, he could not be both, as they were contradictory positions. Nevertheless, Edwards accused him of every heterodoxy at or outside the boundary of a strictly doctrinal Christianity.[23]

---

21   *John Marshall John Locke, Toleration, and Early Enlightenment Culture*, 257–259. Edwards's argument resembles that of many who sought to discredit by showing that heretical ideas derive from people's public positions. In a letter to Pierre Coste, Locke's friend and correspondent Pierre Bayle described the common practice of deriving anti-Trinitarian implications from another person's professed beliefs. Bayle specifically wrote of the abuses lobbed at the Cambridge Anglican (however latitudinarian) Ralph Cudworth. Said Bayle, "No one is unaware that in disputes, one objects to one's adversaries as many inopportune consequences as one can from their principles," qtd. in John Marshall, *John Locke, Toleration, and Early Enlightenment Culture*, 258. In Edwards's hands, Locke found himself treated as Cudworth—labeled an anti-Trinitarian based on seemingly innocuous pronouncements.

22   *Some Thoughts Concerning the Several Causes and Occasions of Atheism, Especially in the Present Age and with Some Brief Reflections on Socinianism and on the Late Book Entitled The Reasonableness of Christianity as Delivered in The Scriptures* (London: J. Robinson, 1795), 121, 64.

23   Jonathan Israel explains the curious connections between Socinianism and radical philosophy in *Enlightenment Contested: Philosophy, Modernity, and the Emancipation of Man 1670–1752* (Oxford: Oxford University Press, 2006), 115–135. Israel's judgment strikes me as quite accurate:

Locke responded to Edwards's allegations in two separate pamphlets, *A Vindication of the Reasonableness of Christianity* and *A Second Vindication*. Edwards responded to Locke's responses in *Socinianism Unmask'd* (1696). This pamphlet war also included several other participants, such as Samuel Bold, an Anglican clergyman and friend to Locke, who authored, among other things, *Some Passages on the Reasonableness of Christianity &c. and its Vindication* (1697).

As my brief gloss of Edwards's argument and Locke's theology intimates, the debate between these two men was prolix and abstruse. Bracketing the theological complexities allows an attention to how Locke argued and also how he argued about argumentation. When we momentarily ignore the content, both the argumentative form and Locke's arguments about "good" argumentative form stand out. In *Socinianism Unmask'd*, Edwards lobbed numerous *ad hominem* arguments at Locke, describing his writing as duplicitous and unreasonable. He accused Locke of having "Angry fits and Passionate Ferments" as well as "Confusion and Disorder."[24] In these cases, Edwards rocketed circumstantial *ad hominem* arguments similar to those that Locke volleyed at Edwards (listed above as examples 2a–2c).

Edwards also argued *ex concessis*, trying to catch Locke in premises and conclusions that contradict one another (thus offering arguments formally similar to those that Locke would present in other debates; see examples 3a and 3b above): "[Locke asserts that] a Multitude of doctrines is obscure, and hard to be understood" and then denies such an assertion in his Vindication; thus, "you [Locke] pretend that you have forgot that any such thing was said by you; which shews that you are Careless of your Words, and that you forget what you write."[25]

Locke disagreed with Edwards's *ex concessis* arguments, though he did not dismiss these as ethically or rationally out of bounds. Rather, in the *Vindication*, while revisiting salient points in his argument, Locke continually noted that Edwards imposed false motives upon him. Edwards, for instance, had accused Locke of omitting discussion of the Pauline epistles because these

---

"while Socinianism assisted the rise of both Enlightenment wings [radicals such as Spinoza and moderates such as Locke], especially as a source of recruits from among those disillusioned with Socinianism, there was little real affinity of ideas, not just between them and the radicals but even between them and [the moderates]," 124.

24 *Socinianism Unmask'd*, 2–3.

25 *Socinianism Unmask'd*, 28.

texts reveal fundamental articles of Christian faith that Locke would deny. Based on this omission, Edwards accused Locke of a Socinian Biblical exegesis, a reading that selectively attended to the Gospels in order to arrive at a minimal catechism.[26] Locke rejoined that Edwards should not presume to see "so deeply into my heart." By Locke's account omitting the epistles was forgivable because "those fundamental articles were in those epistles promiscuously, and without distinction, mixed with other truths" (WJL 6.167–168). In this instance, and in several others, Locke took issue with the evidence and the conclusion premised upon such evidence. Writing as a philosopher, he carefully rebutted and thus laconically approved of Edwards's arguments *ex concessis* and *ad hominem*.

5 The Locke-Stillingfleet Debate

We can witness a similar pattern in the debate with Bishop Edward Stillingfleet, a high-church Anglican who contended that Locke's *Essay* set the groundwork for a range of heresies, anti-Trinitarianism among them. The context for the Stillingfleet debate includes three salient features: First, Stillingfleet was Locke's social superior; second, Stillingfleet had criticized a work publicly associated with Locke; third Stillingfleet was a leader in the established national church, siding theologically with the empowered clergy under William's reign. Edwards, by comparison, belonged to a marginalized theological group of Calvinists, whose religious views eventually cost him a university position at St. John's College, Cambridge. Moreover, *The Reasonableness of Christianity* was published anonymously.

Though Edwards could and did insinuate that Locke had written the work, he could make no outright nor public accusations of heresy. An unimportant voice in the wilderness hurling accusations at an anonymous pamphleteer did not worry Locke. A respected and empowered leader in the state church loudly thundering heretical charges that included Locke's proper name and his proudest work caused significant trepidation. Though the interregnum abuses of dissenters and heretics had abated, no one save high-flying Anglicans enjoyed freedom to profess and practice. Publicly convicted heretics in late 17th century England could be stripped of their property, fined, exiled, and impris-

....

26 *Some Thoughts*, 108–111.

    © Frank & Timme Verlag für wissenschaftliche Literatur

oned. Locke's friend, Matthew Tindale, for instance, saw his works condemned and burned by the House of Commons (1710). Likewise, English and Irish Parliaments burned John Toland's *Christianity Not Mysterious* (1696). Toland lost a government job in Ireland and eventually had to flee the country under charges of being a "public and inveterate enemy to all reveal'd religion."[27] Locke's reputation, his property, his livelihood, his freedom, and his person were at stake in the Stillingfleet debate.

Despite these contextual differences, some notable textual similarities between the Edwards and the Stillingfleet debates remain. To begin with, Stillingfleet, like Edwards, presented *ex concessis* arguments to discredit Locke. To be sure, Stillingfleet qualified and tempered more than his Calvinist counterpart. Rather than calling Locke himself a Socinian, Stillingfleet insisted that Locke's *Essay* presented a series of notions (including a manner of investigation and fundamental presuppositions about substance) that would lead to such heresy. In his *Discourse in Vindication of the Trinity* (1697), Stillingfleet said that Locke's "method of true Reasoning" would "make us reject Doctrines of Faith, because we do not comprehend them."[28]

Locke defended against the *ex concessis* portion of Stillingfleet's argument, saying that the skeptical conclusions that Stillingfleet would draw from the *Essay* are unwarranted: "If by the way of ideas [...] a man cannot come to clear and distinct apprehensions concerning nature and person [...] it will follow hence that he is a mistaken philosopher: but it will not follow from thence, that he is not an orthodox Christian" (WJL 3.68). Stillingfleet's subsequent pamphlet expanded these *ex concessis* arguments to support his claim that Locke's *Essay* leads to heresy. For instance, he maintained that Locke's way of ideas ties consciousness to a material (mortal) substance, which would lead people to disbelieve the "Resurrection of the Dead." Moreover, Locke's ideas about "nature" and "person" would lead to anti-Trinitarianism.[29] Stillingfleet's arguments about "person" and "nature" are far too extensive to encapsulate here. (They require 200 pages of his *Second Answer*.)[30] What's important for our

---

27 Qtd. in Jonathan Israel's *Radical Enlightenment: Philosophy and the Making of Modernity 1650–1750* (Oxford: Oxford University Press, 2001), 97.

28 Edward Stillingfleet, *A Discourse in Vindication of the Trinity* (London: Henry Mortlock, 1697), 267.

29 Edward Stillingfleet, *The Bishop of Worcester's Answer to Mr. Locke's Second Letter*, 32–44.

30 Stillingfleet summarized his position on these matters in the following statement: "the true Reason of Identity in Man is the vital Union of Soul and Body: And since every Man hath a different Soul united to different Particles of Matter, there must be a real Distinction between them,

purposes is that Stillingfleet took Locke's ideas and used them to support heretical notions, thus arguing *ex concessis* that Locke's work was heretical.

Locke's *Reply to the Right Reverend the Lord Bishop of Worcester's Answer to his Second Letter* is a monumental effort at rebutting Stillingfleet's *ex concessis* arguments. His willingness to carefully represent and then refute the textual evidence that underpins Stillingfleet's deductive claims indicates a respect for the form. He found no fault in the manner, only in the execution, saying, "My lord, the words you bring out of my book are so often different from those I read in the places which you refer to, that I am sometimes ready to think, you have got some strange copy of it" (WJL 3.407–408). Though his response is often mordant (as indicated by example 2d above), Locke philosophically engaged Stillingfleet's *ex concessis* arguments.

6   The Locke-Proast Debate

If the evidence culled from the Edwards and the Stillingfleet debates remains insufficient to demonstrate that Locke philosophically and ethically approved of *ex concessis* argumentation, then evidence from the Proast debate decidedly tips the scales. For, in this debate about toleration, Locke offered his most extensive refutations and deployments of argumentation *ex concessis*. At issue in the Proast debate was not Anti-Trinitarianism but the use of public force to encourage religious conversion. Proast, responding to Locke's *Letter Concerning Toleration* contended that some amount of public force should lead people consider true (Anglican) religion. As Proast put it, force is "neither useless or needless for the bringing Men to do, what the saving of their souls may require of them."[31] Furthermore, the magistrate's authority "is not an Authority to compel anyone to his Religion, but onely an Authority to procure all his Subjects the means of Discovering the Way of Salvation."[32] Locke philosophically objected to Proast's *ex concessis* arguments—questioning evidence and infer-

---

without any respect to what is accidental to them [...] the Identity of Man depends neither upon the Notion of Place for his Body; nor upon the Soul consider'd by it self, but upon both these, as actually united and making one Person," *The Bishop of Worcester's Answer to Mr. Locke's Second Letter*, 172–173. For a full review of Stillingfleet's theology as it relates to the "way of ideas," see M.A. Stewart's "Stillingfleet and the Way of Ideas," *English Philosophy in the Age of Locke*, ed. M.A. Stewart (Oxford: Clarendon Press, 2000), 245–280.

31   Jonas Proast, *The Argument of a Letter Concerning Toleration, Briefly Consider'd and Answer'd* (Oxford: George West and Henry Clements, 1690), 12.

32   Jonas Proast, *The Argument*, 21.

         © Frank & Timme   Verlag für wissenschaftliche Literatur

ence, asking for clarification and definition. For instance, in the *Second Letter Concerning Toleration*, he asked Proast to define "force," (WJL 5.111) and Proast replied in his *Third Letter Concerning Toleration* (1691) that by "force," he meant "having sufficient means of Instruction in the true Religion provided for them, yet do refuse to embrace it."[33] In his own *Third Letter for Toleration*, Locke further pressed Proast to define "force" in greater particularity, since past uses of force had ranged from the innocuous to the cruel (WJL 6.287–288). Proast's assurance in his *Second Letter* (1704) that he only intended "moderate penalties" for dissenters never satisfied the philosopher.

The Proast debate lasted twelve years and provided grist for an intellectual mill yielding seven substantial works. Throughout, both Locke and Proast argued *ex concessis*. Two of Locke's *ex concessis* arguments against Proast are presented above as examples 3a and 3b. But perhaps the most memorable comes at the end of his *Fourth Letter*:

Formal Paraphrase: Proast is committed to supporting the magistrate's obligation to enforce the true (Anglican) religion by force, yet Proast is also committed to the belief that many magistrates do not own or even know the true (Anglican) religion; therefore, Proast's commitment to the spread of true religion should not be accepted.

Locke's Natural Language:

(3c) You tell us, it is by the law of nature magistrates are obliged to promote the true religion by force. It must be owned, that if this be an obligation of the law of nature, very few magistrates overlook it; so forward are they to promote that religion by force which they take to be true. This being the case, I beseech you tell me what was the Huaina Capac, emperor of Peru, obliged to do? Who being persuaded of his duty to promote the true religion, was not yet within distance of knowing or so much has hearing of the christian religion, which really is the true [...] Was he to promote the true religion by force? That he neither did nor could know any thing of; so that was morally impossible for him to do.

<hr>

33   Jonas Proast, *A Third Letter Concerning Toleration: In Defense of the Argument of the Letter Concerning Toleration, Briefly Consider'd and Answer'd* (Oxford: George West, 1691), 23.

Was he to sit still in the neglect of his duty incumbent on him? That is in effect to suppose it a duty and no duty at the same time. (WJL 6.573–574)

Likewise, Proast tried to paint Locke into an argumentative corner by asking him to admit conclusions based on Locke's own assertions. Consider the following argument from his Third Letter:

Formal Paraphrase: Locke is committed to the belief that the natural religion is the true and unavoidable religion in all countries. Locke is also committed to the belief that magistrates regularly embrace false religions. Therefore, Locke's commitment to the belief that the natural religion is equally true and unavoidable in all countries cannot be accepted.

Proast's Natural Language:

(3d): But I hope when you have thought a little more of the matter, you will be so far from asserting that the Supposition, that the National Religion is the onely true Religion, is in all Countries, equally unavoidable, and equally just, that you will acknowledge that it cannot be at all unavoidable, or just, where any false Religion is the National Religion. Otherwise, you will be forced to own that men may be bound to embrace false Religions.[34]

Locke and Proast wrangled for over a decade, finding or teasing out contradictory positions, all in an effort to undercut the other's credibility. Neither objected to the other's *ex concessis* or *ad hominem* argumentation. The Proast debate therefore offers one more representative example of a pattern: Locke approved of and engaged various *ad hominem* and *ex concessis* arguments, thus signaling his approval in practical politics.

---

34 *A Third Letter Concerning Toleration*, 12.

Arguing as a philosopher, Locke engaged and deployed arguments *ex concessis* as well as *ad hominem*. Though the debates above were all heated, only two debates became acrimonious: the Edwards and the Stillingfleet debates. To understand why the argumentative tension turned to animosity, we should notice an argumentative form present in these two debates but wholly absent from the Proast debate. Both Edwards and Stilingfleet assaulted Locke with guilt-by-association arguments. And, when then did, Locke did not respond as a rational-empirical philosopher but as a tolerant ethicist. He did not object to their inference or their evidence but to their very manner of argumentation. Furthermore, he premised his objections on an ethical commitment to a tolerant republic of letters where a person's circumstantial identity should not prejudice an audience against his/her ideas. Locke harbored no deep philosophical reservation about argumentation *ad hominem* or *ex concessis*. He philosophically entertained and engaged both forms. When responding to the guilt-by-association arguments, however, Locke shed his philosophical composure and adopted an ethicist's outrage.

8   The Locke-Edwards Debate

Locke refused, out of hand, Edwards's consistent effort to associate him with various heretical sects and thus to damage his credibility. Over the course of *Socinianism Unmask'd*, Edwards accused Locke of being Racovian, a closet Socinian, a person with the faith of a "Turk," and a Unitarian. He did so by loose associations built upon Locke's own premises, his admissions, and his style of writing. He said, for instance, that Locke "follows the Steps of the Racovians, who submit the greatest Mysteries to the judgment of the Vulgar." In *The Reasonableness of Christianity*, Locke asserted unequivocally that "These two, faith and repentance, i.e. believing Jesus to be the Messiah, and a good life, are the indispensable conditions of the new covenant, to be performed by all those who would obtain eternal life" (WJL 6.105). According to Edwards, Locke "trusses up in One Article, that the poor people and bulk of mankind can bear it [...] The plain truth is, he Socianizes here, but will not own it." Moreover, according to Edwards, Locke's doctrinal minimalism reveals a "Lank Faith" like "the Faith of a Turk." (Edwards averred a that Socinianism was rampant in Eastern Europe and Turkey.) According to Edwards, Locke cited Scripture like a Socinian, and he even refused to reveal his name, thus confirming, once and for all, his identity as a Racovian.[35]

Take the following example as paradigmatic of Edwards's many guilt-by-association arguments:

Group 4: John Edwards's Guilt-by-Association Argument

The Form:
a is a member of or is associated with group G which should be morally condemned.
Therefore, a is a bad person.
Therefore, a's argument A should not be accepted.

Example:

Formal Paraphrase: Locke is a Socinian or is associated with Socinians, who should be morally condemned because they are anti-Trinitarian heretics. Therefore, Locke is a bad person. Therefore, Locke's beliefs about minimal Christian doctrine (as well as his denial of Racovian or Socinian sympathies) should not be accepted.

Edwards's Natural Language:

(4a) It is true, he [Locke] tells us that he never read the Socinian Writers, p. 22 but we know his Shuffling is such that there is no depending on his word. But suppose he did not read those Authors, yet he doth not deny that he hath Convers'd with some of them, and hath heard their Notions and Arguments: and this indeed he intimates to us when he lets us know that the generality of Divines he more converses with are not Racovians, p. 22. which intimates that there are some Particular Divines he less converses with that are of another way. What shall we say? The Gentleman is a Racovian, and yet pretends he doth not know it. So we must number him among the Ignoramus-Socinians (as they tell us in

---

35 *Socinianism Unmask'd*, A3 recto, 21, 28, 53, 65–66, 92–93, A3 recto.

their late Papers of Ignoramus Trinitarians) which is one sort of those folks it seems.[36]

That Edwards argued *ex concessis* and by association is nothing remarkable nor interesting. That Locke objected argumentatively to the *ex concessis* arguments but ethically to the guilt-by association arguments is interesting. *Ex concessis* arguments invoked the philosphor's reply. Guilt-by association arguments spurred the tolerationist's condemnation.

Locke declared that, though he would prefer to address the matter at hand, he was forced to "wipe off the dirt he [Edwards] has thrown upon me." He contended that Edwards should focus on "the most weighty and important points that can come into question"; Edwards should not turn this debate "into a mere quarrel against the author" (WJL 183). At several points in the *Second Vindication*, Locke repeated this objection to Edwards's guilt-by-association arguments (WJL 197, 201, 211, 262–263). Locke was no naturalistic philosopher refusing responsibility for his own statements, nor did he proclaim that a need for incontrovertible truth motivated his every argument.[37] He indicated as much by his careful rebuttal of Edwards's *ex concessis* arguments; by his own willingness to engage in argumentation *ad hominem* and *ex concessis*; and by his criticism of Edwards's guilt-by-association arguments. When he rejected Edwards's guilt-by-association *ad hominem*, Locke did so based upon a tolerationist's ethic, not a philosopher's reason. He valued a tolerant republic of letters characterized in part by open debate between reasonable discussants who focus on their ideas and not their allegiances. The guilt-by association *ad hominem* interrupts such debate by fomenting hot rancor and by following red herrings. As Locke admonished Edwards: "[I]t matters not to a lover of truth, or to a confuter of errours, who was the author; but what they contain. He who makes such a deal to do about that which is nothing to the question, shows he has but little mind to the argument; that his hopes are more in the recommendation of names, and prejudice of parties, than in the strength of truth follows that, whoever be for or against it; and can suffer himself to pass by no argument of his adversary, without taking notice of it, either in allowing its force, or giving it a fair answer" (WJL 6.402). In the polite republic of letters to which

....

36 *Socinianism Unmask'd*, 92–93.

37 Henry Johnstone contends that those who formally object to all *ad hominem* arguments often do so based on these presuppositions. "Philosophy and Argumentum *ad hominem*," 490, 496.

Locke addressed his work, the guilt-by-association *ad hominem* deserved outright condemnation for its ability to corrode a tolerant ethos.

9   The Locke-Stillingfleet Debate

Though Stillingfleet's assertions lack the asperity characteristic of Edwards's contentions, many remain guilt-by-association arguments. Stillingfleet associated Locke with others who were considered heretical for their skeptical philosophies, including Renée Descartes whose philosophy was attacked by defenders of traditional Christianity throughout 17th-century Europe.[38] Locke's response to Stillingfleet's initial volley also exhibits telling parallels to his earlier rejoinders. He objected especially to Stillingfleet's practice of associating him with a plural "they," a group of skeptics who "expose a doctrine relating to the divine essence, because they cannot comprehend the manner of it" (WJL 3.45).

In *The Bishop of Worcester's Answer to Mr. Locke's Letter* (1697), Stillingfleet expanded the guilt-by-association argument, tying Locke to Thomas Hobbes and Benedictus de Spinoza.[39] Associating Locke with Hobbes was a bothersome jab. Associating Locke with Spinoza was a full-force roundhouse. Hobbes's writings were arguably secularist and potentially heretical. But Hobbes never openly questioned the Anglican Church's power nor doctrine. In the mid 17th century, as Jonathan Israel explains, Spinoza "emerged as a leader, perhaps the leader, of the 'atheistic' circle which by then had taken shape" in Amsterdam.[40] According to Stillingfleet, "my joyning your words with another's Application" was perfectly legitimate since an infidel had cited Locke's way of ideas when questioning Christian doctrine. The question, then, should be "whether your general expression had not given him too much occasion for it."[41] The infidel in question, the individual who had extrapolated heretical ideas from Locke's Essay, was none other than John Toland, whose *Christianity Not Mysterious* (1696) began with very Lockean assertions about

....

38   Jonathan Israel, *Radical Enlightenment*, 29–58.

39   Edward Stillingfleet, *The Bishop of Worcester's Answer to Mr. Locke's Letter Concerning Some Passages Relating to his Essay of Humane Understanding* (London: Henry Mortlock, 1697), 55–56, 79.

40   Jonathan Israel, *Radical Enlightenment*, 163.

41   Edward Stillingfleet, *The Bishop of Worcester's Answer to Mr. Locke's Letter*, 35–39.

the "agreement and disagreement of ideas." Based on Lockean principles, Toland claimed to have developed a sense of reason that undercuts various Anglican doctrines.[42] In *The Bishop of Worcester's Second Answer to Mr. Locke's Second Letter* (1698), Stillingfleet stated that Toland "saw into the true consequence" of Locke's work.[43]

Based on a comparison to the works of known and convicted heretics, Stillingfleet built a guiltby-association *ad hominem*. The implications of Locke's *Essay* put him in the untrustworthy company of Descartes, Spinoza, Hobbes, and Toland. We can encapsulate Stillingfleet's claims thus:

> Formal Paraphrase: (4b) Locke argues like or provides suppositions that support the arguments of known heretics and atheists, who should be morally condemned. Therefore, Locke is a bad person. Therefore, we should not believe his ideas about person, identity, or the proper manner of reasoning.

Locke lectured Stillingfleet in moralistic terms similar to those he directed at Edwards, saying that ethical argumentation does not include associating one's interlocutors with nefarious company. As he said to Stillingfleet, "when you did me the honour to answer my first letter [...] you were pleased to insert into it direct accusations against my book; which looked as if you had a mind to enter into a direct controversy with me. This condescension in your lordship has made me think myself under the protection of the laws of controversy, which allow a free examining and showing the weakness of the reasons brought by the other side, without any offense" (WJL 3.249). The laws of free and open controversy exclude guilt-byassociation argument.

....

42 John Toland, *Christianity Not Mysterious, or, A Treatise Showing that there is Nothing in the Gospel Contrary to Reason, Nor above it and that no Christian Doctrine Can be Properly Call'd a Mystery* (London: Sam Buckley, 1696), 11–15. Toland never directly cited Locke, a point that Locke himself noted in his *Reply to the Bishop of Worcester's Answer* (WJL 3.114–115). The curious nature of this relationship is emblematic of Locke's relationship to 17th- and early 18th-century freethinking philosophy. He influenced many freethinkers, such as Toland, but he was also opposed many of their skeptical conclusions. As Isabel Rivers explains, "Paradoxically, Locke was both an anticipator and an opponent of free-thinking," *Reason, Grace, and Sentiment: A Study of the Language of Religion and Ethics in England, 1660–1780. Volume II Shaftesbury to Hume* (Cambridge: Cambridge University Press, 2000), 26.

43 Edward Stillingfleet, *The Bishop of Worcester's Answer to Mr. Locke's Second Letter; Wherein his Notions of Ideas is Prov'd to be Inconsistent with itself, and with the Articles of the Christian Faith* (London: Henry Mortlock, 1698), 21.

Notably, Locke never indulged in any guilt-by-association arguments himself. For instance, when discoursing on toleration, he insinuated that Jonas Proast was truly motivated by a disdain for dissenters and not a desire to promote true religion or its critical investigation: "Pray consider whether it be not that which makes you shy of the term dissenters, which you tell me is mine, not your word. Since none are by your scheme to be punished, but those who do not conform to the national religion, dissenters, I think, is the proper name to call them by; and I can see no reason you have to boggle at it, unless your opinion has something in it you are unwilling should be spoke out, and called by its right name: but whether you like it or no, persecution and persecution of dissenters, are names that belong to it as it stands now" (WJL 245–246). Yet the argumentative thread goes no farther. Locke never accused Proast of being a high-flying Anglican clergyman, though he certainly was. He never implied that Proast supported the Blasphemy Act of 1698, though he probably did. He never placed Proast in the company of those who opposed late 17th-century toleration for orthodox Protestant dissenters, though he easily could.[44] Faced with a clear opportunity to advance a credible guilt-by-association *ad hominem*, Locke declined. The absence of guilt-by association arguments in the Locke-Proast debates explains the low level of argumentative spite as well as the want of ethical objection. Locke never voice outrage at Proast, even as he openly detested many of Proast's ideas. Furthermore, Locke never objected to Proast's arguments based on anything more than a rational or empirical quibble. Proast's arguments appeared to him ethically sound, if argumentatively unstable.

---

44 The Blasphemy Act replaced the lapsed Licensing Act, providing prison terms for those who attacked the Trinity as well as for anyone who attacked the divine revelation of the Gospels or the providence of God. The late 17th-century English toleration of orthodox Protestant dissenters was achieved by an agreement among Latitudinarian Anglicans (like Locke) and nonconformist Anglicans against the wishes of high-church Anglicans, like Proast. See John Marshall's *John Locke, Toleration, and Early Enlightenment Culture*, 131–132.

11   Locke on Fallacy and Ethics—Some Conclusions about the Tolerationist

The analysis so far avers that Locke believed in a tolerant republic of letters characterized discursively by argumentum *ad judicium* as well as *ad hominem* and *ex concessis*, but absolutely devoid of any guilt-by-association arguments. Though the philosopher should pursue truth by privileging argumentation *ad judicium*, s/he could reason probabilistically (in practical politics) by other, lesser appeals *ad hominem*. The empirical/rational philosopher, of course, objected to *ad hominem* argumentation because it remained inferior to argumentation *ad judicium*, yet this same philosopher, while principally appealing to judgment and observation, indulged other persuasive tactics. The tolerant ethicist objected to any appeals that interrupt the free exchange of ideas, the guilt-by-association *ad hominem* chief among them. Our understanding of Locke's approach to argumentative fallacy expands.

The *Essay Concerning Human Understanding* presents argumentative fallacy from "alethic" and "epistemic" perspectives, objecting to certain arguments because they lack deductive validity or because they depend on dubious evidence. The Edwards, Stillingfleet, and Proast debates, however, present Locke as a "pragmatic" fallacy theorist, objecting to certain deductive forms because they interrupt a preferred form of tolerant dialogue.[45] The pragmatic perspective, in the eyes of many argumentative theorists, is a contemporary development, the alethic and epistemic both antiquated views. According to C.L. Hamblin, the scholar inaugurating pragmatic fallacy theory over thirty years ago, Locke's theory of argumentation is superannuated. Reading the *Essay*, we might agree. Reading the debates, however, we see a different Locke, one more in tune with Hamblin and his pragmatic disciples.

In addition to this new perspective on Locke the fallacy theorist, these debates also offer a different version of Locke the tolerationist. In his letters on this subject, Locke offered a moderate version of toleration, a belief that some but not all beliefs should be tolerated. As a result, he seems to fall short of tolerance's

....

45 Hamblin labels his preferred approach to fallacies "dialectical," which he differentiates from alethic and epistemic approaches by insisting on a new criterion for determining a fallacy: the agreeableness of the participants. An argument's "dialectical" quality is its likelihood to achieve conviction in a dialogue by appealing to the interlocutors' sense of what is good and true, *Fallacies*, 241. For two recent pragmatic approaches to fallacy that build upon Hamblin's dialogic fallacy theory, see Douglas Walton's *A Pragmatic Theory of Fallacy* and Frans H. van Eemeren and Rob Grootendorst's *A Systematic Theory of Argumentation*.

political potential.[46] Locke's ethical-pragmatic attacks on the guilt-by-association *ad hominem*, on the other hand, make him seem more tolerant than the "moderate" descriptor allows. While Locke-the-philosopher undoubtedly advanced a limited view of toleration, Locke-the-informal-logician advanced a widely tolerant ethic of public debate. As a theorist of argumentation, Locke was more tolerant than he would ever allow himself to appear as a political pamphleteer. In the latter role, he refused religious toleration to Catholics, atheists, heretics, and libertines. In the former role, he insisted that all ideas, regardless of the social ties or political/religious identities of the arguers themselves, deserved to be heard and weighed rationally, empirically, probabilistically, ethically, and carefully. As an argumentative theorist, he insisted that all identities be ignored so that dialogue could attend to ideas. As a political theorist, he insisted that all identities be attended so that some could be tolerated but others excluded if not punished. Locke was a radically tolerant debater if a moderately tolerant philosopher.

Of course, my distinction between Locke-the-informal-logician and Locke-the-politicalphilosopher assumes a distinction between form and content. In essence, I propose that Locke argued in and for a tolerant form of dialogue while advancing a somewhat intolerant philosophical content. This analytic distinction between form and content allows us to understand another facet of his public debates: their reception. For, while Locke's radically tolerant form of argument invoked an ideal audience, his moderately tolerant content invited a different actual audience. Locke's detractors focused on the actual audience's invitation rather than the ideal audience's invocation. And their attention to this actual audience allowed Edwards and Stillingfleet to argue by association.[47]

....

46 John Marshall notes that Locke did not extend toleration to Catholics, atheists, or libertines, *John Locke, Toleration, and Early Enlightenment Culture*, 686–719. Jonathan Israel, based on these limits to Locke's proposed religious toleration, places Locke in the "moderate" toleration aimed at protecting "freedom of worship, theological debate, and religious practice, insofar as these are an extension of freedom of conscience, rather than with freedom of thought, debate, and of the press more broadly, or indeed for that matter freedom of lifestyle," *Enlightenment Contested*, 139.

47 By distinguishing the actual from the ideal (the particular from the universal) audiences, I follow contemporary rhetorical fallacy theorists who focus on the ideal audience invoked by the argument's form, asking, What kind of ideally rational and ethical person would find this sort of argument persuasive and good? Such a question leads to formal argumentative analysis that locates an ideal universal audience lurking in the appeals. Rhetorical analysis, as Perelman speculated, may best be suited for investigation into the universal audience found in textual evidence. According to Alan Gross and Roy Dearin, Perelman relegated investigation into particular audiences to the social sciences. *Chaim Perelman* (Albany: State University of New York Press, 2003), 32. Following Perelman, James Crosswhite suggests that arguments be evaluated based on the quality of their universal audiences: "[T]he worth of an argument is dependent upon the quality of the life to which assenting to it would lead," *The Rhetoric of Reason: Writing and the Attractions of Argument* (Madison: University of Wisconsin Press, 1996), 170.

Attending to Locke's own arguments as well as his ethical objections to any guilt-by-association *ad hominem*, we can conclude that he formally invoked a universally tolerant audience. Yet, when we look closely at the content of his argumentation, we see another, particular audience invited to assent.

Locke's efforts in these debates would likely have appealed to three particular audiences: Whigs, orthodox Protestant non-conformists, and various derided sects (including Quakers, Baptists, and Socinians). Among those who likely read his work, several specific groups not committed to his ethical-rhetorical ideal, not willing to become the posited universal audience of tolerant citizens, would nonetheless find his public arguments appealing. These include latitudinarian Anglicans who were less orthodox in their religious beliefs and more rational in their method of reading Scripture or arguing about religious matters. As a monotype of such people, consider the early 17th-century collection of intellectuals often referred to as the "Great Tew Circle." The Tew Circle included, among others: William Chillingworth, John Earls, George Eglionby, and Edward Hyde, all Oxford intellectuals and all committed Anglicans, though many had doubts about their religion. (Chillingworth had Catholic sympathies and bounced back and forth between the Jesuits and the Anglicans throughout his young life.) These men were committed to rationalism and individual interpretation of Scripture. In Hugh Trevor-Roper's words, their "most distinctive contribution […] was a restoration of the Anglican Church, not merely as an institution of Style, in a particular form, victorious over Calvinism, Puritanism, and the sects, but also with a particular philosophy." Free from a commitment to "prophetic history," the Church could accept "critical reason and humanist scholarship as the interpreter of its own documents."[48] Locke admired Chillingworth's great work, *The Religion of the Protestants* (1637), recommending it to many of his friends.[49] In *The Reasonableness of Christianity*, Locke advanced a similar view of religion, saying God made man a "rational creature" who can follow "the law of reason," to investigate Scripture and nature (WJL 6.11). He himself followed reason's mandate, read Scripture according to its plain and rational meaning, and avoided orthodox bromides.

---

48 Hugh Trevor-Roper, *Catholics, Anglicans, and Puritans: Seventeenth-Century Essays* (Chicago: University of Chicago Press, 1987), 229.

49 John Marshall, *John Locke, Toleration, and Early Enlightenment Culture*, 291.

Locke's arguments would also have appealed to dissenters, who found themselves abused during the Restoration and who wanted a safe space to deliberate matters of faith without risking persecution. These individuals had been maligned as schismatics, traitors, heretics, and sodomites. Arguments for toleration received similar vitriol. Thomas Long, for example, directly refuting Locke's Letter, said, "I know not what to compare the Author of this Letter, but to one of those Locusts that arose out of the smoke of the bottomless Pit, Rev. 9.3, whose smoke darkned the Air and the Sun." He claimed that Locke's version of toleration would "bring the whole Church and State to Confusion, by his absolute Toleration, which is intended to crumble us into innumerable and irreconcilable Sects, that so Popery may not only have a Toleration among us, but get Dominion over us."[50] As dissenters threatened national order, so did religious toleration. A union between such dissenters and latitudinarian Anglicans ended Restoration-era persecution. Both factions welcomed any effort to promote open and tolerant discourse about religion. Though Locke tended to write in an abstract and secular manner, an argumentative stylenot likely to resonate with dissenters, he advanced a political program that they appreciated.[51] Though Calvinists, like John Edwards, may have criticized Locke's religious positions, they supported the opportunity to deliberate such matters with other Protestant Christians.

Finally, Locke's arguments would have appealed to various sects beset on all sides by charges of schism and heresy. Socinians, Quakers, and Anabaptists would likely have appreciated his arguments for toleration in part because argued similarly. Locke, in fact, purchased and studied numerous 16th- and 17th-century Anabaptist and anti-Trinitarian defenses of toleration. During the 1680s, as he was exiled in Holland, Locke intensively considered Quaker tolerationist arguments.[52] Locke furthermore wrote in their fashion. John Edward's charge that Locke cited Scripture like a Socinian was not without merit. Contemporary historians still debate whether Locke was a crypto follower of Faustus Socinus, a closet anti-Trinitarian.[53] If he were an anti-Trinitarian in

---

50 *The Letter for Toleration Decipher'd, and the Absurdity and Impiety of an Absolute Toleration Demonstrated by the Judgment of Presbyterians, Independents, and by Mr. Calvin, Mr. Baxter, and the Parliament*, 1662, (London: Freeman Collins, 1789), 4–5.

51 *John Marshall, John Locke, Toleration, and Early Enlightenment Culture*, 123.

52 *John Marshall, John Locke, Toleration, and Early Enlightenment Culture*, 319, 494.

53 For two articles that neatly capture this debate, see John Marshall's "Locke, Socinianism, 'Socinianism,' and Unitarianism," *English Philosophy in the Age of Locke*, ed. M.A. Stewart (Cambridge: Clarendon Press, 2000), 111–182; and Victor Nuovo's "Locke's Theology, 1694–1704," *English Philosophy in the Age of Locke*, ed. M.A. Stewart (Cambridge: Clarendon Press, 2000), 183–215.

hiding, he had good reason to obscure his beliefs. Even as latitudinarian Anglicans and dissenters conspired to advance toleration, neither group allowed such heretics liberty to express their beliefs. The Blasphemy Act of 1689 provided Parliamentary indulgence of nonconformist practices of worship, thus ending the persecution of Protestant dissenters, but it excluded all anti-Trinitarians. We can conclusively say, despite the controversy, that Locke wrote in a Socinian way. His writing had an exoteric quality (insofar as it appeared benignly Anglican though arguably latitudinarian) and an esoteric quality (insofar as it cited sources, repeated claims, and adulated "reason" in a seemingly anti-Trinitarian fashion). As John Marshall puts it, Locke's writing "was capable of trinitarian as well as unitarian explication."[54]

We can surmise that all three groups—latitudinarian Anglicans, orthodox dissenters, and persecuted, "heretical" sects—would have liked Locke's arguments. They are his particular audience, an amalgam whose interests derived from their very particular investments in the contemporary debate about religious toleration in England. Furthermore, certain groups would not have appreciated his arguments. High-church Anglicans (such as Bishop Stillingfleet), Catholics, and free-thinkers (atheists and deists) would not find him convincing. Locke openly refused toleration to Catholics and free-thinkers on the grounds that they would decline to take oaths and might follow the dictums of someone other than the civil magistrate (i.e. the Roman Catholic Pope) (WJL 5.46–47). Locke vehemently denied any knowledge of free-thinking philosophy. To Stillingfleet, he declared, "I am not so well read in Hobbes and Spinoza, as to be able to say what were their opinions in this matter" (WJL 3.477). Despite these denials, Locke's ability to appeal to these particular audiences left him open to the guilt-by-association arguments that Stillingfleet and Edwards heaped upon him. They did not have to entertain Locke's ethical injunction to argue in a tolerant manner. In the rough-and tumble of public debate, they merely had to ignore Locke's universal audience, to refuse his invocation of a tolerant republic of letters, and to loudly label him a member of his particular audience: a Socinian, an anti-Trinitarian, an ally of free-thinkers, a heretic.

....

54 "Locke, Socinianism, 'Socinianism,' and Unitarianism," 174.

12 The Argumentative Origins of Ethics—Some Conclusions about Tolerance

The form-content division that allows every analytic application in this article suggests that Locke knew what he was doing and simply neglected to adopt the most effective strategy. He knew that he would appeal to a particular audience by presenting certain content and a universal audience by engaging certain tolerant forms, but he failed to see how the particular invitation would undercut the universal ethical invocation. Of course, that is likely not the case. Locke was probably not metacognitively nor super-rhetorically aware of the ethical imperative in his criticisms of guilt-by association arguments. Evidence from the *Essay* indicates that he was hyper-conscious of his effort to argue *ad judicium*, but we find no similar expressed consciousness of an effort to advance a tolerant republic of letters by denouncing the guilt-by-association *ad hominem*. It seems most probable to stipulate that Locke aimed to persuade a particular audience and then feared public association with some in that audience, so he mounted a wide-reaching defense of argumentative toleration. Nevertheless, carefully attending to the distinction between Locke's universally tolerant audience and his particularly religious audiences does help us to understand something about early Enlightenment tolerance in general.

The universal tolerance that 21st-century intellectuals would like to see in Locke's writings and in our own intellectual culture, may have been seeded, in part, by argumentative appeals to particular audiences. In the mid-20th-century, argumentation theorist Chaim Perelman insisted that universal audiences always arise out of appeals to particular audiences.[55] By emphasizing Perelman's qualified assertion that everyone constructs a notion of a universal audience out of what s/he knows and has experienced, we can see the universal

---

55 Of course, the notion of the "universal audience" has drawn some considerable scholarly criticism. Its invocation raises the specter of transcendent norms. Any effort to describe a universal audience, including Perelman and Olbrechts-Tyteca's, risks something like "conventional rationalist models of argumentation," which Perelman himself hoped to avoid. Lisa Ede, "Rhetoric Versus Philosophy: The Role of the Universal Audience in Chaim Perelman's The New Rhetoric," in *The New Rhetoric of Chaim Perelman: Statement and Response*, ed. Ray Dearin (Lanham: University Press of America, 1989), 142. To address such a charge, Chaim Perelman and Lucie Olbrechts-Tyteca opined: "Everyone constitutes the universal audience from what he knows of his fellow men, in such a way as to transcend the few oppositions he is aware of," *The New Rhetoric*, 33. Following Perelman and Olbrechts-Tyteca, more recent rhetorical theorists' turn our attention to what Antonio de Velasco calls the concept's "political dimensions [...] the way in which the universal audience can be seen as a privileged addressee for necessarily and partisan claims about the real," "Rethinking Perelman's Universal Audience: Political Dimensions of a Controversial Concept," *Rhetoric Society Quarterly* 35.2 (2005): 47.

audience not as a normative ideal but as "always potentially contested." Following Perelman, Antonio de Velasco explains, that the universal audience is a "political [...] site of appeal through which facts, and presuppositions emerge in various contexts of symbolic production. From this standpoint, politics can be seen as a fundamentally rhetorical struggle over the form and identity of the universal audience."[56] In his public debates over questions of religion and toleration, in his particular appeals to specific early-Enlightenment audiences, Locke engaged and advocated a form of argumentation that invoked (perhaps unbeknownst to him) a universal audience tolerant of all ideas regardless of identity. His universal tolerationist ethic, argumentatively-formally advanced, grew out of his particular-rhetorical efforts at moving specific groups with peculiar knowledge and interests to accept a philosophical argument for undeniably limited toleration. If we criticize Locke- the-philosopher for not being tolerant enough, then our criticism in part depends upon the appeal to a universally tolerant audience as invoked by Locke-the-debater. And we realize that the early-Enlightenment culture of toleration depended upon both philosophical content (inviting particular audiences) as well as argumentative form (inviting universal audiences). If we object to Locke's philosophical arguments for limited toleration, then we only do so because we willingly enter the role that his argumentative form invokes. If we call him an advocate of "moderate" toleration, then we may do so from the perspective of his universal audience, a group that values all ideas regardless of their associated identities. Undoubtedly, the present-day willingness to find the edges of Locke's philosophically adulated toleration may stem from a wholly different, though undoubtedly more radical, sense of toleration. If so, this new ethic of tolerance likely depends upon a similarly argumentatively-invoked universal audience. Tolerance, then as now, depends upon argumentative content and form.

....

56   Antonio de Velasco, "Rethinking Perelman's Universal Audience," 51.

Dr. Kari Palonen, University of Jyväskylä

The Parliamentary Model of Rhetorical Political Theory

Abstract: In an interview in January 2008, Quentin Skinner said: "I now say to my students on Hobbes's Leviathan…think of it as a speech in Parliament; all of these great works of political philosophy are recognizably contributions to a debate." My thesis is that Skinner formulates a contemporary expression of what could be called a parliamentary theory of knowledge. The procedural rules and rhetorical practices of the Westminster Parliament have offered a model for political thought: not only for William Gerard Hamilton's maxims in Parliamentary Logick (published posthumously 1808), but also for the political theories of John Stuart Mill and Walter Bagehot. Indebted to George Grote's reinterpretation of ancient Greek history, Mill writes in On Liberty (1859): "… if opponents of all important truths do not exist, it is indispensable to imagine them, and supply them with the strongest arguments which the most skilful devil's advocate can conjure up." In a similar tone, Bagehot writes in Physics and Politics (1872): "to our government by discussion, which has fostered a general intellectual tone, a diffused disposition to weigh evidence, a conviction that much may be said on every side of everything which the elder and more fanatic ages of the world wanted." Max Weber's revision of the concept of "objectivity" (1904) as fair dealing of the omnipresent scholarly controversies is similarly indebted to British parliamentary procedure. As a complement to the "rhetorical turn" in parliamentary studies, we need to reactivate this "parliamentary turn" in political theory.

The rhetorical principle that any motion or proposal can be properly understood only if it is confronted with opposed perspectives lies at the heart of this paper. Furthermore, the parliamentary procedure for conducting and regulating debates provides the historical model for a vision of knowledge which will be developed below. While such an idea also renders the research process inherently political, the point is to insist on the heuristic value of parliamentary procedures and debating practices for fair dealing with omnipresent scholarly controversies.

The rhetorical character genre of this essay can be described as a "genealogy" of a cluster of arguments, which I call a "parliamentary theory of knowledge." Such a view is strongly indebted to rhetorical styles of thought. The aim of my genealogy is to illustrate, with some historical examples, how the parliamentary model of debating can also provide a theoretical model for knowledge.

1   A "Parliamentary" Theory of Knowledge and Politics

Allow me to begin with an autobiographical reference to establish the context of this paper. I first make reference to Max Weber's "parliamentary" theory of knowledge in my "Max Weber, Parliamentarism and the Rhetorical Culture of Politics," published in *Max Weber Studies* in 2004 and based on the Uppsala symposium "Max Weber's Relevance as a Theorist of Politics" in May 2003. There, I wrote:

> For Weber expressions such as *Gesichtspunkte*, *Kampf* and *Auseinandersetzung* are not metaphors but indicators of the presence of a rhetorical and political dimension within the research process itself. Weber's view on conceptual change is analogous to the alteration of government through shifting electoral or parliamentary majorities. With an *einseitige Steigerung* we could speak of Max Weber's "parliamentary" view on the human sciences as an extension of the parliamentary politics of controversy (Palonen 2004, 279).

At the end of the same article I summarised this point:

> What I have referred to as Weber's "parliamentary theory of knowledge" rehabilitates the value of the compeition and deliberation in the formation and assessment of knowledge. The parliamentary politician is an ideal typical figure who is competent to use such knowledge against the bureaucratic tendencies and toward monopoly and secrecy (Palonen 2004, 289).

　　　　© Frank & Timme　Verlag für wissenschaftliche Literatur

The last point alludes to my thesis on a conceptual link between Weber's perspectivistic concept of "objectivity" from 1904 and his demand for the parliamentary control over the allegedly superior knowledge held by officials in his pamphlet *Parlament und Regierung im neugeordneten Deutschland* from 1918.

Thus, in 2004, I already named the Weberian link between knowledge and politics, but spoke rather vaguely of a "parliamentary theory of knowledge." However, the article initiated a personal research track that resulted in the book *Objektivität" als faires Spiel. Wissenchaft als Politik bei Max Weber* (Palonen 2010). This research led me to study the parliamentary and rhetorical origins of Weber's view of objectivity as a fair procedure in connection with the history and interpretations of Westminster parliamentary procedure.

My intention in the present study is to recapitulate some of the landmarks in the conceptual genealogy of the parliamentary theory of knowledge and politics. I have intentionally built this narrative around quotes from those authors included in the genealogy of a parliamentary theory of knowledge. Lastly, I have left out of this essay some important examples, above all the tracts on British parliamentary procedure with which I am dealing elsewhere (see Palonen 2014).

2 Renaissance Rhetorical Culture of Disputing in *Utramque Partem*

Quentin Skinner's *Reason and Rhetoric in the Philosophy of Hobbes* (1996) and his other rhetorical writings since the 1990s provide another source of inspiration for this piece. The theses on the "Renaissance rhetorical culture" and on disputing *in utramque partem* (i.e., in both directions) are his most important points. In the introductory chapter, Skinner writes:

> Finally, there is the still more rhetorically minded view associated with Renaissance humanism: that our watchword ought to be *audi alteram partem*, always listen to the other side. This commitment stems from the belief that, in moral and political debate, it will always be possible to speak *in utramque partem*, and will never be possible to couch our moral or political theories in deductive form. (Skinner 1996, 15)

Skinner attributes this idea to Cicero and Quintilian (ibid, 98–99). The idea is already regularly presented in early tracts on Westminster parliamentary procedure as a part of dealing with items in a parliamentary manner. Thomas Smith's De *Republica Anglorum* puts these points as follows: "For all that commeth in consultation either in the upper house or in the neather house, is put in writing first in paper, which being once read, he that will, riseth up and speaketh with it or against it: and so one after another so long as they shall thinke good" (Smith 1583, II.1). The tracts on procedure thus extend the principle to the entire parliamentary deliberation process and to the contrast between plenum and committee rules of debating. In his *Rhetoric, Politics and Popularity in Pre-revolutionary England*, Markku Peltonen has recently identified that arguing *in utramque partem* was recognised in 1593 as a principle procedure for the House of Commons (Peltonen 2013, 139).

Despite the decline of rhetoric in academia, the rhetorical mode of thinking survived in Parliament. However, among the eighteenth-century master speakers in parliamentary oratory, such as Lord Chatham, Edmund Burke, William Pitt Jr., and Charles James Fox, only the last one has a reputation among formidable debate speakers which the school rhetoricians regarded as a lower oratorical genre (see e.g. Hazlitt 1809, Goodrich 1853).

3   Hamilton's Parliamentary Logick

The parliamentary culture of debating *pro et contra* received an explicit eighteenth-century formulation in a work describing the practices of parliamentary speech and debate. William Gerard Hamilton's (1728–1796) maxims were written down during his 42 years as a Member of Parliament and published under the name *Parliamentary Logick* by Edmund Malone in 1808. The former MP, Courtney S. Kenny, published a slightly reorganised edition of *Parliamentary Logic* with a new preface in 1927, which is the edition that I am using here.

For Hamilton, logic is a sub-genre of rhetoric. Referring to the *invention*, he understands the procedural organisation of the parliament on the principle of speaking *in utramque partem*. "The very nature of a disputable question is where some thing plausible or probable may be said on both sides" (Hamilton 1927, 15). *Parliamentary logic* alludes to the justification of debating as "parliamentary reason" based on its operating systematically with opposed points of view as a condition of understanding the questions themselves.

The plurality of meanings is a major topos in Hamilton's maxims: "Consider if a word has not different significations, and if you may not use it advantageously, sometimes in one sense and sometimes in another. Watch this artifice in others" (ibid, 58). This maxim renders an ordinary practice in parliamentary speaking more explicit for members. The parliamentarians were able to alter the meanings of words for political purposes "by a particular author upon a particular occasion or in a particular discourse" (ibid, 59).

In line with the sophistic thought, Hamilton defends a perspectivistic view of knowledge: "In the support of every principle and every measure there will be some excellences and some defects" (ibid, 60). He applies speaking *in utramque partem* to parliamentary debates by recognising that nothing remains outside contestation and some grounds may be found to defend almost everything. The conclusion Hamilton draws is: "[A]nd their comparative merit, not their perfection, is the real question" (ibid). Parliamentary debate is not searching for the best arguments but comparative grounds for and against a motion in order to enable a stand in the vote.

The parliamentary history and the specific Westminster procedural rules and practices are clearly present in these maxims: for instance, "Take into view not only the measures of the session, but of the same men in other sessions" (ibid, 27). An important aspect, here, concerns the partisan agenda-setting and formulation of the question: "Watch the first setting off, and the manner of stating the question at the outset; there, is generally the fraud" (ibid, 32). This formula provides an oppositional device to limit the speaker's scope to manipulate the agenda (cp. Campion 1953, 150).

Hamilton's Logick treats parliamentary speeches as interventions into debates to be judged according to their persuasive force. In this sense, his agenda corresponds to that of deliberative rhetoric.

Hamilton's maxims are written for the use of members of parliament. The *Logick* does not offer an introduction to the rhetoric of parliamentary debates, and it does not discuss any general criteria for debate or the singularity of Westminster parliamentary debates; rather, it presumes them to be already well known to the debaters. An awareness of actual perspectives as well as being able to imagine possible opposed perspectives on the items on the agenda are necessary conditions for participating in parliamentary debates. Hamilton presupposes debating *pro et contra* as a condition of understanding a political question, but he never spells out this principle. His maxims aim at winning debates and votes, but the forms of parliamentary debating are never thematised in their own terms.

4 A Note on George Grote

The work of George Grote (1794–1871), a banker and Benthamite radical as well as MP for the City of London in the reformed Parliament (1832–1841), is an indispensable source on the rehabilitation of the Sophists in the nineteenth-century. Following his career in parliament and banking, Grote became a historian of ancient Greece and of the works of Plato and Aristotle. He was opposed to the dominant "Tory" historiography of Mitford, and he did much for recovering the legacy of Athenian democracy and the Sophists.

I shall not undertake an analysis of Grote's historical studies here. Instead, I shall restrict my discussion to Grote the historian as seen by John Stuart Mill and Walter Bagehot, whom I discuss later. Mill quotes in 1846 from the second volume of *Grote's History of Greece*:

We are thus enabled to trace the employment of public speaking as the standing engine of government and the proximate cause of obedience, to the social infancy of the nation. The power of speech in the direction of public affairs becomes more and more obvious, developed, and irresistible, as we advance towards the culminating period of Grecian history—the century preceding the battle of Chæroneia....The susceptibility of the multitude to this sort of guidance, their habit of requiring and enjoying the stimulus which it supplied, and the open discussion, combining regular forms with free opposition, of practical matters, political as well as judicial, are the creative causes which formed such conspicuous adepts in the art of persuasion. Nor was it only professed orators who were thus produced....Not only the oratory of Demosthenes and Pericles, and the colloquial magic of Socrates, but also the philosophical speculations of Plato, and the systematic politics, rhetoric, and logic of Aristotle, are traceable to the same general tendencies in the minds of the Grecian people; and we find the germ of these expansive forces in the senate and agora of their legendary government (Mill 1846, 104–106).

Bagehot remarks plausibly in *Physics and Politics*: "Grote's history often reads like a report to Parliament" (Bagehot 1872, 124). In his obituary, Bagehot makes the same point that Grote's parliamentary experiences fruitfully shaped his reinterpretation of Athenian political struggles.

> Grote was not a mere literary man, and no mere literary man could have written his history. He was essentially a practical man of business, a banker trained in the city, a politician trained in parliament, and every page in his writings bears witness that he was so. Just as in every sentence of Thucydides there lurks some trace of exercised sagacity fit for the considerate decision of weighty affairs, though by fate excluded from them, so in every page of Grote there is a flavour not exactly of this quality, but yet others only to be learned in the complex practical life of modern times, and equally necessary for it (Bagehot 1871).

Mill wrote two reviews on Grote's *History* (1846, 1853) and one on his Plato (1866, during his membership of the House of Commons). Mill explicitly refers to how the British Parliament is indebted to the ancient Greek views on deliberative politics:

> Yet truth, in everything but mathematics, is not a single but a double question: not what can be said for an opinion, but whether more can be said for it than against it. There is no knowledge, and no assurance of right belief, but with him who can both confute the opposite opinion, and successfully defend his own against confutation. But this, the principal lesson of Plato's writings, the world and many of its admired teachers have very imperfectly learned. We have to thank our free Parliament, and the publicity of our courts of justice, for whatever feeling we have of the value of debate. The Athenians, who were incessantly engaged in hearing both sides of every deliberative and judicial question, had a far stronger sense of it (Mill, 1866).

Mill and Grote probably made of Plato a more "deliberative" thinker than he really was. Nonetheless, Grote appears to have inspired both Mill and Bagehot to defend the parliamentary theory of knowledge. Without his exercise of parliamentary judgment this would hardly have been the case. If Hamilton's exposition of parliamentary debating *in utramque partem* was largely an extension of ancient and Renaissance rhetorical ideas to Westminster, the case of Grote was precisely the other way around: his knowledge of Westminster procedures and rhetorical practices heuristically served his reinterpretation of Athenian political and academic controversies.

5 Mill's Parliamentary Model of Liberty

John Stuart Mill (1806–1873) was a life-long *homo politicus* as well as being an MP for Westminster from 1865 to 1868. Signs of what I call a parliamentary theory of knowledge can be found early in his work. The young Mill became angry with the "Tory historiography" in Walter Scott's *Life of Napoleon*. While admitting Scott's arguments against the French revolutionary parliamentarians, Mill accuses him of for not even trying to understand their original arguments:

> It was surely very foolish in the Assembly to waste so much time and labour in anxious deliberation on points which our author settles so perfectly at his ease. Nothing can be more conclusive than the case he can always make out against them; nothing more completely satisfactory than the reasons he gives, to prove them always in the wrong; and the chief impression which is made upon the reader, is one of astonishment, that a set of persons should have been found so perversely blind to considerations so obviously dictated by sound policy and common sense. But when we examine the original authorities, we find that these considerations were no more unknown or unheeded by the Assembly than by our author himself. The difference in point of knowledge between them and him consisted chiefly in this, that they likewise knew the reasons which made for the other side of the question, and might therefore be pardoned if, being thus burthened with arguments on both sides, they were slower to decide, and sometimes came to a different decision

 © Frank & Timme Verlag für wissenschaftliche Literatur

from that which, as long as we confine ourselves to one, appears so eminently reasonable (Mill 1828).

Without considering that the "losers in history" might also have had a point or that the results of debates cannot be known in advance, Mill maintains that Scott adopts his stand too easily. Here, already, Mill regards the parliamentary debate *pro et contra* as a heuristic tool for historical interpretation. In the second chapter of *On Liberty*, "Of liberty of thought and discussion," Mill extends this parliamentary model from history to philosophy. He refers to Cicero's legal practice of arguing *in utramque partem*:

[H]e always studied his adversary's case with as great, if not with still greater, intensity than even his own. What Cicero practised as the means of forensic success, requires to be imitated by all who study any subject in order to arrive at the truth. He who knows only his own side of the case, knows little of that. His reasons may be good, and no one may have been able to refute them. But if he is equally unable to refute the reasons on the opposite side; if he does not so much as know what they are, he has no ground for preferring either opinion (Mill 1859, 38).

This view parallels the point made by Hamilton that it is always important to listen to the opposite side and to reconstruct the argument. Mill, however, goes further in claiming that we cannot speak of "knowledge" at all without setting it in the process of debating:

Their conclusion may be true, but it might be false for anything they know: they have never thrown themselves into the mental position of those who think differently from them, and considered what such persons may have to say; and consequently they do not, in any proper sense of the word, know the doctrine which they themselves profess. They do not know those parts of it which explain and justify the remainder; the considerations which show that a fact which seemingly conflicts with another is reconcilable with it, or that, of two apparently strong reasons, one and not the other ought to be preferred. All that part of the truth which turns the scale, and decides the judgment of a completely informed mind, they are strangers to; nor is it ever really known, but to those who have attended equally and impartially to both sides, and endeavoured to see the reasons of both in the strongest light. So essential is this discipline to a real understanding of moral and human subjects, that if opponents of all important truths do not exist, it is indispensable to imagine them, and supply them with the strongest arguments which the most skilful devil's advocate can conjure up (ibid, 39).

In other words, if dissenting voices are absent, we still have to imagine what these voices could be. This corresponds to the parliamentary procedure of submitting all thinkable objections to every motion. "Knowledge" requires a confrontation with opposite views: "On any other subject no one's opinions deserve the name of knowledge, except so far as he has either had forced upon him by others, or gone through of himself, the same mental process which would have been required of him in carrying on an active controversy with opponents" (ibid, 46).

In *On Liberty*, Mill practises thought experiments, in which an extreme situation is imagined, as in this initial point:

> If all mankind minus one, were of one opinion, and only one person were of the contrary opinion, mankind would be no more justified in silencing that one person, than he, if he had the power, would be justified in silencing mankind.…But the peculiar evil of silencing the expression of an opinion is, that it is robbing the human race; posterity as well as the existing generation; those who dissent from the opinion, still more than those who hold it. If the opinion is right, they are deprived of the opportunity of exchanging error for truth: if wrong, they lose, what is almost as great a benefit, the clearer perception and livelier impression of truth, produced by its collision with error (Mill 1859, 20).

In other words, Mill has to a remarkable degree constructed what Max Weber later calls *ideal types*, the latter being necessary conditions for understanding the more "regular" cases. The parliamentary procedure of deliberating offers a true paradigm of such an ideal type which not only is applied more or less consistently in existing parliaments but is also applied to analogical situations beyond parliaments, including scholarly controversies.

Walter Bagehot (1826–1877) in his book *The English Constitution* (1867) defends the cabinet government not merely as a technique of revising the relations between parliament and government but also one that inspires a broad culture of parliamentary debating in and beyond parliaments. In contrast, the US type presidential system restrains such debating. Later, in *Physics and Politics* (1872), he also presents a philosophy of history as a support for the debating culture.

In the chapter, "The Age of Discussion," Bagehot opposes the old Eastern and customary regimes to the new Western and "changeable civilisations" based on choice and discussion: "It is that the change from the age of status to the age of choice was first made in states where the government was to a great and a growing extent a government by discussion, and where the subjects of that discussion were in some degree abstract, or, as we should say, matters of principle" (ibid, 115). The point that matters is the form of government; its "principle" is deliberation, both in the form of debate and choice in the parliamentary sense. Referring to Grote, he claims that this transition to "government by discussion" was made in the ancient Greek and Italian republics:

> "But a government by discussion,...at once breaks down the yoke of fixed custom....As far as it goes, the mere putting up of a subject to discussion, with the object of being guided by that discussion, is a clear admission that that subject is in no degree settled by established rule, and that men are free to choose in it" (ibid, 117–118).

In Britain, Bagehot's "government by discussion" refers to the parliamentary sovereignty over the Common Law, based on customs and precedents. The choice of a "government by discussion" is not analogous to a vote. The very presence of deliberation in the form of government makes the difference: there is no return to custom. The politicisation of government cannot be simply taken back or forgotten, for a decision to prevent discussion is also a form of choice. Even so, to discuss politics freely requires habitually practising it. For Bagehot, the free discussion is itself the mark of civilising progress (ibid, 118).

Furthermore, for Bagehot, discussion is opposed to direct or immediate action: "If you want to stop instant and immediate action, always make it a condition that the action shall not begin till a considerable number of persons have talked over it, and have agreed on it" (ibid, 140). The parliamentary procedure of reserving time for debating in several stages provides the historical paradigm for thorough reflection: "But for the purpose now in hand—that of preventing hasty action, and ensuring elaborate consideration—there is no device like a polity of discussion" (ibid).

The contemporary adversary of Bagehot's contemporary adversary was Thomas Carlyle, whose "direct action" contains dictatorial implications. Their great enemy is Parliamentary government; they call it, after Mr. Carlyle, the "national palaver." They add up the hours that are consumed in it, the speeches which are made in it, and they sigh for a time when England might again be ruled, as it once was, by a Cromwell—that is, when an eager, absolute man might do exactly what other eager men wished, and do it immediately (ibid).

Bagehot illustrates how the parliamentary vision of politics requires time and, therefore, enough of it should be provided. Time is an inherent part of both discussion and action, as manifested in the structure of parliamentary procedure as a multi-stage and multi-level process of deliberation. He is vehemently opposed to making rapid decisions: "it is to the incessant prevalence of detective discussion that our doubts are due; and much of that discussion is due to the long existence of a government requiring constant debates, written and oral" (ibid, 142).

Parliamentary government is based on debating, spending enough time, and limiting violence and numerical power. At the same time, it activates the criticism of customs and conventions, including also among the citizens. A choice without debating the alternatives is no real choice.

7   **James De Mille and the Singularity of Parliamentary Debating**

The Canadian professor James De Mille (1833–1880) explicitly defends the parliamentary theory of knowledge from a rhetorical perspective. His *Elements of Rhetoric* is among the first studies that distinguishes between oratory and debate as forms of rhetoric. "Oratory is the discussion of a subject by one; debate is the discussion of a subject by more than one. Oratory considers the subject from one point of view; debate considers the subject from two or more opposed points of view." (De Mille 1878, 471)

    © Frank & Timme   Verlag für wissenschaftliche Literatur

De Mille further divides debates between "controversial" and "parliamentary." The former unites deliberative and negotiating aspects of rhetoric in controversies in which the parties are not swayed from their position, do not seek for compromises, or mediation, but aim at victory. The criterion of parliamentary debate is its procedural and formal character: "The peculiarity of parliamentary debate is that the subject to be examined is presented in a formal statement, called a resolution, or question, to which alone the discussion must refer" (ibid, 472).

The Westminster Parliament has historically been exemplary in proceduralising its debates. For De Mille, the "parliamentary" qualifier of a genre of debate does not depend on the locus where it is delivered. Conversely, not all historical parliaments necessarily conduct their debates in a "parliamentary" manner.

Unlike Bagehot, De Mille separates debate from mere discussion, in which the viewpoints are not "contrary" but merely "different": "The aim of parliamentary debate is to investigate the subject from many points of view which are presented from two contrary sides. In no other way can a subject be so exhaustively considered" (ibid. 473).

This paragraph expresses precisely the conceptual and historical link between parliament and rhetoric, between the political form of parliamentary debate and a rhetorical view of knowledge. The formula contains three aspects: namely, a perspectivistic investigation of the issue on the agenda, a division of the parliament into two sides (i.e., between members with contrary points of view) and a thorough consideration of the items on the agenda.

A parliamentary debate, when carried on by able men is one of the finest exhibitions of the powers of the human mind that can be witnessed. We see well-informed and well-trained intellects turning all their powers to the discussion of a subject from many points of view, in which two opposite forces struggle for the victory. In such a struggle all the highest intellectual forces are put forth. We encounter broad and deep knowledge, quick apprehension, argumentative power, a sharpness of epigrammatic statement, a vehemence of denunciation, a keenness of the quick retort, sharp repartee, biting sarcasm, and a great command of language together with the resources of wit, humor, and pathos (ibid.)

With these conditions stipulated, parliamentary debate reaches an ideal status for expressing and practising civilised dissensus. As such, it may serve as a measure for judging the activities of existing parliaments and other assemblies: that is, how far and in which respects they do deviate from the ideal type. A parliamentary view of knowledge also indicates the political revaluation of debate and dissensus.

Most nineteenth-century professional rhetoric scholars had difficulties recognising that the rhetoric of debate must be judged by different criteria than the oratory of separate speeches. In this regard, De Mille is on this point close to Mill or Bagehot, yet he seems to insist more on the role of the procedure as a mark of distinction. For him, the dissensus between perspectives is no mere instrument for debating but a condition for a parliamentary vision of knowledge and politics.

8   A Remark on Nietzsche

So far my argument has been restricted to the Westminster Parliament. This does not mean that other sources have not given rise to similar ideas. As an example, I quote a long passage on rethinking the concept of "objectivity" in Friedrich Nietzsche's *Zur Genealogie der Moral* from 1887:

Seien wir zuletzt, gerade als Erkennende, nicht undankbar gegen solche resolute Umkehrungen der gewohnten Perspektiven und Werthungen, mit denen der Geist allzu lange scheinbar freventlich und nutzlos gegen sich selbst gewüthet hat: dergestalt einmal anders sehn, anders-sehn-wollen ist keine kleine Zucht und Vorbereitung des Intellekts zu seiner einstmaligen 'Objektivität', – letztere nicht als 'interesselose Anschauung' verstanden (als welche ein Unbegriff und Widersinn ist), sondern als das Vermögen, sein Für und Wider in der Gewalt zu haben und aus- und einzuhängen: so dass man sich gerade die Verschiedenheit der Perspektiven und der Affekt-Interpretationen für die Erkenntniss nutzbar zu machen weiss. Hüten wir uns nämlich, meine Herrn Philosophen, von nun an besser vor der gefährlichen alten Begriffs-Fabelei, welche ein 'reines, willenloses, schmerzloses, zeitloses Subjekt der Erkenntniss' angesetzt hat, hüten wir uns vor den Fangarmen solcher contradiktorischen Begriffe wie 'reine Vernunft', 'absolute Geistigkeit', 'Erkenntniss an sich': – hier wird immer ein Auge zu denken verlangt, das gar nicht gedacht werden kann, ein Auge, das durchaus keine Richtung haben soll, bei dem die aktiven und interpretirenden Kräfte unterbunden sein sollen, fehlen sollen, durch die doch Sehen erst ein Etwas-Sehen wird, hier wird also immer ein Widersinn und Unbegriff von Auge verlangt. Es giebt nur ein perspektivisches Sehen, nur ein perspektivisches 'Erkennen'; und je mehr Affekte wir über eine Sache zu Worte kommen lassen, je mehr Augen, verschiedne Augen wir uns für dieselbe Sache einzusetzen wissen, um so vollständiger wird unser 'Begriff' dieser Sache, unsre 'Objektivität' sein (Nietzsche 1887, 860–861).

Nietzsche argues for a perspectivistic reorientation of the concept of "objectivity." It is easy to see that with this move he wants to transcend philosophy and science with rhetoric. He re-conceptualises here "objectivity" as "… das Vermögen, sein Für und Wider in der Gewalt zu haben und aus- und einzuhängen", that is, as to the ability to influence positions for and against. So, it would seem that Nietzsche takes parliamentary as a point of reference after all. This was explicitly the case with Immanuel Kant, who in Der Streit der Fakultäten speaks of the legitimate (rechtsmäßig) disputes between faculties "in der Parlaments der Gelehrtheit" (Kant 1798, 42).

Nietzsche had read Grote and made an interesting remark: "Die Taktik Grote's zur Verteidigung der Sophisten ist falsch: er will sie zu Ehrenmännern und Moral-Standarten erheben – aber ihre Ehre war, keinen Schwindel mit großen Worten und Tugenden zu treiben…" (NF-1888, 14[147] – Nachgelassene Fragmente Frühjahr 1888). For Nietzsche, the sophists practised a provocative *Umwertung der Werte*, yet not a fair debate in the British parliamentary style, as Grote seems to attribute to them.

Even if Nietzsche barely followed everyday parliamentary debates, they may still have inspired him at this stage of his perspectivistic view on knowledge. Or, there were scholars inspired by Nietzsche's perspectivistic vision of knowledge who were more *homines politici* than he was. The most prominent figure among them was, of course, Max Weber.

In my Introduction to *"Objektivität" als faires Spiel. Wissenschaft als Politik bei Max Weber* (Palonen 2010), I present three quotes from Weber's 1904 essay, which I shall repeat here and situate in the current narrative. Weber's reconceptualisation of "objectivity" can be understood as the result of an unexpected combination of two strains of thought, Nietzsche's concept of "objectivity" and British parliamentary procedure.

The first quote includes an obvious link to Nietzschean perspectivism:

Es gibt keine schlechthin 'objektive' wissenschaftliche Analyse des Kulturlebens oder – was vielleicht etwas Engeres, für unsern Zweck aber sicher nichts wesentlich anderes bedeutet – der 'sozialen Erscheinungen' unabhängig von speziellen und 'einseitigen' Gesichtspunkten, nach denen sie – ausdrücklich oder stillschweigend, bewußt oder unbewußt – als Forschungsobjekt ausgewählt, analysiert und darstellend gegliedert werden (Weber 1904, 170).

This quote contains several points. For Weber, no "facts" independent of interpretative perspectives can exist because as the perspective changes so that the "facts" become different. Thus, we have no grounds to assume the existence of some perspective that is independent "hard facts." Furthermore, there cannot be any "total" or "comprehensive" views, as all perspectives are necessarily one-sided and the point is to oppose them to each other, and to judge their strengths and weaknesses even if the criteria for judgement are liable to change in the course of the debate. It is obvious that, in addition to Nietzsche, this Weberian perspectivism is indebted to rhetorical and sophistic styles of thinking.

The second quote illustrates the necessity and heuristic value of the confrontation between research perspectives:

Das Kennzeichen des sozialpolitischen Charakters eines Problems ist es ja geradezu, daß es nicht auf Grund bloß technischer Erwägungen aus feststehenden Zwecken heraus zu erledigen ist, daß um die regulativen Wertmaßstäbe selbst gestritten werden kann und muß, weil das Problem in die Region der allgemeinen Kulturfragen hineinragt (Weber 1904, 153).

For Weber, political and cultural questions are controversial in principle. For scholars, such "controversies" are omnipresent and are also, for Weber, heuristically valuable in rendering different viewpoints explicit. Such a practice would also systematically use confrontation in a manner that leaves the judgement about stronger and weaker arguments to be decided by the audience. In the academic milieu of Weber's time, this clearly was not the case, in particular not in his own discipline of political economy as we can see from my third quote:

> Daß das Problem als solches besteht und hier nicht spintisierend geschaffen wird, kann niemandem entgehen, der den Kampf um Methode, 'Grundbegriffe' und Voraussetzungen, den steten Wechsel der 'Gesichtspunkte' und die stete Neubestimmung der 'Begriffe', die verwendet werden, beobachtet und sieht, wie theoretische und historische Betrachtungsform noch immer durch eine scheinbar unüberbrückbare Kluft getrennt sind: 'zwei Nationalökonomien', wie ein verzweifelnder Wiener Examinand seinerzeit jammernd klagte. Was heißt hier Objektivität? Lediglich diese Frage wollen die nachfolgenden Ausführungen erörtern (Weber 1904, 160–161).

In this passage, Weber asks what should be meant by "objectivity" in the humanities, and he provides at least an implicit answer to it. Struggles regarding methods, concepts, presuppositions, and viewpoints are permanent, not only between the two schools of political economy at the time, but in the human sciences (*Kulturwissenschaften*) in general. Weber suggests not to "resolve" such struggles in favour of some specific approaches, but to arrange a fair regulation of the controversies between them. Here lies his reinterpretation of the very concept of "objectivity."

In "ordinary" politics at the time, the omnipresence of these struggles was widely recognised, in particular in Britain. My thesis is that Weber suggests using the Westminster procedural regulations as a model for fair regulation of scholarly controversies, after reinterpreting "objectivity" itself as a procedural concept aiming at the fair regulation of scholarly controversies.

This view can be illustrated by knowledge claims that are presented as being beyond dispute. For Weber, the purest examples of such knowledge claims can be found among state officials in imperial Germany, when ministers were also officials and no parliamentary control over the rule of officialdom (*Beamtenherrschaft*) was available. Weber deals with such knowledge claims in his pamphlet *Parlament und Regierung im neugeordneten Deutschland*, published as book in the winter of 1918.

Weber distinguishes three levels of knowledge claims among these officials: *Fachwissen, Dienstwissen, Geheimwissen*—or factual competence, aspects of service as officials, and the requirement of official secrecy. He does not dispute the superior knowledge of officials over parliamentarians. Rather, he regards it as indispensable to construct devices enabling parliamentarians to question the validity, range, and relevance of such knowledge. Here Weber proposes three main instruments: the cross-examination of officials before parliamentarians, the possibility for MPs to conduct on the spot inspections of the sources of knowledge provided by the officials, and the introduction of parliamentary examination commissions. All of these have their model in the parliamentary committees of Westminster (Weber 1918, esp. 236–237, see my discussion in Palonen 2010, ch. 8).

Weber's broader target concerns views of knowledge that are present in parliamentary politics. German officials at the time regarded themselves (à la Hegel) as incarnations of the general interest in contradistinction to particularistic politicians. With his perspectivistic vision of knowledge and "objectivity," Weber militantly opposes all claims for a "total view" of knowledge and thus excludes the possibility of officials embodying the representation of the "general interest." Rather, the relatively superior knowledge held by official is an empirical matter due to their position in the system of bureaucracy, and which also includes, by necessity, the one-sided perspectives mentioned earlier. Such one-sided superiority can be controlled only by confronting the work of officials with that of others, both of those working in other offices with different perspectives and of the parliamentarians who have learnt to deliberate between opposed points of view and invent alternative perspectives, including when none seems to exist. This procedure is analogous to Mill's thought experiments.

In other words, the parliamentarians' experiences with procedural rules and rhetorical practices of debating *pro et contra* constitute an important factor in controlling or mediating the alleged omniscience of officialdom and its

<u>monopolistic claims over knowledge</u>. Weber's view on the tendency to bureaucratisation tendencies makes visible the rise of similar dangers outside the state administration, such as in business, parties, trade unions, and the universities (see his comparison of bureaucratisation in German and US universities, Weber 1911).

Weber does not share the strong belief in progress which underpins the viewpoints of Mill and Bagehot. In his "Der Sinn der 'Wertfreiheit' in sozialen und ökonomischen Wissenschaften" (1917), Weber deconstructs the language of progress and evolution, which cannot itself be beyond a conception of knowledge given by rhetorical conceptual controversies. This is due to Weber's interpretation of bureaucratisation being the historically dominant tendency of the age and requiring the counterweight of parliament (esp. Weber 1918, 222–223). He is suspicious of all teleological figures of change, against which he sets the proceduralism of parliamentary politics which also provides a model regarding knowledge claims and their control and confrontation with each other.

With his views on "objectivity," Max Weber was engaged in a struggle on two fronts. He fought governmentalist tendencies in German universities, in particular in Gustav Schmoller's neocameralist economics. At the same time, he militantly rejected politicians' willingness to follow or even hide behind the authority of "science" in questions that depend on debates and decisions for their very intelligibility, and in which "science" (*Wissenschaft*) could claim no authority. Weber's point is that parliamentary procedures for conducting deliberations can also provide a model for the reconceptualisation of "objectivity" and "value freedom" (*Wertfreiheit* as interpreted by Weber in his 1917 essay). As a life-long *homo politicus*, Weber was not burdened by any of the typical academic objections to learning from the practices of politicians.

The link between his "objectivity" essay and the parliamentary control of claims to knowledge by officials is seldom recognised. Many of the introductory courses in the methodology of human sciences presented in our universities hardly have little, if any, idea of Weber's conceptual radicalism. Few people have really understood how militantly Weber turns against the religion of science in all its forms.

I have not followed the "genealogy" of a parliamentary theory of knowledge beyond Max Weber. Views resembling Weber can be found in the writings of others who defend the necessity and value of professional politicians (a number of them are discussed in Palonen 2012). However, to further illustrate my argument for the presence of a parliamentary theory of knowledge today, I would like to close this scholarly discussion by quoting one scholar who was also particularly indebted to Max Weber.

In an interview in January 2008, Quentin Skinner said: "I now say to my students on Hobbes's Leviathan…think of it as a speech in Parliament; all of these great works of political philosophy are recognizably contributions to a debate" (Skinner 2008).

Skinner's view actualises another aspect of the parliamentary theory of knowledge. When scholarly works are contributions to debates, the contributions allow us to read academic debates in terms analogical to parliamentary controversies. In this sense, Skinner's suggestion resembles the works cited in this study. His proposal could be carried further in more systematically applying the Westminster procedural vocabulary and constructing analogies to such moves as committing, amending, adjourning, or raising the question or order.

References

Bagehot, Walter (1867). *The English Constitution* edited by Paul Smith. Cambridge: Cambridge UP 2001.

Bagehot, Walter (1871). "Mr. Grote". In: *The Works and Life of Walter Bagehot*, vol. 5 (Historical & Financial Essays; The English Constitution) [1915], 93–98, http://oll.libertyfund.org/?option=com_staticxt&staticfile=show.php%3Ftitle= 2263&chapter=213021&layout=html&Itemid=27

Bagehot, Walter (1872). *Physics and Politics*, Introduction by Hans Kohn. Boston: Beacon Press 1956.

Campion, Gilbert (1953). "Parliamentary Procedure: Old and New", in Gilbert Campion et al. (eds.) *Parliament. A survey*. London: Allen & Unwin, 141–167.

De Mille, James (1878). *Elements of Rhetoric*. New York: Harper and Brothers. http://archive.org/stream/elementsrhetori02millgoog

Goodrich, Chauncey A. (1853). *Select British Eloquence: Embracing the Best Speeches Entire, or the Most Eminent Orators of Great Britain for the Last Two Centuries with Sketches of their Lives and Estimate of their Genius, and Notes, Critical and Ecplanatory*. http://www.archive.org/details/selectbritishel00goodgoog

Hamilton, William Gerard (1808). *Parliamentary Logick. To which are subjoined two speeches delivered in the House of commons of Ireland and other pieces*, London: Payne. http://www.archive.org/stream/parliamentarylo00johngoog

Hamilton, William Gerard (1808/1927). *Parliamentary Logic*, with an introduction and notes by Courtney S. Kenny. Cambridge: Heffer.

Hazlitt, William (1809). *The Eloquence of the British Senate being a Selection of the Best Speeches of the Most Distinguished English, Irish and Scotch Parliamentary Speakers from the Beginning of the Reign of Charles I to the Present Time*; vol. II, http://www.archive.org/details/eloquenceofbriti02hazliala

Kant, Immanuel (1798). „Der Streit der Fakultäten". In: *Der Streit der Fakultäten und kleinere Abhandlungen*. Köln: Köhnemann, 5–140.

Mill, John Stuart (1828). "Scott's Life of Napoleon". In *Collected Works XX, Essays on French History and Historians*, ed. John M. Robson, Introduction by John C. Cairns, Toronto: University of Toronto Press, 1985, http://oll.libertyfund.org/title/235/21586/803731

Mill, John Stuart (1846). "Grote's History of Greece [i]". *Collected Works XI, Essays on Philosophy and the Classics*, ed. John M. Robson, Introduction by F.E. Sparshott. Toronto: University of Toronto Press 1978, 271–306. http://oll.libertyfund.org/?option=com_staticxt&staticfile=show.php%3Ftitle=248&chapter=21770&layout=html&Itemid=27

Mill, John Stuart (1853). "Grote's History of Greece [ii]". *Collected Works XI, Essays on Philosophy and the Classics*, ed. John M. Robson, Introduction by F.E. Sparshott. Toronto: University of Toronto Press 1978, 307–338. http://oll.libertyfund.org/?option=com_staticxt&staticfile=show.php%3Ftitle=248&chapter=21773&layout=html&Itemid=27

Mill, John Stuart (1859). "On Liberty". In Stefan Collini ed. *On Liberty and Other Writings*, Cambridge: Cambridge UP 1989, 1–115.

Mill, John Stuart (1866). "Grote's Plato, 1866", *Collected Works XI, Essays on Philosophy and the Classics*, ed. John M. Robson, Introduction by F.E. Sparshott. Toronto: University of Toronto Press 1978, 375–440. http://oll.libertyfund.org/index.php?option=com_staticxt&staticfile=show.php%3Ftitle=248&Itemid=27

Nietzsche, Friedrich (1887). „Zur Genealogie der Mora"l. In: *Werke*, Hg. Karl Schlechta, Frankfurt/M: Ullstein 1981, II, 761–900.

Nietzsche, Friedrich (1888). *Nachgelassene Fragmente Frühjahr 1888*. Nietzsche Source. Digitale kritische Gesamtausgabe Werke und Briefe, www.nietzschesource.org/#eKGWB/NF-1888,14[147]

Palonen, Kari (2004). "Max Weber, Parliamentarism and the Rhetorical Culture of Politics". *Max Weber Studies* 4, 273–292.

Palonen, Kari (2010). *"Objektivität" als faires Spiel. Wissenchaft als Politik bei Max Weber*. Baden-Baden: Nomos.

Palonen, Kari (2012). *Rhetorik des Unbeliebten. Lobreden auf Politiker im Zeitalter der Demokratie*. Baden-Baden: Nomos.

Palonen, Kari (2014). *The Politics of Parliamentary Procedure. A conceptual history of parliamentary ideal type of politics in Westminster procedural tracts*. London: Budrich (forthcoming).

Skinner, Quentin (1996). *Reason and Rhetoric in the Philosophy of Hobbes*. Cambridge: Cambridge UP.

Skinner, Quentin (2008). *Quentin Skinner interviewed by Alan Macfarlane* 10th January 2008, http://www.dspace.cam.ac.uk/handle/1810/197060

Smith, Thomas (1583). *De* Republica *anglorum*, http://www.constitution.org/eng/repang.htm

Weber, Max (1904). „Die ‚Objektivität' sozialwissenschaftlicher und sozialpolitischer Erkenntnis". In: *Gesammelte Aufsätze zur Wissenschaftslehre*, hg. v. Johannes Winckelmann. Tübingen: Mohr 1973, 146–214.

Weber, Max (1911). „Vergleich deutscher und amerikanischer Universitäten". In John Dreijmanis (Hg.). *Max Webers vollständige Schriften zu wissenschaftlichen und politischen Berufen*. Bremen: Europäischer Hochschulverlag 2012, 122–130.

Weber, Max (1917). „Der Sinn der Wertfreiheit in sozialen und ökonomischen Wissenschaften". In: *Gesammelte Aufsätze zur Wissenschaftslehre*, hg. v. Johannes Winckelmann. Tübingen: Mohr 1973, 489–540.

Weber, Max (1918). „Parlament und Regierung im neugeordneten Deutschland". In: *Max-Weber-Studienausgabe* I/15, hg. v. Wolfgang J. Mommsen. Tübingen: Mohr 1988, 202–302.

Dr. Serena Tomasi, University of Trento – CERMEG

Do the "Critical Questions" Have only Dialectic Relevance?
Some Remarks on the Rhetorical Value of CQs
in Legal Argumentation

Abstract: The purpose of this study is to provide critical and theoretical insights into the assessment of legal reasoning, judicial reasoning, and lawyering skills. The Italian Supreme Court has recently set logical standards for evaluating expert opinions. The Court's guideline appears generic and falls short of providing a reasonable justification. I will take into account the tools endorsed by a representative approach to argumentation: namely, the New Dialectics. This theory furnishes a list of options available to users in the current context of everyday language. The discussion entails the risk of a systematic approach. The development of my argumentative position has been influenced by the works of Enrico Berti and Francesca Piazza on rhetoric in the 1990s and by the studies of forensic rhetoric by CERMEG (Centre of Research on Legal Methodology) to which I belong. In this study, I will present the Aristotelian predicable classification as a topical scheme applicable to six critical questions (CQs). According to this approach, topics, dialectic, and rhetoric may be considered jointly as a rational procedure. The CQs would play a rhetorical function as well. This analysis becomes relevant in putting forth a broader framework, one of contemporary studies on argumentation, for the judicial evaluation of scientific evidence.

1 Introduction

The purpose of this paper is to provide some critical theoretical insights for the study of legal reasoning, forensic reasoning and lawyering skills.

The starting point will be a recent clamorous case in Italian law of crimes in which the decision was based on an expert solution: the attribution of legal responsibility was determined by an innovative legal report, which measured the very possibility of a person doing actions intentionally on neurosciences researches and new techniques for mapping the brain.

By this example, I want to explore what are the means of justifying a legal decision based on expert opinion according to argumentation studies. In the current debate of argumentation, there has been a development of researches on legal reasoning, which provides a strict methodology. I argue that the judicial choice, in most cases, however, is not a purely technical one, but a matter of *logos, pathos* and *ethos*. It is rarely preferable to use fixed patterns for reasoning (as argumentation schemes) without making use of persuasive elements.

I will take into account the tools endorsed in the legal context by a representative approach to argumentation: the New-Dialectics by Walton. Moreover, in this contribution, I will turn the centre of attention to a more general topic: rhetoric and the role (which it is expected) to play in legal arguing. Discussing whether an argumentation scheme has rhetorical relevance, my reasoning has been influenced, more particularly, by the works of Enrico Berti and Francesca Piazza on rhetoric in the Nineties and by the studies of forensic rhetoric of Cermeg (Centre of Research on legal methodology).

Finally, this analysis comes in relevance for putting forth a broader framework, the one of contemporary studies on argumentation, for the judicial evaluation of scientific evidence.

2   The Case

In 2011 the Court of Appeal of Trieste reversed a decision made by an earlier Court, influenced by neuroscience research. The case introduces a new scenario in the Italian Legal System with respect to the role of neuroscience in law.

This is the case: a man was stabbed to death at the railroad station in Udine, a city in the North of Italy. An Algerian man was arrested in connection with this death and then convicted of murder and sentenced to imprisonment. The defendant appealed the decision to the Court for requesting a formal change of it. During the appeal process, a neuroscientist was called as an expert witness. He testified, showing a map of the brain, that the man suffered severe brain impairment: a genetic vulnerability affected his mental capacity and changed his personality into violent behaviours in response to specific social adverse stimulus. The Court declared him partially mentally incompetent and reduced the level of punishment (Corte d'Assise d'Appello of Trieste, 1.10.2009, n. 5). The Court upheld that the first decision was unjust because scientific criteria were misapplied in determining the degree of culpability of the accused: neuroscience, in practice, assessed the legal measure of mental competence, which is relevant for criminal responsibility.

The decision of the Court of Appeal to accept the "brain scan" as evidence for a fuller comprehension of behaviour rests upon a case-to-case basis. The Supreme Court has not so far ratified it.

3   Legal Premises

In this case the Court, in forming the decision, drew almost exclusively from the neurosciences.

The decision recalls the legal debate on the standard for admissibility of expert testimony. The background of this presentation mainly consists in Italian legal system: there is an extensive reference to Italian experience.

Many works argue on those leading decisions, which value the scientific support for judge in trial and identify specific factors for reliability (see, in a wider context, the works on Frye v. United States, 293 F. 1013 – D.C. Cir. 1923, Daubert v. Merrell Dow Pharmaceuticals, 509 U.S. 579, 113 S.Ct. 2786, 125 L.Ed. 2d 469 – U.S. June 28, 1993; (Puppo, 2004; Godden & Walton, 2006; Fuselli, 2008).

It is necessary to clarify some legal aspects.

First, it is possible for the judge or the court, both in civil and in criminal law, to come to judgment founding his opinion on an expert opinion. Broadly speaking about the legal order, Italy is a civil law country. Materially, civil law holds case law to be secondary and subordinate to statutory law and the court system is usually unbound by precedent. In Italian jurisdictions the decisions of the Courts are not necessarily binding beyond the immediate case before but, in practice, the decision of higher courts provide a very strong precedent, for both itself and all lower courts. More properly expressed, the Italian Supreme Court decisions represent *grands arrêts*, which give a direction to judicial practice and doctrinal studies, setting certain rules in a chaotic network formed by rules, lower court decisions and regulations. They play an argumentative role as *topoi* suited to orienting the interpretation but also a practical legal role, representing the "living law", the rules that judges apply and create when legal gaps occur (Mengoni, 1996).

In Italian jurisdiction, the Italian Supreme Court has recently set the outcome of a Daubert-like standard to expert opinion testimony. It focuses attention not upon the requirements for acceptability of expert testimony but upon the criteria that would lead judges in grounding their discretional decision.

"Within the legal order in force, based on the principle of the free belief of the Judge, the Judge can found his decision upon an expert survey, although it has been opposed by the opposing party, as long as he will provide appropriate grounds for his decision" (Supreme Court, Civil Law, section VI, 12.12.11, n. 26550, Agenzia delle Entrate vs. Ericson Telecomunicazioni S.p.A).

"According to the principle of the free belief of the Judge and lacking legal evidence, the Judge can choose among different theories propounded by different experts, nominated by the Judge or by the parties, the one which is the most sharable, as long as he will explain carefully and deeply the reasons of his disapproval or the reasons of his choice and he will specifically confute the opposing deductions of the parties. The Supreme Court will not interject about major or minor plausibility of scientific theories; it will not decide whether the thesis which has been approved by the lower court is true or not, but it will examine the grounds of the decision which needs to be *reasonable* and *logical*. The Supreme Court is not the judge of the science because it does not have scientific knowledge: it will assess the methodological correctness of the lower court approach with regard to the expert opinion and it will critically verify its trustworthiness" (Supreme Court, Criminal Law, section IV, 13.5.12, n. 24573).

The guidelines of the Supreme Court recalls the gatekeeping role of the judge as defined by *Daubert*: the judge has not a passive role limiting himself to attributing weight to the expert opinion; he plays an active role focused on the methodological check. Especially: 1) the judge provides appropriate grounds for decision; 2) he explains carefully and deeply the reason of his choice (approval / disapproval); 3) he confutes the opposing deduction; 4) he assesses the logical correctness of the procedure; 5) he cannot judge science in the merits.

In short, the Italian Supreme Court's decisions highlight, first, that the judicial decision is governed by the principle of free belief. The judge is partially free in the sense that, despite his personal conviction, the verdict needs to be justified on the evidence of the trial. The judicial discretion is not unlimited. It does not consist in a personal conviction but in the rational determination based on critical discussion of the parties (see Manzin and Puppo, 2008).

Secondly, the core of the judicial experience is the dialectical and reciprocal *ex*change of the parties, which is going to be an effective *inter*change (for the concept of *trilogue*, see Plantin, 1999, 2001, 2011).

Third, the judge can disregard the arguments propounded by the parties as long as he will give *justification*. The duty of justification plays an important role for the public determination of the decision making process. This duty is established at the highest level of Italian legal order (see art. 111 co. 6 of Constitutional Act) and confirmed by the Code of Civil Procedure (art. 132 c.p.c.) and by the Code of Criminal Procedure too (art. 546, 192 c.p.p.). Legal justification consists in explaining the *logical* and the *legal* procedure that lead to conclusion.

According to the common experience of the courts, the best way of justification is formed by a syllogism, in which the major premise (the s.c. judgment in law) is the rule to apply to the case; the minor premise (the s.c. judgement in fact) is determined by the reconstruction of the fact as an historical event; the conclusion is the final decision. The s.c. *judicial syllogism* is founded on two following operations: one is duty-bound to law; the other one is based on the judicial discretional power over choosing and evaluating evidence (see Manzin, 2011, 2012a, 2012b). For instance:

P.M. A person who kills a man commits a murder
p.m. An Algerian citizen killed a man
Dec. An Algerian citizen committed a murder

In logical terms, the judicial syllogism is an argument: the first two statements are the premises; the third statement is the conclusion. If an argument is offered as a justification of its conclusion, two questions arise. First, are the premises true? Second, are the premises properly related to the conclusion? The logical correctness or incorrectness of the argument depends upon the relation between premises and conclusion: it is independent of the truth of the premises. But a logically correct argument may have one or more false premises; a logical incorrect argument may have true premises; indeed, it may have a true conclusion too.

Respecting this, a key tool for legal practitioners is offered by contemporary argumentation theories: they provide a baseline to recognize arguments, to identify premises and conclusions, to supply the missing premises of an incomplete argument. They can serve a theoretical framework for implementing the Italian Supreme Court's logical standards for evaluating expert opinions.

4 Evaluating Expert Opinion: The New Dialectics' Standard of Proof

In this paper, I will adopt the theoretical framework for the analysis and evaluation of arguments propounded by Douglas Walton (Walton, 1995, 1996, 1998). The challenge is twofold: 1) presenting a normative model to check the grounds for judicial decision; 2) evaluating the process-view presented.

According to a (simplified) account of this new method in use in argumentation theory and informal logic, there are two main basic concepts to be presented: dialogue types and argumentation schemes.

A dialogue (or conversation) "is a sequence of exchanges message or speech acts between two or more participants" (Walton, 1989: 3). It is a necessary condition for an argument, identified by five characteristics: the issue, the viewpoints of participants, the politeness, the opposition of viewpoints and the use of arguments. According to this definition, an argument always involves a claim, advanced by a party, and a question put forward by the other party.

A dialogue type is "a context or setting in which argumentation occurs in everyday argumentation" (Walton, 1995: 98). It can be used as a normative model for evaluating arguments in different types of cases, even legal cases. According to this approach to fallacies, to evaluate an argument as correct or incorrect, it is necessary to examine the argumentative moves by the participants in the context in which the dialogue occurs. A fallacy occurs as an illicit dialectical shift from one type of dialogue to another; some contexts support moves which can be considered fallacious in other contexts.

The dialogue-type of legal case is viewed, in the model of the new dialectic, as a kind of persuasion dialogue in which there is a central thesis to be proved by a party. Inferences are chained together to aim at proving an ultimate conclusion of the dialogue.

Another basic concept is identified by the use of argumentation schemes, which are, in a broad sense, general and abstract patterns used to create, classify and evaluate arguments. In a conventionalized way, argumentation schemes show the internal organization of each single argument and the way by which the argument can be employed.

Depending on the argument scheme used, various types of argumentation can be detailed; each type of argumentation involves a set of critical questions. They include deductive, inductive and defeasible forms of argument (see Walton & Reed & Macagno, 2008: 1–2). In this recent book, the authors provide a menu of argumentation schemes, a complete taxonomy, bringing together a large number of schemes that occur in everyday argumentation. They develop a method of classifying schemes in a formalized way based on logic and artificial intelligence. Their project of classifying argument schemes is prior to classifying informal fallacies.

In new dialectics, fallacies are closely related to argument schemes: most of informal fallacies are associated with misuses of schemes. Specifically, argument schemes can be classified under three broad headings: reasoning, source-based arguments, applying rules to cases (Walton, 1998; 2006).

Legal reasoning requires a variety of argumentation schemes to be used together. The legal case I have presented in the beginning can be modelled in an argument from expert opinion. This kind of argument is dependent to the source: an agent is in a position to know something; so the argument depends on the characteristics of the source (its credibility, its expertise). Walton has indicated the constitutive elements of such argumentation scheme as follows.

Appeal to expert opinion is an argument found on (see Walton, 2002: 49–50):

Major *Premise:*	*Source* E *is an expert in subject domain* S *containing proposition* A
Minor Premise:	E *asserts that a proposition* A *(in domain S) is true (false).*
Conclusion:	A *may plausibly be taken to be true (false).*

There are six basic critical questions matching the appeal to expert opinion; they indicate the way by which an argument can be criticized, by analysing the relation between premises and conclusion.

1. Expertise Question: *How credible is E as an expert source?*
2. Field Question: *Is E an expert in the fields that A is in?*
3. Opinion Question: *What did E assert that implies A?*
4. Trustworthiness Question: *Is E personally reliable as a source?*
5. Consistency Question: *Is A consistent with what other experts assert?*
6. Backup Evidence Question: *Is E's assertion based on evidence?*

In a practical view, adopting a scheme-based approach can be useful.

The argumentation scheme and the CQ associated with it can be used as inputs into the judgement. The list of CQ may be a tool for judges and lawyers (participants at the legal dialogue) to represent premises and conclusion and the link between the premises and the conclusion: they are simple, accessible and selective. They indicate the key assumptions on which the correct argumentation depends.

Walton and Gordon have recently implemented a software library for building argumentation tools. To give an example, Carneades, which is free available on line, provides a computational model for representing, diagramming and evaluation arguments. Within the European Estrella Project, it has been used in legal domain as a device to help lawyers and judges to build a wide variety of arguments, improving their ability to argue the issue of a case.

In closing, in the new dialectic model, argumentation schemes and the appropriate CQ related may be used as a *logical tool* to check the application of an argument in conversational contexts and to evaluate the strengths or weakness of an argument. *Logical* means *dialectical*: applying argumentation scheme, an argument can be analysed as a *process* in which different types of rules are used (from deductive logic, inductive and abductive form of reasoning) in a dialogical sequence of acts.

This process view is well illustrated by informal logic approach: "to say that argumentation is dialectical, then, is to identify it as a human practice, an exchange between two or more individuals in which the process of interaction shapes the product" (Blair and Johnson, 1987: 46). In order to identify the dialectical conception of argumentation, four elements come to relevance: a) argumentation is a product / process link; b) argumentation is originated by a conflict between at least two arguers; c) the starting point of argumentation consists in a question or a doubt; d) the argumentation is a purposive activity in the peculiar sense that the parties have a goal towards which their moves turn.

If New Dialectic theory is right and practically useful, then it offers a topic to discuss: does it imply rhetoric? Do the "critical questions" have only dialectic relevance? New Dialectic provides a pragmatic framework for identification, description and evaluation of arguments: does rhetoric make its contribution?

The solution I argue in this paper is supported by Enrico Berti's work on rhetoric. For what his solution implies, rhetoric is the one identified by Aristotle. Referring to Aristotle involves assuming rhetoric as the ability "not to simply succeed in persuading, but rather to discover the means of coming as near such success as the circumstances of each particular case allow" (*Rh.* 1355b 27). Discussing this definition, Berti emphasizes that rhetoric is not the art of persuasion but the (fallible) attempt of choosing a way (*methodon*) to persuade. Nothing is persuasive *per se* but it is always *to* someone. This is the real challenge for rhetoric: to find out something, which can be persuasive in each argument *to* someone.

There are three means of effecting persuasion: "The man who is to be in command of them must, it is clear, be able (1) to reason logically, (2) to understand human character and goodness in their various forms, and (3) to understand the emotions-that is, to name them and describe them, to know their causes and the way in which they are excited" (Rh. 1356a).

From the perspective of philosophy of language, Berti argues, all the participants in a dialogue are *within* the discourse: they are constitutive elements of it and not just external users.

Logos is made of three parts: the speaker, the topic, the man towards whom a speech is directed (see. *Rh.* 1358a 37-b1). The outcome of such this statement is that argumentation develops within the *logos*. The *logos* is not just a component of the model: it may simply be a part of it if argumentation is figured as a communicational system. But *Logos* cannot be reduced to the "message" because it is not neither external to the participants, nor neutral to them. *Logos*, *pathos* and *ethos* cannot be represented as devices for emotional persuasion: they consist in essential components of the persuasive process.

In order to fully understand the traditional concept of rhetoric, it is necessary to collect the pieces into which it has been fragmented. Francesca Piazza, an Italian philosopher of language, discussing on the revival of rhetoric in the Nineties, recognizes that rhetoric has been performed in two directions: valuing the rules of *inventio* (s.c. rhetoric of proof) or valuing the rules of *elocutio* (s.c. rhetoric of trope). For the rhetoric of proof, rhetoric is assimilated to the art of dialectic and reduced to a general theory of argumentation. For the rhetoric of the trope, rhetoric is assimilated to poetics.

A united conception of rhetoric has been expanded by Cermeg (Centre of Research on Legal Methodology) in various work on forensic rhetoric.

The most peculiar aspect of the studies of Cermeg on legal argumentation is the bottom-up approach, moving from a legal case study to the metaphysical foundation of the argumentative procedure (see Manzin, 2010, 2012; Tomasi, 2011). The aim of the Cermeg research on legal argumentation is not limited to the practical aspect of providing for legal practitioners an easy-to-use handbook for being successful in circumstantial cases. The idea is to recover classical studies on rhetorical procedure, getting rid of the neo-platonic influence, in order to understand the principle by which each party may argue and check it.

In this view, the critical questions of the new dialectical theory may be interpreted as a *topical* scheme functional to the argumentative procedure.

To evaluate the plausibility of the expert argument, it is necessary to use criteria based on *endoxa,* opinions generally accepted (Luzzati, 1990). In a critical discussion, the opposing party does not confine himself/herself to acknowledge what the expert says but criticizes tit. The CQ assign to the party an active role: the party is considered not to be a passive user of the expertise of someone else, but an active judge who has to evaluate what the expert source communicates.

In *Topics*, Aristotle presented a method "whereby we shall be able to reason from opinions that are generally accepted about every problem propounded to us, and also shall ourselves, when standing up to an argument, avoid saying anything that will obstruct us" (Arist., *Topici,* I, 100a 18–21). This method moves from statements. Each statement in which there is a predication reveals a definition, a genus, a property, an accident. The Aristotelian classification may be briefly explained.

The *definition* of anything is the statement of its essence, i.e. that which makes it what it is. *Genus* is that part of the essence which is also predicable of other things different from them in kind. A *property* is an attribute, which is common to all the members of a class, but is not part of its essence (i.e. need not be given in its definition). An *accident* is an attribute, which may or may not belong to a subject.

The predicable classification provides a topical scheme, which emerges from the set of the critical question too. The topical scheme may be considered a way to read and interpret the Critical Questions.

For example, the *Expertise Question* is functional to establish whether the expert assertion can be drawn into the genre of "expert discourses". So the expertise question plays a role that is on a par with the one of the genus. It provides a necessary element for evaluating the argument.

Once established that E is an expert source, the *Field Question* confines the field of expertise. E's assertion is relevant only if he is competent in the specific field within the subject is included. It corresponds to the property's role: it allows identifying the subject in an unambiguous way.

The *Opinion Question* allows to clarify E's theory in relation to the argument A: the question plays the role of the definition, because it specifies the essence of the discourse.

The *Trustworthiness Question* can check a relation similar to the one of the accident: the personal reliability cannot be considered as a decisive standard to evaluate an assertion. So trustworthiness is a possible element, not an essential one. Too many variables can affect the judgment of trustworthy.

The *Consistency Question* aims to put E's opinion in relation to what other experts have argued in the same field and to check its compatibility. The idea is to make a comparative judgment: this function is the one served by the property because the kind of compatibility does not describe the essence of the object but a relation.

Through the *Backup Evidence Question*, it is possible to assess the limits of E's assertion beyond which the theory is neither informative nor grounded. It corresponds to the definition's role.

By reading the CQ into a topical classification, it becomes clear that the kind of critical control carried out by questioning is *doxastic*: it regards the relation between the expert opinion and the topic at issue. Moreover, argumentation schemes provide not only a dialectical guidance for conducting the discussion, but assume topical and rhetorical functions.

Topics are functional to the use of *dialectics,* which correspond to the praxis of confutation (*elenchos*): having recovered the premises, it becomes necessary to verify that a certain proposition lacks opposition because the parties share it or because its opposition is contradictory. The proposition defended by confutation of the opposite thesis within the controversial context is true: this conclusion is rationally guaranteed by the logical principle of non-contradiction.

Lastly, *rhetoric* is an indispensable part of the argumentative procedure: it does neither replace nor coincide with dialectics but it pursues a purpose complementary to it, which is to support persuasively the dialectic conclusion. Though without excluding but rather underlining the importance of a careful study of words, voice, gestures, rhetoric must not be reduced to the mere practice of techniques to move the inspiration of the audience. The employment of rhetorical means leads to cogent conclusions as the objections are overcome.

In short, see the following table

New Dialectic	Forensic Rhetoric
Argumentation schemes are forms of argument (structure of inferences) that represent structures of common types of arguments used in everyday discourse	CQ represent a topical scheme: the kind of critical control carried out by questioning is doxastic; it regards the relation between the expert opinion and the topic at issue
Classification of informal fallacies	*Predicables*
DIALECTICAL RELEVANCE	RHETORICAL RELEVANCE

I argue that the two perspectives are compatible.

According to the Aristotelian conception, dialectic may not be considered as an analytical procedure geared to an ordered composition of arguments.

"The more we try to make either dialectic rhetoric not, what they really are, practical faculties, but sciences, the more we shall inadvertently be destroying their true nature; for we shall be re-fashioning them and shall be passing into the region of sciences dealing with definite subjects rather than simply with words and forms of reasoning" (*Rh.* 1359b).

The border between dialectics and analytics has been discussed since medieval time and, namely, as Petrarca reported it, it emerges in the epistemological conflict between *dyalectici* and *scholae dyalectici* (see Manzin, 1994). The former apply the Aristotelian methodology based on confutation (*elenchos*); the latter apply a method affected by scholasticism, more inclined to classification[1]. A misconception of dialectics would be determined by scholastic epistemology, which tended to simplification, to reduction to unity by splitting into identical parts, classifying and reordering.

The scholasticism mixed up dialectic with eloquence, granting a privilege to the procedure able to persuade the audience. But the cogency of dialectic may not be measured upon the effects on the audience: it implies non-contradiction in premises and coherence with the conclusion. In modern thought, scholasticism would be responsible for favouring analytical procedure, by adopting deductive procedure, aiming at persuasion, forgetting the truth.

So here is a passage in which Aristotle warns against people, like sophists, think and act thinking of dialectics as a practical science:

"Still we ought not to be ignorant of that which occurs in this treatise... For the beginning of every thing is perhaps, as it is said, the greatest thing, and on this account the most difficult; for that is the hardest to be perceived, which, as it is the most powerful in faculty, is by so much the smallest in size; yet when this is discovered, it is more easy to add and co-increase what mains, which also occurs in rhetorical arguments, and in almost all the other arts" (Arist. *El. Sof.* 183b 15–30).

Dialectics is described as an art, not a mere matter of skills: if it were a technique, it would be automatically applied. Qualifying it as an art implies practising it, caring about not its effects but the reason why certain effects are produced. Learning what comes from art is easier, faster and effortless: it helps if necessity but it doesn't increase knowledge.

The Aristotelian example is also very forceful:

"As if a person professing to deliver the science of keeping feet from injury, should afterwards not teach shoemaking, nor whence such things (as safe-guards for the feet) may be procured, but should exhibit many

---

1   I am referring to Manzin'work on the interpretation of the concept of order in a legal philosophical perspective (Manzin 2008). Neo-platonism has influenced the modern and static order: Plotinus and his scholars were first responsible for denying the ontological dimension of difference, by reducing the difference into unity. This idea derives from Anassagora and Zenone and their conception of principle: qualifying the principle of everything always just alike itself, they removed difference from the horizon.

kinds of shoes of every form; for he would indeed afford assistance as to use, yet not discover the art" (Arist. *El. Sof.* 184a).

Dialectic is an *ars logica*, founded on principle of non-contradiction, which implies confutation. Dialectis involves searching for truth (*inquisitio very*); true is what appears as undeniable in a context. Pseudo-dialectic abstracts from this element (*telos*): truth is out of consideration; what is required is audience's persuasion. We could say that persuasion is the condition of efficiency in pseudo-dialectic view.

Using a pseudo-dialectic procedure could take many advantages: practically speaking, it helps cutting the difference by providing a ready-made scheme of order; the scheme of order is functional to a concrete goal pursued by a party; the goal is automatically achieved following the instructions given; the scheme of order is rational, based on the principle of coherence. But what is missing? The theoretical component of the theory, the research of the principle by which it is possible to increase or decrease the knowledge.

> "The sophist does not differ from the good rhetorician for a matter of knowledge or a matter of skills, but for choosing a different way of life: the sophist makes a bad choice which consists in ignoring or hiding the truth and bending the other party to his will. In this context, persuasion is apparent: not in the sense that it doesn't exist, but in the sense that it is not grounded because it turns to be a mere subjection to a power" (Cavalla, 1992: 725).

The consequent issue would be: how is possible to pass on a true discourse? The starting point of argumentation is, in its basic form, an option formed by *possible* opposite discourses of the parties. But how can be declared the truth?

The solution is represented by that methodology composed by topic, dialectic and rhetoric. Rhetoric cannot be excepted: rhetoric and dialectic are complementary. Both regards controversial situation: dialectic plays a preliminary role checking the opposition; rhetoric makes the discourse effective by persuasion. The rhetorical procedure is a complex procedure, which is addressed to a pragmatic goal (arousing audience's attention) and to the more general goal (winning the opposition by confutation of the opposing argument). A party prevails against the other by following acquisition of approval about controversial *topoi*. The first act for the rhetorician is finding out the most effective *topoi*: they will represent the starting point of discussion for getting the other party's approval. A reference book regarding the topical potential to consult would be useful: but it would not be enough. The discourse needs to be assessed by a logical check, rationally guaranteed by principle of non-contradiction.

6   Conclusion

In this final section, from the points made in the essay, I will finally draw the conclusion discussing the practical legal side of it.

As I have stated in the beginning, in 2011 the Italian Supreme Court has ruled the judging in those cases where an expert witness, voluntarily or under compulsion, provides testimonial evidence. Both in private law and in criminal law, the expert survey is required for providing scientific or technical information to the solution of the legal issue.

What is the role of the judge? The guidelines of the Supreme Court recall the gatekeeping role as defined by *Daubert*: without spotting criteria of admissibility of evidence, both the decisions emphasize the duty of justification. It is supposed to be a distinction between scientific/technical or other specialized knowledge and rhetorical skills: the judge, and so the parties in trial, are not required to have scientific knowledge but they need to apply argumentative skills.

However, the Court's guidance appears quite generic and doesn't avoid the most practical difficulty of a reasonable justification. How do judges operate when they evaluate the admissibility of scientific evidence and come to judgment?

The argumentation schemes are fruitful tools to this purpose. A careful reading of the Court's decisions shows the applicability of argumentation schemes in Italian legal experience.

What does it mean to provide appropriate grounds for decisions? The decision could not be unjustified and unreasonable. The duty of justification obliges the judge to make public his/her decision-making process. Unreasonable is the decision that has no valid connection to the case.

What are the conditions at which an argumentation is reasonable or logical? Argumentation schemes capture common patterns of reasoning and perform a practical function: to check the logical consistency of argumentation. If there is an expert witness, the scheme is the one from expert opinion as defined by Walton (Walton, 2002: 49–50). This argument is defeasible: it is subject to defeat in light of new information, which can come out in the argumentative dialogue (Walton and Godden, 2006: 277). This is why the critical questions are so important to verify the validity of the argument. Following the list of six critical questions sketched in the pattern, many doubts / oppositions can feed the discussion. For instance, the judge (and the parties too, in force of due process principle) may ask: how credible is the expert source? What qualifications does he/she hold? What are his/her publications? Is the field of expertise the one of his/her knowledge? Is he/she up-to-date in relation with the developments of the area? Is his/her assertion clear? Is he/she personally reliable as a source? Is his/her assertion consistent with what other expert assert? Can the expert provide good reasons in opposing other experts conclusions? Does his/her assertion belong the major opinion in the scientific community (general acceptance)? Is his/her assertion based on evidence?

All these critical questions "codify some of the background information that is assumed by (or implicit in) the argument from expert opinion. As questions, they function to request the background information on which the success of the argument depends. As objection, they challenge the acceptability of the original argument until the additional information is found to be favourable (to the initial argument)" (Walton and Godden 2006: 279).

As maintained by Cermeg'work and by the reported studies on rhetoric, the relevance of argumentation scheme is not only dialectical but also rhetorical: the content of the critical questions can be reconstructed by the predicable theory. The answers to the questions represent possible discourses, which need to be checked by confutation in order to be true.

How can be checked the methodological correctness of the decision? After having selected the *topoi*, the controversial arguments are subject to the dialectical assessment. The conclusion, which stands to opposition, is true. Therefore, rhetoric is a fundamental part of the process: it regards the way to express a true discourse. In legal context, for instance, the ritual formulas (for instance, "in name of the Italian people", "*salvis iuribus*", …) have a rhetorical meaning because they convey a message in a shared linguistic form. The use of specific legal expressions corresponds to a rhetorical choice.

Is it exhaustive to make a legal syllogism? The deductive inference of the practical judicial syllogism doesn't use up legal argumentation: after having sketched the premises, major premise and minor premise need to be linked to conclusion in a coherent way. The final deduction implies a more complex process in which the participants move in a strategic way.

In concluding, I want to add a critical remark on the use of argumentative schemes. Argumentation theories may not be reduced to provide a list of options available to users in the current context of everyday language.

It is theoretically possible to distinguish two lines of developments: on the one hand, providing more and more complete schemes which sum up the logical and conversational operations; on the other hand, recalling the classical tradition, acquiring skills without forgetting but researching the principle by which the truth emerges (*aletheia*). According to the former, argumentation theory is thought to be a system: the risk is to confuse dialectic with the analytical procedure and consider it not only a tool for practical utilities but also a guarantee for a rational procedure. According to the latter, the theoretical framework is different: the check's demand cannot avoid a foundational investigation of the argumentative structure. In other words, arguing reasonably and effectively cannot be reduce to the use of practical skills, without knowing the principle by which the techniques applied are valid.

The risk of adopting a systematic approach to argumentation produces methodological consequences: the discourse is split into units and organized by schemes relating to a static and totalizing concept of order; if the system of rules is violated, a fallacy occurs and the argumentation cannot come to its reasonable outcome.

Indeed, the second way of thinking of argumentation is characterized by putting in relevance the difference, which is the real source of the controversial situation: the difference is not resolved through fixed standards but discussed and checked through the principle of noncontradiction.

So, here are two possible attitudes towards the use of argumentation schemes: an automatic application *vs.* a critical use; a systematic procedure *vs.* a rhetorical one. This second way, I argue, parties in trial must act using topics, dialectics and rhetoric.

References

Berti, E. (1989). *Le ragioni di Aristotele*, Laterza: Bari.

Berti, E. (2002). "La dialettica antica come modello di ragionevolezza". *Ars interpretandi. Annuario di Ermeneutica giuridica*, 7: 17–27.

Blair, A.J., Johnson, R.H. (1987). "Argumentation as dialectical". *Argumentation*, 1, 41–86.

Breton Ph., Gauthier, G. (2000). *Histoire des theories de l'argumentation*, La Découverte: Paris.

Cantù I., Testa P. (2006). *Teorie dell'argomentazione. Un'introduzione alle logiche del dialogo*, Bruno Mondadori: Milano.

Cantù, P., Testa I., Cattani, A. (2009). *La svolta argomentativa. 50 anni dopo Perelman e Toulmin: 1958-2008*, Loffredo: Napoli.

Cavalla, F. (1992). "Topica giuridica". *Enciclopedia del diritto*, XLIV, 720–739.

Feteris, E. (1999). *Fundamentals of legal argumentation. A survey of theories on the justification of legal decisions*, Kluwer: Dordrecht.

Fuselli, S. (2008). *Apparenze. Accertamento giudiziale e prova scientifica*, FrancoAngeli: Milano.

Garssen, B. (1997). *Argument schemes from a pragma-dialectical perspective*, IFOTT: Amsterdam.

Goddon D.M., Walton D. (2006). "Argument from expert opinion as legal evidence: critical questions and admissibility criteria of expert testimony in the Legal American System". *Ratio iuris*, 19, 3, 261–286.

Lo Cascio, V. (2009*). Persuadere e convincere: manuaale dell'argomentazione*, Academia Universa Press: Milano.

Luzzati, C. (1990). *La vaghezza delle norme: un'analisi del linguaggio giuridico*, Milano: Giuffrè.

Manzin, M. (1994). *Il petrarchismo giuridico. Filosofia e logica del diritto agli inizi dell'umanesimo*, Cedam: Padova.

Manzin, M. (2010). "Per un approccio multidisciplinare al principio di non contraddizione". Puppo, F. (ed.), *La contradizion che nol consente. Forme del sapere e valore del principio di non contraddizione*, FrancoAngeli: Milano, 9–20.

Manzin, M. (2011). "Rhetorical vs. Syllogistic Models of Legal Reasoning: the Italian Experience". Eemeren, van F.H., Garssen. B., Godden, D., Mitchell, G. (eds). *Proceedings of the 7th Conference of International Society for the Study of Argumentation*. Amsterdam: Rozenberg / Sic Sat, 1165–1174.

Manzin, M. (2012a). "Quale logica per il processo penale? Ragionamento giudiziale e forme di controllo argomentativo della sentenza". Comi, V. & Dominici, G. (eds.). *L'argomentazione giudiziale e il suo controllo in Cassazione*. Roma: Aracne, 63–79.

Manzin, M. (2012b). "A Rhetorical Approach to Legal Reasoning. The Italian Experience of CERMEG". Eemeren, van F.H., Garssen B. (eds.). *Exploring argumentative contexts*. Amsterdam: John Benjamins, 137–148.

Manzin, M., Puppo, F. (2008). *Audiatur et altera pars. Il contraddittorio fra principio e regola*, Giuffrè: Milano.

Mengoni, L. (1996). *Ermeneutica e dogmatica giuridica*, Giuffrè: Milano.

Mortara Garavelli, B. (2008). *Manuale di retorica*, Bompiani: Milano.

Piazza, F. (2000). *Il corpo della persuasion. L'entimema nella retorica greca*, Novecento: Palermo.

Piazza, F. (2004). *Linguaggio, persuasion, verità*, Carocci: Roma.

Plantin, C. (1999). "La interacción argumentativa". *Ecritos*, 17/18, 23–49.

Plantin, C. (2001). "L'argumentation entre discours et interaction". *Lingua, discours, texto*, 71–92.

Plantin, C. (2011). *Les bonnes raison des emotions. Pricipes ed method pour l'étude du discours émotionné*, Peter Lang: Bern.

Puppo, F. (2004). "La 'nuova prova' scientifica nel processo penale. Alcune riflessioni sul rapport tra retorica e scienza". Ferrari, G., Manzin, M. (eds.). *La retorica tra scienza e professione legale. Questioni di metodo*. Giuffrè: Milano, 355–372.

Taruffo, M. (2007). *Precedente e giurisprudenza*, Editoriale Scientifica: Napoli.

Tindale, C.T. (2004). *Rhetorical Argumention. Principles of Theory and Practice*, Sage Publication: Thousand Oaks.

Van Eemeren, F.H. (2001). "The State of the art in argumentation theory". Van Eemeren, F.H. (ed.). *Crucial concepts in argumentation theory*. Amsterdam University Press: Amsterdam.

Van Eemeren, F.H. et. al. (1996). *Fundamentals of argumentation theory: a handbook of historical backgrounds and contemporary developments*, Lawrence Erlbaum Associates: New Jersey.

Van Eemeren, F.H., Grootendorst, R. (1992). *Argumentation, communication and fallacies*, Lawrence Erlbaum Associates: New Jersey.

Van Eemeren, F.H., Grootendorst, R. (2004). *A systematic theory of argumentation. The pragma-dialectical approach*, Cambridge University Press: Cambridge.

Walton, D. (1995). *A Pragmatic Theory of Fallacy*, University of Alabama Press: Tuscalosa.

Walton, D. (1996). *Argument Structure: A Pragmatic Theory*, University of Toronto Press: Toronto.

Walton, D. (1998). *The New Dialectic*, University of Toronto Press: Toronto.

Walton, D. (2002). *Legal argumentation and evidence*, Penn State Press: University Park – Pennsylvania.

Walton, D. (2006). *Fundamentals of critical argumentation*, Cambridge University Press: New York.

Walton, D., Gordon, T.F. (2009). "Legal reasoning with argumentation schemes". Hafner, C.D. (ed.). *Proceedings of the 12th International Conference on Artificial Intelligence and Law. Association for Computing Machinery*: New York, 137–146.

Walton, D., Reed, C., Macagno, F. (2008). *Argumentation schemes*, Cambridge University Press: Cambridge.

DR. CAROLE LIPSYC, UNIVERSITY OF PARIS

Can Rhetoric Help in Creating a European Episteme for the Digital Age? The Example of Publication Processing and Analogical Semantics

Abstract: Rhetoric offers an inspiration for solving some of the challenges that digital publishing faces when treating complex semantic objects. Such is indeed the case of publication processing and analogical semantics, respectively a production method and a semantic model for complex digital publishing. On a descriptive level, this study explains their similarities with the arts of memory and process of compositio. On an epistemological level, it examines the influences that both a rhetorical approach to digital publishing and a non-rhetorical one could have on our cognition and on our social interactions—that is, on our episteme. The critical analysis in this study uses the philosophical tool of symbolic form. Ultimately, this study proposes that a rhetorical approach to digital publishing could inspire a European way of building the emerging digital society, a way that would take ethical and responsible dimensions into account.

1   Introduction

Rhetoric and computing have something in common: both are technics that treat information. Unlike computing, rhetoric does not treat any kind of data. Rhetoric specializes in producing efficient semantic objects. Subsequently, rhetoric could offer an inspiration to solve select challenges that computing faces when treating complex semantic objects and situations. In particular, the tools and processes of digital publishing could benefit from the influence and tradition of rhetoric. Such is indeed the case of publication processing and analogical semantics, respectively a production method and a semantic model for complex digital publishing.

In this study, we explore the influence of rhetoric on publication processing and on analogical semantics on descriptive and epistemological levels. On the descriptive level, we discover publication processing and its similarities with the arts of memory, most especially with the process of *compositio*. We also compare publication processing, which is information-centred, with its alternative, information architecture, which is user-centred. On the epistemological level, we'll use the conceptual tool of symbolic form to analyse the possible consequences of these two different approaches on cognition and social interactions: in other words, on episteme. Ultimately, this line of critical analysis will lead us to wonder whether a rhetorical approach to digital publishing and complex digital content could inspire a European way of building the emerging digital society.

2 Symbolic Form and Intellectual Technology

Symbolic form is a conceptual tool developed within the fields of philosophy of art and philosophy of culture. It refers to the means and strategies we use to objectify the world. Defined by Ernst Cassirer, this tool can be traced back to the works of Konrad Fiedler.[1] Konrad Fiedler considered that art was a way to get to know the world[2] and that each work of art expressed a unique sensitive intuition about reality [1].[3] This distinction between the process and the product ultimately led to two different types of symbolic forms: one is phenomenological, the other sociohistorical. [2]

The phenomenological symbolic form has been explored and described by Ernst Cassirer when he explained that each domain of culture (myth, art, science, technique) corresponded to a specific activity of the spirit [3]. This type of symbolic form is centred on the subject: it distinguishes the specificities of the different operations of the mind. The sociohistorical symbolic form, developed by Erwin Panofsky, originally aimed to understand a society through its art, architecture, and visual perspective techniques [4]. For Panofsky, these cultural and technical domains revealed the substrate of a civilization, what Foucault would have called the episteme [5], which is to say the underlying order that comes into action when we think, relate, and act as individuals and contemporaries—as a body.

---

1   In the introduction of his fourth unpublished volume on symbolic form, Cassirer pays tribute to Fiedler "who clearly understood the necessity to build the aesthetic system on a foundation that would be more serious in terms of a theory of knowledge." Quoted by Cohn in [1], p. 106.

2   For instance: "Art has and can only have one task which is to take part to the immense work of objectifying the world". Aphorism 57, [1], p. 29.

3   For instance: "The work of art has no idea; it is the idea." Aphorism 77, [1], p. 39.

A similar assumption has been used and developed in the study of technics and most especially in the study of the techniques dedicated to knowledge and memory. Anders asserts that instruments determine the kind of relationships we have with others and with things [6], McLuhan that the medium is the message [7], Goody that the invention of writing has generated a certain kind of reasoning (a *logic of writing*) [8], Eisenstein that printing has made positive science possible [9], Canadian philosopher Feenberg that the future of human beings is decided as much by the form of our tools as by the action of states-men and political movements [10], French philosopher Stiegler that technolo-gy constitutes what he calls a *pre-individual milieu*, an environment that condi-tions everything else [11], and Carr that Google is making us stupid [12] …

In this second epistemological life, the tool of symbolic form changes its name to *intellectual technology* [13]. Intellectual technology studies the cognitive processes, the social order, the kind of rationality, and the episteme that are in-duced by the technologies of knowledge and memory. Like symbolic form, it can focus either on the phenomenological dimension or on the sociohistorical one.

In this study, symbolic form and intellectual technology are used to under-stand the consequences of the different digital publishing approaches but also to offer guidance in their development. Consequently, they have an operating as well as a critical purpose. Symbolic form and intellectual technology consti-tute the general background and frame for this study on the digital age and its information technologies.

3   The Digital Age, Computational Rationality, and Their Challenges

A major shift happened in everyday available technologies in the 1980s and 1990s when computing and telematics entered into everyone's life.[4] The con-junction of these two developments marked the beginning of our digital society. The conjunction transformed our everyday life and impacted, with respect to documents, the way we think, teach, learn, communicate, relate, create, and so on.

The French engineer of knowledge Bachimont provides the name of *logic of computing* to this cognitive transformation [14]. *Logic of computing* follows

-----

4   Computing deals with the treatment of information, telematics with its transmission.

Goody's *writing rationality* [raison graphique] and can be considered the phenomenological symbolic form of the digital age. Logic of computing is forged by the fact that digital content can be fragmented, combined, enriched and transformed in a continuous and unplanned circulation. This particularity divides into four factors:

1) The arbitrariness of interactivity[5];
2) The inflationary, even entropic, profusion of documents and data;
3) The existence of different types of participatory authorships that makes it hard to trace the origins, modifications, and intentionalities of the content;
4) The variable and proteiform use, shaping, and display of content according to the different publishing choices available and compatible.

These four factors create a complex informational context and induce three major challenges:

1) the emergence of knowledge instead of the production of noise;
2) the creation of coherence and of meaning instead of the development of chaos and of senselessness;
3) the establishment of what pragmatics calls shared meaning[6]—in other words, a dialogical capacity where original intentions are acknowledged and understood, instead of the reign of solipsism where everything is integrated into a self-justified monologue.

To resolve these difficulties, there are two main approaches. The first one is user-centred, the second one information-centred.

4   The User-Centred Solution to Digital Complexity

The user-centred approach to digital complexity strives to satisfy the user. Consequently, it aims to keep things simple, effortless, and quick: that is, to give the user what he is looking for, nothing else and nothing more. To achieve these

----

5   The arbitrariness of interactivity relates to the fact that the creator of a digital informational object cannot know beforehand what the user will choose to read, watch, or listen.

6   Shared meaning [*sens commun*] designates the ability to understand correctly what has been expressed thanks to different kinds and levels of norms or topics. [21]

    © Frank & Timme   Verlag für wissenschaftliche Literatur

goals, any impression of complexity must be avoided even if it means to ignore and erase what could be, and sometimes what should be, complex.

A word has even been created to describe this ability to give the user what he's looking for: namely, *findability* [15]. And, another word has been created to express an effortless and intuitive user experience: voila, *usability* [16].

Findability and *usability* are the two keys of a successful user experience.[7] A *successful user experience* is currently the basic requirement for any digital project (websites, mobile apps, software products, browsers, operating systems, platforms, etc.). All the stakeholders of any project expect a successful user experience: users, designers, owners, evaluators, financiers, etc. To achieve *findability*, *usability*, and a *successful user experience*, two complementary solutions emerge: information architecture (the design and structuring of pleasant information spaces) and data mining (the automatic quest for the proper information through the use of algorithms).[8]

The need to keep things simple, intuitive, and attractive must be examined in the light of symbolic form. What does it reveal about our relationship to effort and to learning? Can we reduce all stakes to attractiveness, which is to say, ultimately, to success and profit? Is the user-centred approach really compatible with literacy and digital literacy? Indeed, can we reasonably expect digital literacy to be spontaneous?

Of course, we could also consider that the question of digital literacy is irrelevant and that we only need to rely on beautiful devices, excellent algorithms, and agile thumbs until, ironically, we no longer need our thumbs because something easier than writing and typing has been invented.

This effortless vision of accessing knowledge and information might well contribute to what is often denounced as a loss of the attention ability and as a fading of thorough and structured knowledge in favour of a more superficial one in the digital age. Nevertheless, there is an alternative that could have more positive effects on computational rationality: specifically, the information-centred approach.

---

7   The expression "user experience" is usually replaced by a fashionable acronym: UX. This popular nickname reveals the symbolic power given to the concept as well as its scope. It is also interesting to note that the second letter of the acronym is not the initial, as requires the tradition, but the shortcut used in texting to transcribe the entire first syllable, thus inscribing the expression in a culture that does not take literacy in writing into account.

8   Data mining is also connected to what is called *Big Data and Smart Data*, which correspond to the analysis of massive amounts of information to profile customers, predict needs and events, and help in decision making or problem solving.

5 The Information-Centred Solution to Digital Complexity

In the information-centred approach, what matters is to respect the complex nature of digital information and to make the best of it. The primary purposes of publication processing are not simplicity, findability, or usability but coherence, meaning, shared meaning, relevance, comprehension, and traceability. To achieve these ambitions, it is necessary to prepare the data as soon as it is created or when it is introduced into the information system. In other words, creating content includes creating metadata. *Metadata* refer to information about the content or what is also called *secondary information*. Metadata help contextualize information as well as trace it, combine it, channel it, use it, find it, cross-reference it, etc.

This treatment of information is what the French School of Documentation Science calls *éditorialisation* [17], translated here as *publication processing*. Publication processing covers the entire chain of digital publishing. At each step of this production cycle, it resolves the issues due to the main characteristic of digital content mentioned earlier: that is, the potential of fragmentation-combination. Publication processing guarantees that this potential does not result in decontextualisation, untraceability, incoherence, etc.; instead, it prepares combinations that actually build new coherent media objects. In a sense, publication processing is similar to speech. Though, unlike expression, instead of producing utterances, it produces media objects. Publication processing is thus a process of mediatisation. In short, publication processing relies on knowledge and requires efforts, even learning and training from content creators and content users. Why? How does publication processing work? What is it exactly?

6 Overview of Publication Processing

Publication processing covers the entire chain of production of informational objects, using digital tools to collect, store, prepare and display the content. It includes six phases: metamodeling, modeling, creating, enriching, publishing, and performing.

a. Metamodeling
A metamodel is a typical structure of information—an organization that works for all projects because it relies on general epistemic norms. Analogical semantics proposes a metamodel inspired by pragmatics, rhetoric, cognitive sciences,

and the semantic web. Others can exist. The field of metamodeling is open to research and development.

b. Modeling

When a project is launched, the metamodel must be adapted to fit its needs and subjects. This activity is called modeling. Modeling produces one specific model that matches one specific project. This model aims to structure and determine the body of data related to the project (i.e., the content matrix). In analogical semantics, this content matrix is called topos.

c. Creating

Digital content matrices are composed by digital assets that can be specifically created for the project, collected, or recycled. They are managed by an information system. In a publication processing approach, these documents need to fit the model's requirements and so does the information system.

d. Enriching

When the documents enter the information system, when they are added to the matrix, they are enriched by metadata and by links. The metadata classify and tag the documents in order to adapt them to the model and information system. The links create new knowledge that are abductive and heuristic.

Analogical semantics has determined rules for linking documents that are based on rhetoric and cognitive sciences. These rules assure that the links rely on cognitive reasoning processes shared by everyone and not merely on subjective and personal associations [18]. These links can be construed as rhetorical figures. A *rhetorical figure*, like metaphor or irony, can be defined as what creates a secondary meaning that is added to the first and literal one [19]. The science of connecting data is, like metamodeling, an interesting and new field of research.[9]

e. Publishing

Well indexed and linked, the content can be easily and coherently combined in order to be displayed. Different apparatuses can then be conceived: sites, apps, and non-digital solutions such as books, speeches, exhibitions, and so forth. During this phase, and then only, information architecture is needed to build attractive and efficient display apparatuses.

....

9   This field of research could even extend to Artificial Intelligence (AI).

f. Performing

When the publication processing cycle is completed, the content is available to the user.[10] Among all publishing options that could have been displayed or have been displayed, among all combinatory possibilities offered by the interactive platforms that have possibly been designed, the user performs one single path and has one single experience.

Nevertheless, thanks to the whole modelled process, his experience is meaningful.[11] It is also faithful to the intentionalities of all mediatisation agents. The mediatisation agents are all the persons who have contributed to the publication processing cycle. Each one of them has actually expressed a certain intentionality that bears significance. Publication processing guarantees that these intentionalities are not lost and that they can be acknowledged, used, interpreted, and even questioned.

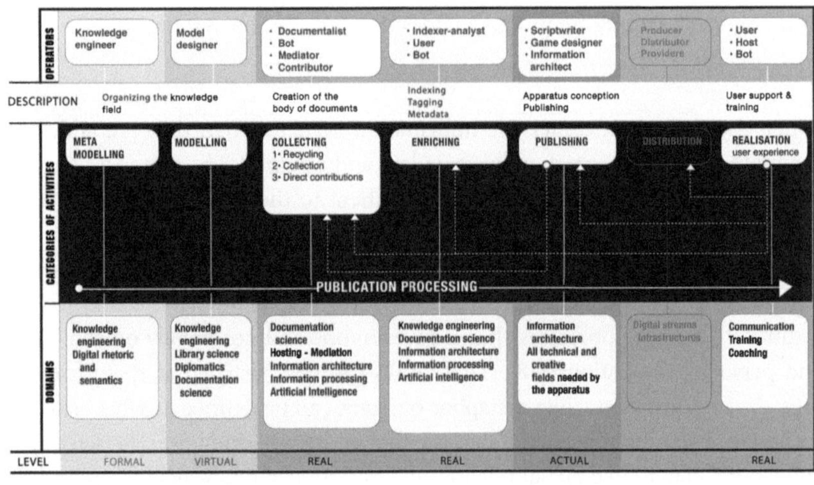

Fig. 1: The Cycle of Publication Processing [20]

---

10   The process is not as linear as it seems since the user can in fact intervene at any phase of the publication processing. S/he can contribute to modeling, creating, enriching, and publishing through cooperative actions.

11   Actually, in science, a model is a guarantee. It assures that a set of rules will lead to certain results. [18]

7 Rhetoric and Publication Processing

a. Metamodeling and Digital Rhetoric

The first phase of publication processing is metamodeling. Metamodeling can be seen as an activity that belongs to the field of digital rhetoric. A metamodel indeed offers what could be considered as a rhetorical vision of how digital content matrices should be organized in order to be exploited in their fullest potential. A formal epistemic knowledge provides optimal solutions, just like the art of rhetoric does.

In Analogical semantics, the metamodel follows a framework designed in pragmatics by Georges-Elia Sarfati and, more precisely, in what he has called *general topic of communication* [21]. A *topic*, in this context, refers to a set of norms that allows shared meaning.

Topic level	Social	Configura-tional	Discursive	Generic	Textual
Linguistic context: Speech process – General Topic of Communication (Sarfati)					
Description	Normative possibilities of a language	Norms of a field of practice	Norms of the common knowledge of a specific group	Conditions of an utter-ance	Utterance
Digital content context: Mediatisation process (Analogical semantics)					
Description	Semantic and document-tary norms Standard documentary structures	Norms and standards of a given infor-mation field or knowledge field	Needs and practices of a group of persons or of a project	An appa-ratus and its structuration	User per-formance
Activity	Metamodel-ing	Modeling		Publishing	Interactive reception
Epistemo-logical level	**Formal:** epistemic structuring	**Virtual:** the information that can exist within a given frame and purpose		**Actual:** the information as it is made available by an apparatus	**Real:** the in-formation as it has been combined by a user in a definite state

Tab. 1: Speech and Mediatisation

b. Publication Processing and the Arts of Memory

Besides the similarity between metamodeling and rhetoric, publication processing can be considered at each of its six phases as the digital equivalent to the arts of memory. *Digital content matrices*, or *digital topos*[12] as they are called in analogical semantics, are actually the equivalent of memory palaces. Memory palaces were mental spaces where rhetoricians kept their knowledge and ideas [22]. Like memory palaces, digital topos store in an organized manner argumentations, documents, texts, and all kinds of content to provide them when needed in an appropriate way. On the epistemological level, memory palaces and digital topos are both virtual objects because they are built from information which is not yet final and manifested: that is, as Bergson suggests, still out of reach.

The French philosopher indeed describes virtuality as a distance between a body and a danger requiring an action. As long as the danger is out of reach, the action is virtual. When the danger happens, when there is no distance left, the action is real. As such, "the real action passes and the virtual action lasts" [23]. This metaphor allows us to understand how virtuality designates a state, out of space and time, when an object or a situation is not yet manifested but already exists. It can still take many forms, but not any form. It is unknown but neither undetermined nor undefined.

As there are rules to build memory palaces, there are also rules to build digital topos. In publication processing, these rules correspond to the metamodel. The specific memory palace built by one person, following the rules of the arts of memory, corresponds to the specific model built by a knowledge engineer for one project, according to the metamodel. During this modeling phase, the engineer determines, defines, and prototypes categories just like the rhetorician created specific places in his palace, the famous *topoi* or *loci*, and designed paths called *itinerari*.

The collecting phase happens then, just the same way in both the arts of memory and publication processing. Thus, content can be created or recycled. In both domains, the content then needs to be prepared. The rhetorician chooses a locus to keep it and an *imagen* to symbolize it. Similarly, the publication processing agent chooses the proper categories to mark it, then enriches it with all necessary secondary information, and decides to link it with other existing data.

Actually, this phase is very important. It determines the future interpretation, combinatory use, and findability of the content. Indeed, the significance

....

12   When used in analogical semantics, the Greek plural form of *topoi* does not apply.

of digital content is as much determined by the content itself as it is by its mark-ups and links. If this step is skipped, if it is poorly or wrongly executed, future meaning and coherence will be altered. Proper metadata are the key to the significance of digital content. They are part of its rhetoric.

Furthermore, the publishing phase in publication processing is the equivalent of *compositio* in the arts of memory. *Compositio* designated the creation of a speech or document with the argumentations and texts that were stored in the memory palace [24]. First, the rhetorician needed to meditate in order to choose a subject and determine a perspective. This phase was called *cogitatio*. In the same way, in publication processing, the publisher of a specific informational project must now decide what will be published on which specific subject(s), for which audience, displayed on which platforms, and so on.

In *compositio*, after *cogitatio* came *inventio*. *Inventio* was a hunt. The rhetorician had to find in his or her palace the proper information that matched the purpose. Mary Carruthers stresses that two things were very helpful in finding the proper information: the structure of the palace (*loci* and *itinerari*) and the emotional power of the *imagenes* [24]. In the hunt for the proper data, the digital publisher can rely on two equivalents: the structure of the model and the emotional and heuristic power of the links—on condition that the links rely on solid motivations and are really rhetorical figures, as is the case in analogical semantics.

After inventio, came formalization. All the hunted elements had to be assembled. Often, memory palace practitioners used determined patterns to operate the formalization phase. These patterns were really precise. They were designed as maps or schemes. They were called *dispositio*ne. In publication processing, this is the work of information architecture. We could say that the information architect designs *dispositio*ne that display the content properly and efficiently. Indeed, information architecture is not put aside in publication processing; rather, it is given a specific role at a precise moment. It exists, is necessary, yet is not all encompassing.

Finally, both in *compositio* and in publication processing, the polishing and embellishing phase takes place. On an epistemological level, the phase of *compositio* corresponds to the moment when the virtual object that was out of reach, because it was stored in one's memory or in an information system, comes into reach ("à portée") [23] because all conditions are now present to display it. This phase is called *actualization*. The virtual object is now actual. It is no longer virtual, out of reach. The virtual object is not yet real, performed, passed, and fixed in contact: it is within reach.

At the end, when the speech is released by the rhetorician or performed by the user, the object is real, takes form, and exists as it is. And, this is the last phase of the mediatisation process in both domains.

Hence, in *compositio* and in publication processing, there are four epistemological phases:

1. The formal level (the metamodel, the rhetorical rules),
2. The virtual level (the memory palace, the digital topos),
3. The actual level (the *dispositio*, the display apparatus)
4. The real level (the creation of the rhetorician, the realization of the user).

In sum, we can conclude that both operational and epistemological processes are similar in the arts of memory and in publication processing.

Arts of Memory	Publication processing
Operational process	
Rhetorical general principles	Metamodel
Memory Palace	Digital Topos
Topoi/Loci	Topical categories
Elements transformation into *imagenes* Elements location in the *loci*	Tagging – Indexing – Linking
Compositio	Publishing
Cogitatio	Editorial & publishing choices
Invention (hunt) • based on *loci* and *itinerari* • based on the emotional power of the *imagenes*	Selection – Data-mining • based on the structure of the digital topos • based on the emotional power of the analogical links (rhetorical figures)
Dispositio	Information Architecture
Polishing, embellishing, producing	
Epistemological process	
1. Formal knowledge (rhetorical rules, metamodel) → 2. Virtual object (memory palace, digital topos) → 3. Actual devices (*dispositio*, apparatus) → 4. Real information objects (rhetorician's creation/user's performance)	

This common operational and epistemological construction between publication processing and the arts of memory does not exist in the user-centred approach of digital informational. Indeed, the user-centred approach does not take into account the virtual object. It does not even acknowledge its existence. In fact, information architecture only deals with apparatuses—with the actual level. And data mining only deals with informational matter—with the real level.

8 Symbolic Forms of the User-Centred and the Information-Centred Approaches

Based on these epistemological elements, we can now try to understand the symbolic forms of the two different approaches to digital content. The user-centred approach refuses complexity; it promotes effortlessness and user satisfaction in all matters, including knowledge acquisition. The user-centered approach focuses all attention on the individual, ignores the virtual object, and concentrates on the interactions with the actual object (the apparatus) and on the production of the real object (data mining).

This is very close to what Jean Piaget has called the *sensorimotor stage of cognitive development*. At this stage, the child has not yet developed the ability to represent the objects and the spatial environment. The child is trapped in a string of detached and meaningless interactions with things and is still in a kind of solipsist state [25]. Besides, Jean Piaget has also stated that when the environment changes, humans—as a species—need to accommodate. They need to shift, collectively, their cognitive abilities and processes [26].

Thus, we can make the assumption that the user-centred approach corresponds to an early stage of accommodation to the new digital environment in which we are living. Indeed, this environment is quite different from the phenomenological milieu we have been inhabiting so far. Constituted by information, displayed by media, generated by mathematics, it is, in Bachelard choice of term, *phenomenotechnical*. This phenomenotechnical environment does not follow the natural rules of the phenomenological environment and it does not take any solid and stable form.[13] It is virtual and its objects are virtual.

---

13 In analogical semantics, this phenomenotechnical environment, manifested through the media, generated by mathematics, and generating an editorial space is called the *digimedia environment*. [18]

However, to become a mature society, people must live together: not only self-centred individuals but responsible persons having a dialogical ability. To be able to deal with complexity, to really acknowledge the digital environment and its virtual objects, we need to go beyond the sensorimotor stage of the user-centred approach. We need publication processing and rhetoric.

9   Conclusion

Nevertheless, is it plausible to develop, alongside the dominant user-centred approach, which keeps us in an underdeveloped cognitive state, an information-centred approach, which favours cognitive maturity and social dialogue? Indeed, two major obstacles exist: 1) The user-centred approach is the mainstream paradigm in academics, in business, in *doxa*, in funding, in the evaluation criteria of committees and buyers, in the making of law, and most particularly in the making of the Intellectual Property laws; 2) The information-centred approach demands hard work and users just do not want to meet the information challenge. To overcome these obstacles, it is necessary to use information architecture to build more attractive and acceptable information-centred technologies. Yet, it will not be sufficient. Above all, political decisions are needed in two areas: research and development funding policies and digital literacy policies.

Such decisions are possible, if and only if, there is an acknowledgement of the importance to create technologies of knowledge and of memory that are beneficial to the development of our cognition and to our common social existence—and, not only technologies that are attractive and profitable. When it comes to building a society, its reasoning patterns, its cognitive abilities, and its models of interactions between individuals, all does not sum up to a mere financial return on investment. The design of technologies can and should also integrate an ethical dimension.

An ethical design of technologies rests on understanding symbolic forms. It chooses not only to witness and observe what computational rationality evolves into being but also to influence it consciously and willingly. The choice to engage in an ethical design of the digital technologies of memory and of knowledge could define a European way of developing digital technologies: Firstly, because Europe is the seminal source of rhetoric and rhetoric would be the corner stone of this ethical design; Secondly, because Europe needs to create business alternatives where the Americans are not yet the leaders and where European companies can be. The user-centred approach has indeed been developed by emblematic American companies, such as Apple (information architecture) and Google (data mining). It is also well promoted by American structures, such as the Information Architecture Institute. And, finally, because Europeans have a tradition of valuing education, culture, and literacy. Undeniably, ethical digital technologies of knowledge will require ambitious educative policies and actions. Since they do not rely on spontaneity and intuition, they require a knowledge that would be the equivalent of what grammar has been to writing and rhetoric to expression. In conclusion, ethical digital technologies of knowledge will require literacy.

References

[1]   K. Fiedler, *Aphorismes.* Paris: Editions rue d'Ulm, 2013.

[2]   A. Rieber, "Le concept de forme symbolique dans l'iconologie d'E. Panofsky," *Rev. Appar., 2013.* Retrieved December 20, 2016 from: <http://appareil.revues.org/436>.

[3]   E. Cassirer, *La philosophie des formes symboliques. 1. Le Langage.* Paris: Editions de Minuit, 1972.

[4]   E. Panofsky, *La Perspective comme forme symbolique.* Paris: Editions de Minuit, 1975, p.13.

[5]   M. Foucault, *Les mots et les choses.* Paris: Gallimard, 1966.

[6]   G. Anders, "L'obsolescence de la sphère privée. Conférence à Hanovre. 1958," in *L'obsolescence de l'homme. Tome II. Sur la destruction de la vie à l'époque de la troisième révolution industrielle,* Paris: Fario, 2011, pp. 209–243.

[7]   M. McLuhan, *Understanding Media: The Extensions of Man.* New York: McGraw-Hil, 1964.

[8]   J. Goody, *La raison graphique. La domestication de la pensée sauvage.* Paris: Editions de Minuit, 1979.

[9]   E. Eisenstein, *The printing revolution in early modern Europe.* Cambridge: Cambridge University Press, 1983.

[10] A. Feenberg, *Transforming Technology: A Critical Theory Revisited.* New York: Oxford University Press, 2002.

[11] B. Stiegler, "Chute et élévation. L'apolitique de Simondon," *Revue philosophique,* vol. 3, 2006. Retrieved December 20, 2016 from: <https://www.cairn.info/revue-philosophique-2006-3-page-325.htm>.

[12] N. Carr, "Is Google Making Us Stupid?," *Atl.,* no. 2008/07/01, 2008.

[13] J.-L. Weissberg, *Présences à distance – Pourquoi nous ne croyons plus la télévision.* Paris: L'Harmattan, 1999.

[14] B. Bachimont, "Arts et sciences du numérique: Ingénierie des connaissances et critique de la raison computationnelle. Habilitation à diriger des recherches.," Université de Technologie de Compiègne, 2004.

[15] P. Morville, *Ambient Findability.* Sebastopol, CA: O'Reilly, 2005.

[16] C. Wodtke, *Information architecture: Blueprints for the Web.* Indianapolis, IN: New Riders.

[17] M. F. Peyrelong and B. Guyot, "Quelques résultats pour les sciences de l'information. In : Holzem M. et Labiche J. (coord.) (2005). Rapport final Action Spécifique « Document et organisation ». RTP Document (RTP 33).," 2005.

[18] C. Lipsyc, "La sémantique analogique: une solution pour l'éditorialisation complexe (interactive, coopérative, transmédia, géomobile, pervasive).," Paris 8, 2012.

[19] G.-E. Sarfati, "Figures de pensée," in *Le dictionnaire du littéraire.*, P. Aron, D. Saint-Jacques, and A. Viala, Eds. Paris: PUF, 2004, pp. 236–237.

[20] C. Lipsyc, M. Ihadjadene, G. Chartron, and S. Chaudiron, "Architecture de l'information et éditorialisation," *Études Commun. langages, information, médiations*, no. 41, pp. 103–118, Dec. 2015.

[21] G.-E. Sarfati, "La théorie linguistique du sens commun et l'idée de compétence topique.," in *De Babel à la Mondialisation.*, Paris: L'Harmattan, 2005, pp. 81–98.

[22] F. A. Yates, *The Art of Memory.* Chicago: University of Chicago Press, 1966.

[23] H. Bergson, *Matière et mémoire. Essai sur la relation du corps à l'esprit.* [Digital edition according to the 72 yh edition, Paris, PUF, 1965], 2003, p.32. Retrieved December 20, 2016 from: <http://classiques.uqac.ca/classiques/bergson_henri/matiere_et_memoire/matiere_et_memoire.html>.

[24] M. Carruthers, *The book of memory: a study of memory in medieval culture.* Cambridge: Cambridge University Press, 2008.

[25] J. Piaget, *La construction du réel chez l'enfant.* Neuchâtel: Delachaux et Niestlé, 1967.

[26] J.-C. Bringuier, *Piaget va son chemin: la maison de Pinchat.* France, 1970.

DR. NORBERT GUTENBERG, SAARLAND UNIVERSITY /
DR. RICHARD FIORDO, UNIVERSITY OF NORTH DAKOTA

"One Speaks To Be Listened To": Schleiermacher's Philosophical View of Rhetoric and Orality

Abstract: The rhetoric of Friedrich Schleiermacher is reviewed in this paper in terms of modern speech communication theory and didactics. Schleiermacher focuses our attention on attention: that is, we speak to be heard, to be listened to, to be provided with attention, and to be confirmed existentially. The tradition to which Schleiermacher belongs, his hermeneutic, his fame in language philosophy and literary studies, his contemporaries and those similar to him in thought, and his theology are not developed in this study; rather, Schleiermacher's non-theological writings which embrace grammar and psychology are stressed. As the totality of linguistic, social, psychic, physical, material and other rhetorical dimensions, speech communication and education employ a holistic approach to a philosophy of understanding. To date, Schleiermacher's contributions to speech communication and education have been undiscovered and unidentified. In this study, his theoretical and educational contributions to oral communication are revealed and demonstrated. Three themes from Schleiermacher's philosophy of understanding are explained: the unity of speech and thought; the accent on activity, productivity, and receptivity in rhetorical, poetic, and artistic contexts; and, the elaboration of rhetoric as the process and content of teaching and learning that is unified epistemologically through communication and receptivity. Thinking is treated as inner speaking, speaking as the conveyance of thoughts via language, and understanding as a function of a dialog of commonized thinking. Toward the close of the study, Schleiermacher's rhetorical perspective of a teacher as someone who "disposes of high-grade knowledge" and advances "the principle of communication" is delineated.

The approach taken in this paper to Schleiermacher's ideas of speech communication and education represents a singular apercu. One of our aims is to elucidate Schleiermacher's philosophy so that we might better grasp what he meant when he affirmed: "One speaks to be listened to." The authors do not explain the tradition to which Schleiermacher belongs, his Hermeneutic, the praise he gained in language philosophy, literary studies, and so on (cf. Birus, Dilthey, Szondi). Furthermore, the authors do not deal with Schleiermacher's contemporaries and kindred spirits (e.g., Herder, Humboldt (cf. Geißner, 1959), Schlegel, or the recent renaissance of hermeneutics (cf. Frank, Biere)). We have not taken Schleiermacher's theological writings into consideration for the simple reason that being members of the audience to whom he directed his "Reden über die Religion an die Gebildeten unter ihren Verächtern" ("Speeches on religion to the educated among its despisers"), these writings reveal nothing to us. Yet, surprisingly, we find his non-theological writings most instructive and eye-opening. Rather, we interpret Schleiermacher's methodological views on biblical exegesis as being more grammatical and psychological, as he says himself, than theological. It appears that Schleiermacher had two distinct ways of thinking and, as it is, we understand just one. The question whether Schleiermacher as a philosopher divides his thinking in this way or not may be answered by others.

Schleiermacher received a pietistic education and studied in Halle from 1779–1789; he aligned himself with hermeneutic and a rhetorical approach to communication in a tradition which may be designated 'Hallian'. With respect to Schleiermacher's hermeneutical approach, the works of Alexander, Greisch, and Schnur give a precise trace of the line Baumgarten-Sender-Ernesti-Meier-Fr.A. Wolf-Chr. Wolf-Ast-Schleiermacher; and, as regards his rhetorical concepts which focus on school and university education, the works of Melanchton-Weise-Thomasius-Francke-Nicolai-Zinzendorf-Schleiermacher are applicable (cf. Schmölders, Fauser).

The overview on Schleiermacher's non-theological works reveals theoretical and didactic concepts of oral communication. Though these concepts can be assigned to philosophical-hermeneutical origin, they cannot be reduced to this, unless one conceptualizes the term hermeneutic to designate as hermeneutical all that which links communication to the category of understanding. To do this, however, would exclude hermeneutic as the methodology of understanding. Philosophy as the discipline of principles becomes relevant when it strives to establish empirical knowledge and find underlying methodological and paradigmatic principles. Dealing with meaning and understanding, hermeneutic exemplifies this paradigmatically and methodologically: (1) paradigmatically because understanding each other is characteristic of oral communication—making sense encompasses all events in oral communication;

and, (2) methodologically through reconstruction and understanding in speech communication and educational analysis—meaning being the processes in oral communication that concern the scholars and teachers who participate in these processes. In so doing, hermeneutic turns out to be a philosophy of communication and a methodology for reconstructing meaning and developing understanding. A discussion of this issue should include Schleiermacher's own definitions of hermeneutic that pertains mostly to rhetoric and dialectic, is attributed to a dimension of reception within the realm of speech communication principles where the discussion may be oriented to the dual nature of hermeneutic, and is to address both paradigmatic and methodological impacts.

Beyond all cursory reviews assigning individual passages out of Schleiermacher's entire work to speech communication and education systems, three strands of thought can be traced as outlines of a theory and didactic of oral communication:

- The first strand accentuates the unity of speech and thought in language (PS, HuK) in both communication theory and epistemology. As the fundamental thought of philosophical hermeneutics, Schleiermacher elaborates it in his dialectic with an epistemological emphasis grounded in communication theory; in his Hermeneutic as Art of Understanding, this idea is applied methodologically.
- The second strand accentuates activity, as explained in his Aesthetic. In his Aesthetic and Hermeneutic and Critic, the dimensions of 'productivity', 'receptivity', and 'activity' are delineated. He also elaborates on the rhetorical and hermeneutical aspects of language insofar as it concerns poetry (Ae, 8) and, by analogy, other arts.
- The third strand of thought develops rhetoric as the process and content of pedagogic activity. In regard to the pedagogic objective, teaching and learning depend on "the common property of language" (E,26) while communication (or discourse), knowledge, (E,29), productivity, and receptivity form a unity (PS, 234).

While Schleiermacher's pedagogical approach is a concept derived from constructs formulated in Hermeneutic and Critic, Ethic, Aesthetic, or Dialectic, it is also of independent origin. It can be designated sociological, political, and religious (cf. 3: Speech on Religion). The pedagogical approach in education may be seen as "the natural utterance of the survival instinct of the community" (PA, 25) while political goals will not be achieved "unless pedagogy becomes an integrating part of it" (PA, 42). This allows us to focus first on the reconstruction of the pedagogic concept as the "idea of language formation" (E. 115) and to continue the reconstitution of subject-theory more than of pedagogy. This does not preclude finding pedagogic insights in his Ethic and insights in subject-theory in his Pedagogy.

As mentioned earlier, Schleiermacher's pedagogical position is quoted only in part. The complete wording is: "the mutual dependency of teaching and learning through the common property of language and, conversely, that of the common property of language on teaching and learning" (E. 263). This interdependency makes speech education a principle of teaching and promotes it as a subject of teaching in Schleiermacher's entire pedagogy as well as in those parts not treating "language formation": "This is obviously a principle *for organizing everything concerning formation in a way that every activity be also seen as having a proper purpose and bearing its satisfaction in itself*" (PS, 297, emphasis Schleiermacher's).

This applies also to infant language acquisition which requires that adult reactions to children's communicative offers (219f) not be added on as a sort of instruction but rather followed-up or continued with what was offered (220) in the sense of Spitz' "dialogue" or Vigotsky's "principle of the next higher level." Whatever the case may be, adult reactions should take seriously the infant definition of the situation. Schleiermacher anticipates Drach's principle to follow 'the way of natural language acquisition': "Education has to observe the way development takes itself" (564). Furthermore, "this purely natural way" implies that mother-child communication "is based on the tendency to lure language out" (200).

Interpreting the above in the context of Schleiermacher's concept, language "comes into being only by the process of function", which makes the idea of language identical to the "idea of language *formation*" (Ethik, 115, emphasis ours). Consequently, as for the rhetorical curriculum in schools, it becomes clear that Schleiermacher makes "teaching in dialogue" (PS) necessary and central in school and across subject areas. Teaching in dialogue constitutes the "connecting point" to "exercises in free speech." Yet, the "immediate speaking may not occur in any other way than with reference to a subject which belongs truly to the field pupils are able to talk about." This is valid for teaching German (that is, the "mastery of language can only be developed by continuing education in the mother tongue" (PS, 372)). This is also valid for teaching as a whole: "Only those tasks may be given which are connected to that what is done in school or which refer to something occurring in common life and have something to do with youth and belong to their circle that they have a right to talk about" (ibid. 371).

The above cited mutual relationship between language and teaching and learning are not pedagogical in a narrow sense: "Teaching and learning are here conceived in its broadest sense and give expression to the very act of transferring a thought from one individual consciousness to another" (E, 263). In terms of the theory of subject, it is a question of the interaction between language, speaking, and thinking: that is, the strand of thought concentrating on communication and cognition. Schleiermacher develops his concept of an interdependent interaction of speaking and thinking in his writings on pedagogy, ethic, hermeneutic and, predominantly, in his treatise of dialectic.

This subject matter treats the following three aspects:

1. Thinking as inner speaking
2. Speaking as conveyance of thoughts on the basis of and by the medium of language
3. Understanding as the compliment to the act of speaking, and speaking as the dialogue of common thinking

1. Thinking as Speaking. Schleiermacher's conception of the first aspect is radical: "Speaking means turning knowledge to the outside. For the speaker/thinker himself, the identity is fundamental since cognition only comes about as inner speaking" (E, 30 f). Schleiermacher even goes further: "Thinking which cannot be expressed in words is necessarily unclear and confused". In other words, "There is no thinking without words; thinking and speaking are one and the same. If there is no speaking aloud, there is inner speaking. Before thinking becomes speaking, it is rather a mere desire to think than thinking" (PA, 114). In the "Dialectic" this thought is given a further precision. The unit (that is, identity and difference between speaking and thinking) becomes more distinct: "the words are formed with the idea." Furthermore, speaking is "nothing but the completion of thinking." Since "speech and thought are so closely linked", "thinking without speaking is not possible" (D, 126 f).

Wittgensteinian "complaints about the inadequacy of language" are not accepted (E, 67, similar also in E, 256 about the "coexistence of *thinking* and *speaking*" (emphasis Schleiermacher's). Nonetheless, Schleiermacher concedes different levels of adequacy in expression: "Indeed, there is no thought without word, but there are thoughts in different degrees of expression; we might have an idea without having simultaneously its suitable expression" (HuK, 225). Schleiermacher, however, grants that thinking is a social phenomenon:

> "Knowing, with validity and content being the same for all, is thinking."
> This is why he considers all thinking "inner speaking" (BzE., 361).

There is a compelling closeness between Schleiermacher's and Vigotsky's concepts of language and inner language in children's language acquisition with an exception. Schleiermacher does not note the development from external language to internal or inner language which Vigotsky described. Instead Schleiermacher stresses the contrary: "all inner speaking tends to be turned to the outside" (ibid.). He emphasizes the sociality of thinking and not merely speaking which he sees from an individual point of view: "This coming out of one's personality and expressing oneself is called speaking" (ib.). It leads to the second aspect.

2. Speaking as Conveyance. Such sociality of thinking is given with language: "The community is in the language" (E, 307). It is at once a prerequisite and a medium of speaking. In short, thinking is "done only by means of language" (PS, 505). This is already granted through the primacy of "speech" as suggested in Schleiermacher's dialectic or the "condition to complete thinking" (127). Language itself is essential to thinking since the individuals develop consciousness with language and have to consider their thoughts "as imitation and those thoughts designated by language as models", while by definition "these have been entered into language for common usage" (E, 263). In a sense, "human beings are delivered to a certain language": "all that has been thought [...] has its natural location only in the language in which it has been thought [and] communicates itself originally only in this language" (PS, 505). In this context, Schleiermacher's terse statements about knowledge and language are to be understood: thus, "without language there would be no knowledge and without knowledge there would be no language" (HuK, 364). Still, emphasis is always given to the social, epistemological, and communicative aspects of language at once. Language exists equally with knowledge as a necessary func-

tion of human beings sharing in community (HuK, 367). Schleiermacher definitely talks about "the proper language" (PS, 506) as being rooted "firmly in the human being" (505) and not about "language in general."

At a glance, language relativism seems distinctly apparent: "Because every language is a proper way of thinking [...], what was thought in one language cannot be reproduced in another language in this very same way" (505). Still, opposed to all possible Whorfian interpretations is Schleiermacher's effort "to search for the transcendent" (170) through the "difference in thinking" (D., 168) residing in the "difference of language". He stresses the "idea of a universal philosophy valid for all languages" (169) being objective with its justification based on insight: "The identical construct of thinking founded in language does not completely guarantee that it is right" (347). He endeavors to justify the "possibility to go beyond language" (Holenstein), to define "knowledge as the type of thinking which ceases the impulse to continue thinking" (i.e., gives room to *convincing*") (D, 172, emphasis Schleiermacher's). This can end in subjectivist aporiae and circular reasoning.

However, in the chapter on "Content of Truth in Language," Schleiermacher observes that the "relativity of knowledge is caused by the genuine difference of physical impressions. This in turn justifies the deviation in the schematizing process of the different peoples which creates the variety of languages" (375f). Thus, he solves the problem in a historical, not a subjectivist way. The difference in "forms of thinking" (168) can be constructible itself and overcome through "approximation" (169). Subsequently, we can say: "In everyone's thought truth is only inherent as long as it is present in language, and it is only inherent in language as long as word and thought of an individual are one and the same" (E, 263). Language being both source and medium of knowledge is grasped dynamically: "Of course, we have to take language for granted; still, to a minimum only, and it comes into existence by the process of function. All that is done in this process will pass over into language, and its total outcome may be reduced to the idea of language-forming" (E, 115). In other words, language involves primarily the process of its emergence in speaking, thinking, and understanding.

With the simultaneity of language forms, the "speaking, thinking, and understanding of the speakers/listeners" and the "speaking, thinking, and understanding of subjects" provides the ground for the possibility of deliberately forming by pedagogic action the speaking, understanding, and thinking of the subjects as well as the language itself. From this perspective, pedagogy involves speech education in its methodical performance; speech education is simultaneously a pedagogy that forms human beings through a process of language-forming. Now, the line of thought returns to the initial citation of the "mutual dependency" between "teaching and learning" and the "common property of language."

3. Understanding, Speaking, and Thinking. The two aspects treated so far require the aspect of understanding for completion. Speaking as the "conveyance of thoughts for the individual", speech as "the thought which has become language" (HuK, 76), "formed language" as a condition (77) of speaking as the "complexity of the common property of thinking" (77), and the simultaneous creation of language imply "correspondingly" the act of "understanding." "Each act of understanding is the reverse of the act of speaking": that is, thinking as "underlying speech has to be brought to awareness" (76). What was said on the relationship between speaking and thinking applies "correspondingly" to the relationship between understanding and thinking.

With respect to the relationship between speaking and understanding, similarities and differences apply: "For in each case, there is always a certain difference in thinking between the speaker and the listener, but this is not insoluble" (HuK, 178). Language becomes a source of knowledge. "Pure thinking can only come into being" by the very same "language elements" (24) "which also occur in common usage" (25). Therefore, using language is the prerequisite (27). Language is considered a part of the "organism"(140) (or the material-physical side of language) and "the openness of human beings towards other beings is the *organism*" (140, emphasis Schleiermacher's). Subsequently, "reason becomes our subject only by organization, namely, by language" (141). This "organic" aspect is elaborated in Schleiermacher's "Aesthetic." Language takes root in interactive speaking and understanding, in communication between "two different and separate forms of mental activities [...] reciprocally referred to each other" (5). Schleiermacher develops his dialectic as a dialogical epistemology and methodology of "pure thinking" or "thinking for the sake of knowing" (7). Practical and creative forms of thinking move smoothly from one to the other: that is, "pure thinking develops itself from those" (10) so that "if anything in either practical or creative thinking belongs equally to pure thinking, dialectic is applied, too" (23). From this point of view, the dialogue represents, in its various forms, the source of knowledge. The dialogue becomes dialectical when "pure thinking is sufficiently differentiated from the others" (10) and when "doubt" or "argument" present an "obstacle to pure thinking" (9). In other words, "only these circumstances have brought about and formed dialectic" (10). Schleiermacher develops dialectical rules which are the "same for all and are appropriate for all arguments designed to lead one interlocutor to the side of the other and to transfer split thinking into the unity of knowledge" (13).

Please note, however, that we will not elaborate on these 'rules'. Schleiermacher recreated Platonic-Aristotelian dialectics (cf. Gutenberg, 1994b) and topics pertaining to the development of logic during his time. His new perspectives on dialectics and logic put him on a par with Hegelian logic, yet free from the ontologisms of the latter. We will focus instead on viewing his dialectical logic as a "discipline of art" (12J43) or an "instruction" (3). In brief, "leading dialogues in the proper way of art" (5) follows "rules according to a theory or discipline of art, and this is science" (74). This is what was conceived with varying connotations in antiquity by the terms téchne, ars or scientia. Téchne refers to the "coherence between rhetoric and hermeneutic and their common relationship to dialectic" (HuK, 76). The relationship between speaking and understanding in dialogues and the inherently occurring thinking is "pre-technical/pre-art": a reality to be grasped in a theory. Téchne shapes the relationship. The resultant skill or art is the "highest level of science" (D, 75). In a sense, "Interpretation is art" (HuK, 80). Rhetoric and hermeneutic are mutually corresponding parts of dialectic and are 'arts' in the narrow sense. Therefore, the "theory of art in the arts has to become science, and the methodology in science has to become art" (Dialectic, 76). The subject matter and pragmatic objective of the science/art of rhetoric are on the side of speech production and those of the science/art of dialectic on the "construction of knowledge" side (55).

Relating these thoughts to the pedagogical starting point, the idea of "language formation" appears in a brighter light. Speech education is seen as a principle as well as a teaching subject. Rhetoric is seen as a subject of teaching and of content. More, however, can be deduced from the confluence of rhetoric, hermeneutic, and dialectic to which Schleiermacher refers in his writings on pedagogy under the title of "the exercise of mind." He conjectures: "Supposing that we cannot separate language and thought [...] because there is no other organ of thinking and conveying thoughts than language, we obtain already here the first essential point which matters [...]: *the practical logic* or *dialectic* of the people to be educated" (PS, 286, emphasis Schleiermacher's).

                223

Consequently, the "exercise of mind" consists in a pedagogic unity of "forming the ability of judgment, mastery of language, and knowledge of natural things" (287), including the "practice of memory" (288): "whereby, at the same time, the moral and social judgment is formed" (287). It is the program also underlying Quintilian's Institutio Oratoria. Schleiermacher's view of language formation as personality formation is implied in his conception of "the setting of the ME is particularly pre-eminent with the acquisition of language" (PS, 200); "the significant in language" would then be reached "when the child accepts the ME in language and consciousness" (PS, 584)—an insight which heads again to the psychological findings of Spitz. Language now traces distinctly the unity of education to dialogue and thinking as well as the unity of education to dialogue and ethics. In terms of the latter, Schleiermacher's initial theory of communication in his "Essay of a Theory of Societal Behavior" will have to be considered. The union of education with dialogue and thinking implies speech and listening education, both in turn involve educating people to think.

The interrelation of speech-thinking and listening-understanding and the formerly outlined fundamental coherence between speaking and understanding in communication as modes of linguistic existence may be conceived as models of intrasubjective and intersubjective processes in speech-thinking and listening-understanding. Although this representation might suggest that Schleiermacher equates thinking and speaking, it would be a coarse simplification: that is, unity is not identity. For Schleiermacher, there is "no thought without word, but there are thoughts in different degrees of wording" Referring to expression, the process of accomplishing elements begins with the composition" (HuK, 225). This describes a process of speech-thinking producing words and thoughts in unified and interdependent components, but still not identical. Schleiermacher describes two operations: "that of thinking [...] and that of speaking" (252). He does this for the purpose of explaining how "slips of tongue (occur) in communication"—a lapse at least partly caused by coordination problems between the two operations.

The combining force that generates unity incorporates grammar which provides that "everything thought correctly is simultaneously directed towards correct speaking" (HuK, 77). Finally, it is grammar, or possibly "position in being," that hermeneutic serves in "making out what the speaker actually intended to say" (HuK, 249). As Schleiermacher puts it: "he who produces a slip of tongue speaks differently to that what he thinks" (ibid.). This is precisely the practical starting point of hermeneutic: "to reveal the thought behind that what has been heard" (HuK, 253). Again speaking and listening are reciprocal, indeed only to be grasped as interdependent processes in communication. However, listening is not limited to receptiveness: "If the listener's perception is to be an activity, it will have to affect something in the speaker as well; passivity must be active [...] Speaking itself must already be an effect of the listener" (Tagebuch XXVIII). Seen from the epistemological aspect of the "Dialectic," the unity of thinking, speaking, and understanding in communication originates in the reciprocity and intersubjectivity of communication. Consistently,

Schleiermacher develops both sides in his pedagogy: "When treating the mother tongue we have, right from the beginning and closely connected to it, the comprehension of another's thoughts and the skill of expressing one's own thoughts" (PS, 369).

Again, the unity of speech-education and think-education is stressed, for "exercise" is required—an exercise "which relates to the living logical understanding of language in order to practice comprehension through the living word" (PS 309). In this context, he argues against the primacy of writing and the accompanying mechanization of language teaching (235ff, 302, 471), even though he recognizes reading and writing as requirements for civil rights (275f, 238f). From a pedagogical point of view, he gives primacy to spoken language: his way of thinking leans toward exercises used "in spoken presentation [...], declamation [...], and recitation" supplemented by "the presentation of one's own deliberations in free speech" (369). Thus, to introduce "rhetoric" in school education was a challenge since "rhetoric" was by many seen as a "branch of science which is not designed for school education and which is not at all suitable for everyone" (371). This naturally includes the faculty of "critical listening-understanding": that is, "the ear shall be particularly active concerning everything pertaining to language; one speaks to be listened to, so, everyone should listen to his own speaking" (373).

Listening thus becomes critical in learning and teaching in the early stages of human development: "for the effects of hearing impressions influence considerably the mood of the child" (210). It emphasizes the affective-emotional part in that the "sense of the ring is also the sense of the feeling." However, insofar as it is the "sense of love it is the sense of fear" (463). It is also the dialogical aspect "because the entire longing for proper human communication originates in this sense" (ibid.). Returning to the conception of speech-education as a principle, "Affective-emotional" means we are to be careful that the "child never fears the human voice, so [he or she] will not fear anything else" (ibid.). This is why Schleiermacher rejects punishment, in particular corporal punishment, for being "wrong at all levels" (530). He postulates: "Reasons shall always be the mean to guide [human] wills" (PS, 245). Schleiermacher bases this respect on an insight which is ethically and pedagogically fundamental: "The first formation area [...] we are given is the human body [...]; thus, life as the accomplished and non-negotiable property" (E, 253). At the level of "cognitive formation," it is important that "children learn gradually to understand their parents." So, "convincing is required", "persuading" as a "means to distract" is rejected, yet one "does not try to convince if the child is to obey." The "circumstances which do not permit convincing—which will decrease along with becoming mature—[...] should not be mixed up with others" (464). Here, the ethical and political implications tie into Schleiermacher's concept of communication and his (speech) education principle. Both anticipate in regard to educational contents and communicative forms of teaching the final purpose of teaching: that is, "their own production [...] with respect to working life and business activity" (370) and "the success of (settling) common affairs" which "depends on speaking" (579), "since humans are human only when they take part in governing" (239). Teaching rhetoric and the rhetoric of teaching is political education!

Rhetoric means in this context speech as well as dialogue. Incidentally, Schleiermacher reconstructs speech from dialogue in an almost Platonic way. Please note the following citation:

"Let us remain with the most natural, with the dialogue. If a dialogue gives rise to a longer speech, the listener has been prepared while it is conceived; the time the speech of the other takes place is already the time of developing one's own counter speech; it is a successive development, just in smaller spoils of time. If we bear in mind that practicing language skills also involves virtuosity in dialogue and if we are simultaneously aware of what we have said on the steadily progressing civil influence of the middle estate, the importance of this teaching subject is brought to light. Only in common discussions may political influence be exerted; only to the extent proficiency in speech is present may the influence be exercised. However, proficiency in speech is only then pre-

   © Frank & Timme   Verlag für wissenschaftliche Literatur

sent when one is able to follow the course of thinking of the other, to take up the essential and to concatenate one's own thoughts to it. When subsequent to the Instauration War [...], the hope of a new frame of the German constitutional circumstances was elicited, all of the experts shared the opinion that there would be a lack of persons [...] who were able to take part in public debates to a certain degree [...]. Though even today, this hope has not yet been fulfilled, public debates of people's representatives will definitely be constituted" (PS, 334).

This background gives reason for the "necessity of teaching in one's mother tongue" with the objective of "practicing free speech" (335). Schleiermacher bases his entire theory of education on a political footing. Whether or not influenced directly by Plato, to him it seems that "the theory of education belongs to a completely different field, namely to politics" (37). Since, "the state is the source of general communication," (PA, 171) it is its task to organize education. As for the contents of education, the decision on "the balance of differences relating to various existing communities and their share in education is made by science and art alone" (PA, 171) because there is "nothing better that settles conflicts than knowledge" (170). It follows then that "science and art have to be free" (172). Ergo, the state should not direct the "academic education." If it does, it would "be judged at the highest level [...] and everything would, as a natural consequence petrify" (171). Schleiermacher postulates that the "true being of science and art, the living spiritual development, the trust that every conflict can be balanced out posit on the grounds that the government frees science and art, though it supports institutions for keeping up the tradition of science and art and maintains them, but refrains from directing them, from exerting any sort of influence on their methodology and from imposing any partial participation." This, however, is a difficult task. Let us think of a certain scientific system in philosophy which has generated in a country and which maintains an ideology of human life. To everyone who has assimilated this system, it appears to be the only truth; for, as soon as the construct has reached a certain degree of accomplishment, conviction can become something very firm in such realm. If those who assume by state office the responsibility of directing and organizing education are involved in their function as adherents to the system, they tend to strive for shaping everything according to this particular view of life and inasmuch as it is within the responsibility of the state, to form education likewise. If this advances to the extent that only those who adhere to the system are entitled to influence education, further development is hindered and other existing types of philosophy are suppressed. What is right in the convincing of individuals becomes wrong by being neutralized without reason. What "applies to the state applies to the church, too [...]. Either the church is not in the need of science and science should not be bothered by it; or it needs science and so must release it. The need for social life and science needs further discussion. Free social life proves itself to be free to the degree that it will not reject the freedom of science" (PA, 172ff).

This is especially valid for universities: "Also, there is nothing more hated [...] than a government taking sides in matters of philosophy by excluding or redrawing one or the other of the conflicting systems" (U, 121). If this appears too idealistic, please be advised to study Schleiermacher's examples of the "quiet accord [...] between state and church concerning the direction of education [...] in the Austrian Empire" (171) or examples in recent history not so far in time.

If such postulates are at least tendentiously met regarding a "government's patronizing the people" (163), the more will the educational system be organized as a subsidiary from bottom to top (cf. 163f). "It has become clear that the manner applied by the state in taking care of education [...] can be seen as a sensible and fine barometer for the proper condition of the state" (165). Equally, it is "not the task of the state to determine the end of pedagogic efficiency" (46), for "Pedagogic efficiency ends with the effective maturity of a human being" (45). "Maturity" is not to be defined in legal terms (that is, "to declare someone of age" (46)). Rather, it is to be defined in the sense of "personal independence" without "guardian or representative" (PS, 275). "Social life is the medium used for gradually developing the political attitude" (PA, 203). Apart from "enlarging the scope of societal interactions", presupposing "a public life" which has to be "reflected and discussed in the family" (PA 204), it involves the "usual interactive form of teaching" (PS 372, s. above) and the non-school "community of free activities" (399). Its "true existence will not come into being but is dependent on the formation of public life, or at least an orientation towards it" (ibid.). "If our public life was similar to that of England" (PS, 406), schools would not be obliged to take over pioneering: "The more practice-oriented schools are equipped, the more deeply should the idea of public life be already evoked in schools" (399).

Schleiermacher's notion of societal interaction is the critical opposite of the German status of "approaching the caste system" (PA, 203) (in his time: end of 18th, beginning 19th century). England, in contrast, "has achieved the shaping of a free citizen system" (PS, 406). This implies the notion of emancipation for which Schleiermacher prefers "the people in Athens" as a model: that is, the "perfection of language" of the Greek society "roots in public life [...] in big public gatherings where language was used to influence minds" (PS, 578)—the language use found in political culture.

Schleiermacher doubts the emancipating efficiency of "learning reading and writing," for this does not offset "the difference between the higher and lower estates." It might serve "equally as a tool for working against the intellectual formation." Schleiermacher promotes the command of spoken language. Where we "approach each other we have to provoke the vital interaction in language" (PS, 578). Certainly, this concept has to be questioned critically. Schleiermacher does not endorse the possibility of a dependent verbalism. In contrast, he ignores the "court eloquence" (Braungart) and imperial rhetoric while concentrating on the Athenian polis: namely, its rhetoric and the Platonic-Socratic dialogue in search of truth.

Today, in the époque of audio-visual re-oralization, it is not possible to share his hope: namely, that "the rest will find its way automatically" (PS, 578). The first step would rather be to realize his fundamental premise in the pedagogic endeavor to orient education towards maturity (Adorno), rather than towards a secondary orality. This fundamental idea, in its pedagogic context explicitly worded as a target-idea, is to be consequently and solely implemented pedagogically. Schleiermacher asserts that occasionally "the state observes with a certain distrust the free, societal interaction of humans" (B.A., 62). Instead, he holds a moderate emancipating claim that "education [...] be designed in a way" that young people will "become efficient and competent if they step into that which prevails" (that is, into conditions of repression), but also "competent in engaging themselves to take up the possibilities of improvement" (PA, 64). Taking his afore-cited observations on convincing and persuading into consideration, the postulated orality may well be critically supplemented.

Schleiermacher extends the category of "free societal interaction" to include the question of whether "the theory of education is based on nationality" (PA, 55). He opposes the "tendency of the state to isolate itself" (PA) and proposes the position that "free societal interaction" be not ruled by the state on the issue of national education. Schleiermacher's conclusions may compensate for the negative feeling we might have when reading him as a political preacher: that is, his strong devoutness to the Prussian state, his German-nationalistic love for the Fatherland, his nationalist-religious identification of Protestantism and 'Germanity'—giving rise to his willingness to enter into war with the Catholic France, a propensity intimating almost a longing for religious war and martyrdom. This is not to follow Dilthey's affirmative-evaluation, but his report in the 4th book on "Schleiermacher's life". Here is another Schleiermacher:

"All such circumstances originate in the area which we called 'free sociability'. Free sociability or free societal interaction implies cosmopolitanism. We cannot ask more from the government than that the influence of this area be not hindered. For example, the interaction of individuals of different nations is limited by the difference of language. It is by all means not the question of extinguishing the diversity of languages, but only of overcoming the separation. This can only be done by the communication of languages. The same distinction as exists between active and passive trade may be applied to active and passive communication of languages. In a country where exclusively passive communication occurs, its position in the community of countries will be subordinate. Communication is active when a country introduces various languages into its realm and becomes familiar with these; communication is passive when a country admits people from other countries but leaves it up to them to acquire the official language. In this case it is not possible to become familiar with life conditions in other countries and to acquire the various languages." (P.A., 168)

Schleiermacher's notion of "societal interaction" in his pedagogical writings connects—due to the years between the two writings, maybe not immediately but comparatively—to the notion of "sociability" in his very first theory of communication in his 1799 "Essay on a Theory of Societal Behavior." This perspective exists in his approaches to the ethics of communication and may also be traced in the above mentioned concepts on rhetoric in school education (as preparation to political action), in "intercultural education," and in his notes throughout the "Ethic."

The epistemological aspect of Schleiermacher's position, "that we preferably trace the roots of ethical life and knowledge in speaking" (P-S, 582), had been demonstrated, even if his "Dialectic" has by far not been exploited completely (cf. Gutenberg 1994 b). The ethical aspect will be explained, in particular, by referring to the "Theory of Societal Behavior" (TB). It is Schleiermacher's first theory of communication. We do not share Fauser's position that this theory tentatively failed; and, that prior to the "Dialectic," he had not devoted himself to a "scientific analysis of communication" (Fauser, 442). Rather, Schleiermacher investigates in the "Theory" a completely different type of dialogue from his "Dialectic" with the latter also relating to a completely different aspect.

In his "Dialectic," the type of discussion becomes the issue: that is, the factual dimension of analyzing problems and debating on a theoretically controversial issue of argumentation. In the "Theory," the type of personal dialogue becomes the issue: that is, from the noncommittal to the committed subtype (based on Schleiermacher's demand). This does not mean that Schleiermacher's notion of 'sociability' excludes problem analysis and debating on theoretically controversial issues. Instead, communication centres on the personal dimension. Communicaton explicitly concerns sociability "free from any external purpose and determination." Schleiermacher searches for "a condition which puts the sphere of an individual in a position that it can be cut by the spheres of others in the most volatile way [...] with emotions and conditions [...] near to him [...]. This is the ethical purpose of free sociability" (TB, 3f). The category dominating his "Theory" is reciprocity or "mutual influence." "If we sunder the notion of free sociability, of society in its true sense, we find that several human beings shall influence each other and that this influence should be in no way whatsoever one-sided" (TB, 8f). The "mutual influence" determines the nature of society; it's "notion contains the shape as well as the purpose of sociable activity" (TB, 10). Schleiermacher then discusses "laws" or "rules" suitable for shaping the societal behaviour to correspond to what he calls "the decent befitting" (TB, 12). Replacing the expression 'society' by 'group', Schleiermacher's treatise concerns that type of personal dialogue which moves from contact to acquaintance. He attempts to resolve the contradictions in the subject of dialogue or between spontaneity and authenticity ("to give expression to his entire individuality") and conventionality ("smooth surface") (14), between generality ("that which is common") (20) and particularity ("the best that an individual may give"), (22) and between "entertaining" and "educating" (27).

Schleiermacher transforms select contradictions into rules:

- an individual's manner, personal style of thinking, personal ability to use the language and speak should be kept: "to let free [our] very own manner" (19)
- as far as the "factual matter" is concerned, "it is a question of finding limits within which the society be included" (17). This is the "total sociable content [...] with the exception of that to which someone in the society might be necessarily almost ignorant" (24)
- "everything that I do to entertain the society [...] must be, at the same time, intended to have an educational effect" (27).
- This allows an organic link to the Dialectic (3rd maxim) and formulates an Ethic of Communication which simultaneously reinforces the "claim for validity" in truthfulness: or, in psychological terms, genuineness (1st rule). The ethics of dialogue protects the other from proneness to injury (2nd rule). In later writings on ethics, the rules become more abstract and connect more closely with personal and factual dimensions:
- "Keeping thoughts closed means neglecting duty. Yet, this applies only to thoughts truly believed to be real knowledge" (E, 307)—rule 3;
- "Enter the universal community with the reserve to preserve your entire individuality" (E, 308)—rules 1 and 2;
- In terms of the philosophy of language: "The community is in language, but only one who produces is in language; otherwise one is just included in the community" (307)—rules 1 and 3;
- "A language lacks perfection inasmuch as it restricts individual usage" (309)—rules 1 and 2.

In the early stage of his theory of dialogue, which centres on "mutual influence", Schleiermacher displays pedagogic thinking: that is, the, perhaps, imperfect "manner" of an individual can be "improved" (TB, 17f) by exercise and solely through it. Though it still means empeiría, and not téchne, the seed for a rhetoric of personal dialogue has been sown. Schleiermacher alludes to téchne through the social behaviour theorist who transcends status represented by "every exercise being nothing but blind incoherent empiricism" (6). In contrast to this, he "wishes to construct social life as an artwork" (6f). What was said about science and art relating to Dialectic has already been covered, and it refers to Schleiermacher's "Aesthetic."

In the conception of science or dialectic, the element of téchne (i.e. the theoretical penetration and methodological systematics) prevailed. It is valid to have this transferred to the canonical arts: that is, "in all arts theory follows experience [...]; so, all consequences valid for the artists have to be drawn from their performances" (Ae, 182). In so doing, professionalism is made teachable. It is equally valid for "arts" outside of the canonical ones, like literature and music, to underline the decisive criterion of what is called aesthetical: namely, enjoying the accomplishment of human productivity! Therefore, we have to keep in mind the "technicality" of dialectic, rhetoric, hermeneutic, pedagogic etc.: these "being art" is only then achieved when Schleiermacher's criterion is met. In short, this practice is "art which features the correct usage of theory by someone who has the faculties of practicing or of productivity." (PS, 516). The sufficient condition is the "faculty of invention." "Theory" is the necessary condition, for it delivers the "criterion for judgment [...] for finding the right" by way of the methodological. It delivers the reasons for mistakes in practice but does not contain "the formula for application" (516). It is not téchne which provides the basis for the specific aesthetic; it is the usage, the very 'productivity'. Though it comes about by learning it cannot be reduced to the content of learning. The relationship between art and science being developed out of the téchne aspect of hermeneutic, rhetoric and dialectic may equally be deduced from Schleiermacher's theoretical writings on aesthetics.

Schleiermacher's theoretical approaches to aesthetics and art confirm the concept of the nature of aesthetics which was put forth in Gutenberg 1994a (346–388), Gutenberg, 1994b, and Gutenberg 2001.

- Schleiermacher's criterion for determining aesthetics significantly exceeds one-sided aesthetics focusing on content, production, work or reception.
- His perspective allows us to consider phenomena as 'art' or aesthetics: members not necessarily of the canon of art disciplines, such as painting, writing, music, or crafts; and, to conceive the relationship between rhetoric and poetry as a unity, systematically and historically.
- His concept of aesthetics, due to his hermeneutics, projects beyond the narrow realm of art theory into deliberations on theory and prac-

tice of education, state, and society; and, it allows surprising empha-
ses in these latter areas.

- His views on poetry and theatre supplement, intensify, and differen-
tiate notions of the arts of reading poetry and acting.

Schleiermacher starts, just as Kant, Schiller, and later Gadamer do, with taking literally the 'aesthetic': it is perception of 'pleasure with the beautiful'. He develops this understanding from the complementary aspects of the 'activity' category: specifically, their "productive" and "receptive" aspects. At some other points, he designates "playing" the "ground [...] for all arts" (PS, 240; Ae, 26). He searches for the aesthetic characteristic outside the realm of the canonical "arts." Schleiermacher follows consistently this approach and finds the aesthetic "everywhere in human productions [as] accidens" (Ae, 6): 1) "scientific work" can be "artwork" (40), and art can be present in "business speeches" (130); 2) "art of life" becomes the "epitome of free actions of an individual, seen as art" (Ae, 185); 3) "fantasy" is one of its forms (E, 73); and, 4) "all human activity" can be art (Ae, 6). Notably, he declares that "also life itself is art" (Ae, 73) and asserts: "There need not be a human relationship which cannot be treated artfully" (PS, 525) because "everyone participates in art in the broadest sense just as everyone takes part in knowledge in the broader sense" (Ae, 77). Pointedly, Schleiermacher "denies" that "not everybody is an artist [...] for there where active life is present [...], where the misery of life leaves just a little space for free play, [...] there will be also art" (Ae, 177).

What turns artful and other activities into the aesthetic or art? According to Schleiermacher, pleasure and perfection do this:

- "my activity should be my pleasure; i.e., it is better the more it approaches an artwork" (TB, XXVIII). In the context of this contribution, he considers also conversation and societal behaviour as being "capable of art".
- The aesthetic refers to "all human activities in their highest perfection" (Ae, 6): not artworks alone, but also "scientific works, state constitutions, social events" (ibid.).

If not in "perfection," in what should we have pleasure? Logically, Schleiermacher stipulates that: "Art is productivity" (Ae, 42). This definition also converts a "scientific work" into "artwork" if the criterion "perfection of the construction [...] in the artistic sense" is present (40). "The objective element of art" (8) or "the beauty of free human production" (4) consist in "occupying oneself with oneself." In other words, it is "play" (26). It exists in "the actual area of art" as well as in a mode of activity "everywhere in human productions" (6). The "pleasure in the beautiful" (3) depends on the "mastery of execution" (156). The mastery is revealed in mastering the functional relationship between proportion and purpose. We get proportion out of purpose, for the sense of "beauty" arises when "proportion and rule" (162) are functional (cf. also 160) (cf. HuK for "proportion" and "rule" as regards scientific works). This is why the aesthetic moment can also be present outside the actual area of art, as may be the case with "rhetoric": "this moment of aesthetics as attached at something else" (148) perhaps also outside the realm of the canonical arts. Just in this case, it is the matter of "fulfilling the purpose, a process which also depends on the artful" (Ae, 129). This does not mean that art is being reduced functionally because play is a "ground [...] for all art" (PS, 240), but all that which is functional is subject to the "art as the governing principle" (PS, 289). This overcomes the one-sided view of aesthetic works: "Art is only there present where an artwork exists; and with reference to skills that such may be presented in its proper way. It appears as artwork if all skills are developed and formed in all respects." (PS, 128).

Art is the "governing principle" on both the productive and the receptive sides of the activity which exists only "where productivity takes on the form of receptivity" (HuK, 204). So, it applies to the "actual area of art": "All those who perceive artworks in one way or the other are considered to be artists themselves. Sense and productivity are just two different steps: the art is the same in both the connoisseur and the artist [...]. Therefore, the impulse is general" (Ae, 178). It is even the "productive organ of music [...] the voice, yet, not the external singing voice, but the inner sounding voice" (Ae, 51); "poetry [...] needs the ear" (46); and, in theatre, "the spectator himself is the third artist who has to invent" (60). This also "renders" hermeneutic "understanding and interpreting into art" (E, 116). If we take this as a possible mode of being, it applies also to other activities requiring the aesthetic to be present on the receptive side: not only in speaking, but also in listening and understanding. Rhetoric becomes art "in order to exploit our aesthetic, to add to rhetoric the poetic" (HuK, 345, cf. also Ae 129). Hermeneutic and dialectic become the referential and integrative disciplines of both.

Now, the line of thought has arrived at a point where, developed from the téchne aspect, art metamorphoses into "the highest level of science." Yet, art is only such because skill and perfection may appear in the successful "technical" shaping of rhetorical, hermeneutical, and dialectical processes (speaking, understanding, and thinking on the basis of methodological-theoretical rhetoric, hermeneutic, and dialectic). As Schleiermacher stresses: "my activity should be my pleasure: that is, it is better the more it approaches artwork" (TB, XXVIII). Before continuing this thought it remains to be clarified what specific features make up the professional arts, except for the fact that they are professional. This allows at the same time a better understanding as to how the aesthetic develops from non-art forms of human activity and provides also an insight to one aspect of Schleiermacher's notion of language and speaking which has not yet been explained.

Viewing aesthetics as specific activity, as form, but not as mode of other activities, is determined by the subject matter which becomes its task. So, aesthetics is not emotionality, underlying of course all producing, "the natural expression of an inner excitement" (Ae, 170) because this makes aesthetic too specific. "It seems to be impossible [...] to deduce all other arts from these natural elements" (ib., cf. also 188) since "art (does not pertain) to the mood alone", but to the "free production arising out of the mood" (Ae, 18). "Certainly, sound and movement (arise) from being affected", but "art" comes into being "only there where the link between emotional state and external appearance does not exist anymore" (Ae, 177). Nor is it the nature of aesthetic to determine the different "media": music, language, image etc. The arts are just differentiated according to the means "whereas art is an occupation of oneself with oneself, a play" (Ae, 26).

Human beings possess the means of their productivity, the media of their activity. So, poetry is the type of art whose subject is language as form and as medium of activity. Hence, the "natural view of language" becomes the focus of attention: "the fluctuating, elementary in the designation, articulated sounds" (HuK, 365). The natural aspect of language does not contradict the epistemological aspect concentrated on thus far. In "Dialectic" Schleiermacher assigns the term "organisation" to the physical aspect of knowledge, the perception. He sees it as the "sensual aspect" in language. "Material for thinking arises out of the organisation, form aided by reason"; the "reason" itself becomes "subject matter by the organisation [...] through language" (D,141, cf. also 358, 362).

Language has two sides: "the lyrical and the musical". Both build an interdependent unity. Skills other than "purity and clarity and appropriateness of sounds and relevancy of accents" causes "the concatenation of thoughts" and "everything grammatical." Yet, there is a "unity of acts" since "the musical follows always the logical if there is a command on the organism". An exception to this might be an "event when someone has to present something which has been thought by someone else, for it is not the production out of one unity" (P8, 579). Language thus becomes the unity of the "sensual" and the "intellectual" (0, 141). The sensual consists in the material of poetry as a form of art (the intellectual remains with the dialectic as téchne with an aesthetic potency as mode!). The deciding factor is that besides the possibility of individual expression, given the "combinatory system" (see (HUK, 78)), the "natural side" of language determines its expressive character.

Schleiermacher summarizes this unity of intellectual and sensual, general and individual as follows: "The system of organic movements which are equally expression and symbolic of acts of awareness [...] subjected to the schematic character of grammar and logic *is language*" (E 65, emphasis Schleiermacher's). Its being "a language of sounds based on an organic system" (E, 66, almost literally in HuK, 380) serves as the subject of poetry and the basis of the unity of the grammatical-Iogical and individual-subjective aspects of communication. The categories of the "organic side" are predominantly developed in the "Aesthetic," even though they are important also for the language practice of non-professional artists. The psychological dimension of the hermeneutical procedure strongly depends on them. Schleiermacher's "Aesthetic," precisely the "music" chapter (Ae 69–73), elucidates numerous parameters of "oral delivery"—to use a term known in speech communication. He maintains that since "language mimics" (Sprachmimik), it may not be missing in "poetry" since it "comes into being only by performance" (Ae, 69). Language needs "the ear and it bears in itself an inseparable musical element" (46): namely, Schleiermacher's criterion for perfection as fundamental to the aesthetic pleasure. Furthermore, "proportion" derives physically from music, poetry, and dance for "proportions inherent in all merely corporeal movements: walk, breathe, pulse" (64). Schleiermacher insists that poetry as a form of art is not an addition of thought, "content", or "poetic enveloping": "only then" is it a form of sound or "metrum." First and foremost, it is a unity brought to life through the "natural side of the language." Without the "sensual side of language, the poetical composition cannot be thought of" (Ae, 145). "The organ of poetry is the language (i.e., the sounded thought)" (Ae, 52): "poetic speech [...] does not belong to the logical side of language, but to its musical" (Ae, 176).

Referring to art education in its narrow sense, Schleiermacher interprets language formation as a model: "The best scheme for educating performing skills in fine arts is that of language education" (PS, 574). It leads, as we have seen, to education in rhetoric and places its art characteristic above the pedagogic aspect. It is through the "musical side of language [...] by which we render language into a general type." The principle of supporting natural development is to be applied for language formation as well as for all other arts being goals of education. Schleiermacher refers to that which, also relating to the notions used, is part of the starting point of his "Aesthetic" and pedagogical play ("education has to assist this play") demonstrated in language acquisition: "the free production, the acquisition of which language is engaged in, [...] is first of all just a play, partly with articulated sounds, partly with imaginations, yet first of all a play using the organic tools of language and then a play with fantasy: but still the fundamentals of all future productions and of all arts, too" (PS, 240). If, as we have seen, language formation is necessarily speech education, then speech education, including education in rhetorical art and dialogical discourse, is necessarily aesthetic education. This line of thought applies to other professional arts.

Allow us to summarize:

- The affective-emotional side serves as the impetus and content of any activity and, thus, also of art: "to be affected in the productive" (Ae, 18);
- The sensual side, language in poetry, is the material of the arts;
- Material serves as the basis for unfolding the definiens of the aesthetic: the pleasure of perfection in reception and production;
- Education in the fine arts, like the theory of aesthetics, starts from play and assists in developing it into artful "productivity";
- "Productivity" in turn occurs as a mode also outside the canonical arts; everything can "approach becoming artwork" and is achieved when the element of pleasure turns up; its prerequisite is téchne (a complicated unity of practice, theory, and art); its explication has already begun.

Therefore, a non-aesthetic "canonical art" may exist as well as a highly aesthetic non-art. To the latter, Schleiermacher assigns, as pointed out before, rhetoric, hermeneutic, and dialectic; but he also includes the "state, theory of state, and wisdom of state [...] [since] all sensual production may be considered art"

(E, 13). Schleiermacher insists on "practice as the field of experience" being
the first: "theory follows the first only when one realizes that the outcome of
the one is good and of the other bad, and when one reflects why such has come
about" (PS, 516). He considers this relationship, similar to his notion of truth,
to be circular or spiralling: "practical thinking" starts "from an interest to
which thinking is nothing but a means [...]. All practice must be put to rules,
to technical terms of the subject, and this again, is assigned to pure thinking"
or theory (D, 400; cf. PS, 421).

Téchne does not simply appear as the second step following the empeiría
and being overtaken in the epistéme, but as a mediating process—starting
from practice, moving to pure theory, and returning to practice, which "becomes more conscious through theory" (PA, 40): in other words, both as theory and (pedagogical) practice. Each step and the relationship between the steps
constitutes a critique: "that which determines all operation of critique gives
rise to the suspicion that there is something which should not be so" (HuK,
255). This sentence, meant to be hermeneutical and referring to "mistakes in
communication" (ibid), represents a most lucid definition of "critique." In his
"Ethic," it directs acts while in his "Dialectic" it is epistemological and methodological. On this basis, Schleiermacher explicitly asserts that art be assigned
to education: "Forming man is also an art" (PS, 516). As we have seen, this
practice becomes art when productivity exceeds theory-directed methodology.
Regarding its share in téchne, Schleiermacher states: "If we consider education
to be art, we presuppose that this art can be learned." (PS, 128) (cf. also PA, 39
ff).

Rhetoric, subsequently, belongs to this art. In the chapter on "Special Training Institutions for Primary School Teachers," Schleiermacher defines a
"teacher" as a person who not only "disposes of a high-grade knowledge but
also of the principle of communication." Of course, "there are many who cannot be denied to have scientific knowledge but who, as we must say, are not
able to convey it to the others": in short, "the skill to communicate is a special
gift" (PS, 317). He then proposes: "The art of communication has to achieve
greater perfection; the methods have to be improved" (375). Thus, it is logical
to relate the formulated didactical rhetoric to a "dialogical form of teaching."
In this way, the success of teaching rhetoric depends on a didactical rhetoric of
the person teaching a given subject and on the "art of communication" of the
teaching person in general.

Although Schleiermacher does not develop in detail a rhetoric of teaching for schools, he treats more profoundly the academic eloquence in "Occasional Thoughts on Universities in the German Sense" (U). While Schleiermacher thinks "the dialogue never gained the status of a general teaching form" and promotes "coherent speech" and the "desk lecture" (U, 106), to the "gift of communication" he adds "conversations, repetitions and examination lessons […] [and] private contacts of the teacher with the audience where the actual communication prevails." Here, he promotes the ability of leading debates between "contesting parties" […] to leading the "course of their debates in a way that the subject would become clear" (136). The desk lecture is considered to be a dialogue "because it primarily brings ideas to the awareness […] though it does not have its outer form" (106). Schleiermacher designates as "dialectical" the procedure to start with the obvious "non-knowledge" of an audience. The "productive" speaker is able to "relate what he knows" and "re-produce his own insight." Also, the productive speaker is in the position to have the audience "immediately recognize and recognizably imitate the activity of reason in producing knowledge" (107). Schleiermacher names this faculty or power "the very art of the university teacher" (ibid.) and places the "nucleus of this art of presentation" in philosophy. However, "it should penetrate all academic teaching" (ibid).

In light of Schleiermacher's opinion that "the truth and very sense the university teacher generates is in direct proportion to his skill of such an art" (108), academic rhetoric would also be part of the "greater perfection in the art of communication". Following Schleiermacher, university education assumes the task of "initiating a process" (95) leading to the comprehension of "philo-sophical principles" of all science (94). To this end, a "dialectically productive art of communication" plays a decisive role. For those who strive for the "at-tribution of honours in studies" (134), the studies should include a 'Collegium styli' as was established by Thomasius in Halle in the 18th century. If Schlei-ermacher's dictum is right, that in university the philosophical faculty is the basis (PS), then the basis of the philosophical faculty is rhetoric!

(*Nota bene*: all citations from Schleiermacher are translated by the authors.)

References

Adorno, Th.W. (1972). *Erziehung zur Mündigkeit*, Frankfurt/Main.

Alexander, W. (1993). *Hermeneutica Generalis: zur Konzeption und Entwicklung der allgemeinen Verstehenslehre im 17. Und 18. Jahrhundert.* Stuttgart.

Birus, H. (ed.) (1982). *Hermeneutische Positionen: Schleiermacher – Dilthey – Heidegger – Gadamer*, Göttingen.

Boehm, G. (Hrsg.) (1978). *Seminar: Die Hermeneutik und die Wissenschaften*, Frankfurt/Main.

Braungart, G. (1988). *Hofberedsamkeit. Studien zur Praxis höfisch-politischer Rede im dt. Territorialabsolutismus.* Tübingen.

Dilthey, W. (1968). *Leben Schleiermachers.* Göttingen (Gesammelte Schriften XIII und XIV).

Drach, E. (1969). *Sprecherziehung. Die Pflege des gesprochenen Wortes in der Schule.* 13th unchanged ed. (1st ed. 1922), Frankfurt/Main.

Drach, E. (1977). *Grundgedanken der deutschen Satzlehre,* (photo-mech. reprint of 3rd ed.), 1963, Frankfurt/Main.

Fauser, M. (1990). *Das Gespräch im 18. Jahrhundert, Rhetorik und Geselligkeit in Deutschland*, Stuttgart.

Frank, M. (1977). *Das individuelle Allgemeine*, Frankfurt/Main.

Gadamer, H.G. (1975): *Wahrheit und Methode. Grundzüge einer philosophischen Hermeneutik*, 4. Aufl. Tübingen.

Geißner, H. (1959). „Sprache und Sprechen bei Wilhelm von Humboldt". In: *Sprechkunde und Sprecherziehung*, Bd. IV. Emsdetten, 16–26.

Geißner, H. (1968). „Zur Hermeneutik des Gesprochenen". In: the same and others (eds.), *Sprechen – Hören – Verstehen. Tonträger und sprachliche Kommunikation* (Sprache und Sprechen 1). Ratingen, 13–30.

Geißner, H. (1975). „Rhetorik in der Schule". In: the same, *Rhetorik und politische Bildung.* Kronberg/Ts., 21–35

Geißner, H. (1983). „Über Hörmuster". In: Gutenberg, N. (ed.). *Hören und Beurteilen* (Sprache und Sprechen 12). Frankfurt/Main, 13–56.

Greisch, J. (1993). *Hermeneutik und Metaphysik: eine Problemgeschichte.* München.

Gutenberg, N.(1981). *Formen des Sprechens. Gegenstandskonstitution und Methodologie von Gesprächs- und Redetypologie in Sprach- und Sprechwissenschaft.* Göppingen.

Gutenberg, N. (1994 a). *Grundlagenstudien zur Sprechwissenschaft und Sprecherziehung.* Göppingen.

Gutenberg, N. (1994 b). "On the Category of the Controversial: An Approach through Schleiermacher's Dialectic". In: *Philosophy and Rhetoric* 17, 4, 347–358.

Gutenberg, N. (2001): „Über das Rhetorische und das Ästhetische – Ansichten Schleiermachers". In: Pankau, J. (Hrsg.): *Rhetorik. Ein internationales Jahrbuch.* Bd. 19: Literatur – Rhetorik – Poetik. Tübingen, 68–91.

Holenstein, E. (1980). *Von der Hintergehbarkeit der Sprache. Kognitive Unterlagen der Sprache*. Frankfurt am Main.

Kant, I. (1966). *Kritik der Reinen Vernunft*, ed. Ingeborg Heidemann, Stuttgart.

Schleiermacher, F.D.E. (1845). *Die Lehre vom Staat. Aus Schleiermachers handschriftlichem Nachlasse und nachgeschriebenen Vorlesungen*, ed. Chr. A. Brandis. Berlin.

Schleiermacher, F.D.E. (1876). *Pädagogische Schriften*, ed. E. Platz, 2nd Ed., Langensalza. (PS)

Schleiermacher, F.D.E. (1913). „Versuch einer Theorie des geselligen Betragens", in: *Schleiermacher's Werke*, 2nd vol., ed. O. Braun and D.J. Bauer, Leipzig, 1–31. (TB)

Schleiermacher, F.D.E. (1924). *Über die Religion. Reden an die Gebildeten unter ihren Verächtern*, introduction H. Leisegang, Leipzig. (RR)

Schleiermacher, F.D.E. (1957). „Gelegentliche Gedanken über Universitäten im deutschen Sinne". in: Schleiermacher, F.D.E. , *Pädagogische Schriften*, ed. E. Weniger, 2nd vol., Düsseldorf-München, 81–139. (U)

Schleiermacher, F.D.E. (1959). *Ausgewählte pädagogische Schriften*, provided by E. Lichtenstein, 3rd ed., Paderborn. (AP)

Schleiermacher, F.D.E. (1973). „Aus Schleiermachers Tagebuch", in: *Schleiermacher's Werke*, ed. O. Braun and D.J. Bauer, 2nd vol., Leipzig, XV–XXX. (T)

Schleiermacher, F.D.E. (1976). *Dialektik*, ed. Rudolf Odebrecht, Darmstadt. (D)

Schleiermacher, F.D.E. (1977). „Brouillon zur Ethik", in: *Hermeneutik und Kritik*, ed. and introduction M. Frank, Frankfurt/Main, 361–370. (BzE)

Schleiermacher, F.D.E. (1977). *Schleiermacher – Hermeneutik und Kritik*, ed. M. Frank. Frankfurt/Main. (HuK)

Schleiermacher, F.D.E. (1984). *Ästhetik. Über den Begriff der Kunst*, ed. Th. Lehnerer, Hamburg. (Ae)

Schleiermacher, F.D.E. (1990). *Ethik (1812/13)*, ed. H.J. Birkner, Hamburg. (E)

Schmölders, C. (ed.) (1986). *Die Kunst des Gesprächs. Texte zur Geschichte der europäischen Konversationstheorie*, 2nd ed., München.

Schnur, H. (1994). *Schleiermachers Hermeneutik und ihre Vorgeschichte im 18. Jahrhundert: Studien zur Bibelauslegung, zu Hamann, Herder und F. Schlegel*, Stuttgart; Weimar.

Spitz, R. (1982). *Vom Dialog. Studien über den Ursprung der menschlichen Kommunikation und ihre Rolle in der Persönlichkeitsbildung*. Frankfurt am Main, Berlin, Wien.

Szondi, P. (1975). *Einführung in die literarische Hermeneutik*, Frankfurt/Main (Studienausgabe der Vorlesungen 5).

Vigotsky, L.S. (1977). *Denken und Sprechen*. Frankfurt/Main.